Deanna Durbin, Judy Garland, and the Golden Age of Hollywood

Deanna Durbin, Judy Garland, and the Golden Age of Hollywood

Melanie Gall

Guilford, Connecticut

An imprint of Globe Pequot, the trade division of
The Rowman & Littlefield Publishing Group, Inc.
4501 Forbes Blvd., Ste. 200
Lanham, MD 20706
www.rowman.com

Distributed by NATIONAL BOOK NETWORK

Photos courtesy of Hisato Masuyama unless otherwise credited

British Library Cataloguing in Publication Information available

Library of Congress Cataloging-in-Publication Data available
Names: Gall, Melanie, author.
Title: Deanna Durbin, Judy Garland, and the golden age of Hollywood / Melanie Gall.
Description: Guilford, Connecticut : Lyons Press, an imprint of Globe Pequot, the trade division of the Rowman & Littlefield Publishing Group, Inc., [2022] | Includes bibliographical references and index.
Identifiers: LCCN 2022001937 (print) | LCCN 2022001938 (ebook) | ISBN 9781493064335 (cloth) | ISBN 9781493069040 (ebook)
Subjects: LCSH: Durbin, Deanna. | Garland, Judy. | Motion picture actors and actresses—Canada—Biography. | Motion picture actors and actresses—United States—Biography. | Women singers—Canada—Biography. | Women singers—United States—Biography. | Women singers in motion pictures. | Musical films—United States—History and criticism. | Motion pictures—United States—History—20th century.
Classification: LCC PN2287.D873 G35 2022 (print) | LCC PN2287.D873 (ebook) | DDC 791.4302/8092 [B]—dc23/eng/20220308
LC record available at https://lccn.loc.gov/2022001937
LC ebook record available at https://lccn.loc.gov/2022001938

CONTENTS

Prologue

"Winnipeg's Sweetheart"

It is an old story, that of the Cinderella girl. And it is a new one, too. The quick trip from poverty to riches used to be taken in a silver slipper and a coach-and-four. Now it is on the magic carpet of the silver screen.

—FREDERICK LEWIS, *LIBERTY MAGAZINE*

THE CROWD BEGAN TO GATHER AT THE CANADIAN PACIFIC RAILWAY station shortly before eight. The morning had dawned crisp and chill, with the thermometer hovering just above thirty-four degrees. April 2, 1937, was a Friday—a weekday, usually filled with work and school—but several excited Winnipeg citizens were taking an unofficial holiday for this momentous event.

By the time the 8:45 a.m. Soo Line train arrived at the Higgins Street CPR station, hundreds of people were jamming the rotunda and crowding the train shed. Photographers checked their flashbulbs; reporters held their notepads at the ready. An incredible array of people—schoolchildren clutching autograph albums and Brownie cameras, businessmen, housewives, and railway workers—were gathered together, with no regard to the usual separations of age and social class.

The train pulled in right on schedule. After the regular passengers disembarked, a welcoming party, led by Mayor Frederick Warriner and Alderman Thomas Flye, boarded the train. Crowding into the private Pullman car reserved for prominent travelers, the men greeted Hollywood manager Jack Sherrill. Warriner and Flye were respected notables—leaders of the city—but they appeared awkward and provincial beside Sherrill.

The manager was slight and balding, unassuming at first glance, but he wore a fine tailored suit with a crisp handkerchief folded in his breast pocket. And Sherrill had an air of glamour. Of importance. Even in the dazzling world of Hollywood, Jack Sherrill was *somebody*. Standing beside him was a small, smiling woman with glasses, a simple dress, and smooth dark hair. She was accompanied by her daughter, a girl of fourteen.

The passengers were tired. They had been on the road for weeks, traveling from Los Angeles to New York, to Philadelphia and now up to Canada. They had come hundreds of miles overnight, and just a few days before, their train had been derailed in the Philadelphia railyard causing a scare and further delays.

After politely greeting the mayor and his staff, the girl followed them to the door of the train. She was neatly dressed in a trim navy frock, a light blue coat, and an off-the-face hat topped with a jaunty pom-pom that danced with each step. Pinned to the coat was a spray of fresh hot-house orchids. The flowers, kept cool during the journey, had been delivered by a porter just prior to arrival.

This was not the girl's first trip to Winnipeg. When she was twelve, she had traveled to Canada with her parents, unimportant and unnoticed, to visit her grandmother. Now, just two years later, she was a movie idol whose golden voice had gone straight to the hearts of film and radio fans worldwide. And this time, as the girl stepped onto the station platform, she turned to face the most extraordinary demonstration that quiet Winnipeg had ever seen.

"There she is!" came the cry from hundreds of throats, as the throng pressed forward and almost swept away the official welcoming party. Albums and handkerchiefs waved as a surging mass of delighted humanity lunged toward the railcar. The crush was so heavy that for a time, the CPR staff, police officers, and plainclothesmen were barely able to hold back the crowd.

Everyone at the train station adored this young girl. They were thrilled to see her in person and proudly celebrated her arrival. And why shouldn't they? For this was Deanna Durbin, "Winnipeg's Sweetheart," and she had come home.

Nowadays, if you ask people if they remember Deanna Durbin, the answer isn't usually encouraging. Some describe a flash of nostalgia, the image of a wide-eyed girl from a black-and-white film or the ringing sound of a soaring soprano voice. Others admit to being vaguely familiar with the name, but nothing more. Some primarily recall Deanna as the lesser-known rival of immortal star Judy Garland. In truth, Deanna Durbin was far more than that. She was the most important and universally loved movie actress for over a decade. Called the "Cinderella of the Silver Screen," she burst into Hollywood almost overnight, waltzed her way through a dozen hit pictures, and when her clock struck midnight—when her ball was drawing to an end—she escaped into the night with her prince. And, unlike so many child actors of Old Hollywood, Deanna did, truly, live Happily Ever After.

Today, even those who remember Deanna have little understanding of the unprecedented impact she had in the 1930s and 1940s, after her first film launched her overnight to the pinnacle of Hollywood stardom. She was a beacon of hope during the Depression and wartime years with an uninterrupted string of box-office blockbusters. She commanded a salary that made her one of Hollywood's most expensive actors and, in 1947, was the highest-paid woman in America. She made classical music appealing to modern youth and inspired several iconic classical singers, including Maria Callas, to pursue opera careers.

Deanna's studio-mandated persona largely defined youth popular culture during the late Depression years. Her transition to adulthood was embraced and emulated by millions, and her first kiss made front-page news around the world. Her clothes, hobbies, even her diet were assiduously reported upon by the leading newspapers in America and followed as gospel by a generation of young women.

When at the age of twenty-seven Deanna made the decision to leave Hollywood, she wanted to be forgotten. She had given her childhood to the people of America. She had allowed them to see her grow up and to watch as she fell in love for the first time. She had been daughter, sister, sweetheart, and friend to a generation of moviegoers. And perhaps because everyone adored her—from fans to photographers to gossip columnists—Deanna was one of the few stars who achieved this dream: a long and happy life off-screen, something so rare for a Hollywood juvenile.

Throughout Deanna's career, her name was continually linked with Judy Garland. The two girls were close in age, were both exceptionally talented and, for several years, their personal and professional lives seemed to run parallel. But while Judy's short, often difficult life launched a timeless legacy that made her an icon, during the Golden Age of Hollywood she was considered just one of several talented juvenile actors, while Deanna was lauded as a shining star of the silver screen. Yet it is Judy's name that has endured, with Deanna often relegated to a mere footnote in Hollywood history.

Those who recall Deanna are found at unexpected moments and in far-flung corners of the world: the librarian in New York whose eyes lit up as he described watching *One Hundred Men and a Girl*; the bookstore owner in Adelaide, Australia, who excitedly described his love for Deanna; the actor in California who has collected Durbin memorabilia for decades. Staunch fans are scattered across oceans, on far-off continents, their devotion a mere echo of the love the world once felt for this talented girl.

To fully understand the impact that Deanna had on music, society, and even on the movies of today, it is necessary to read beyond the superlatives, to look for glimmers of truth in the carefully crafted publicity department copy fed to gossip-hungry reporters. So for the first time in the century since Deanna's birth, her story is being told. And really, Deanna's story can't be told without Judy Garland: childhood friend, professional rival, and possibly the only one who could truly understand the pressures Deanna faced in Hollywood. And although this is primarily the tale of Deanna's life, Judy Garland's story is interwoven throughout.

But this is more than just a biography of a successful film star. This is the story of a Hollywood miracle: a young girl's meteoric ascent to stardom after a single feature film; a teen-aged singer achieving astounding success at a time when adolescence was anathema to a movie career; a major Hollywood studio saved from ruin by a girl mistakenly fired by its biggest rival.

This is the story of a symbol: an ideal of girlhood with a wholesome quality and a fresh singing voice who entranced audiences during some of the darkest days of America's history; a favorite of Winston Churchill, Anne Frank, even Benito Mussolini; a household name in almost every country, including Soviet Russia.

This is the story of a mystery: a young woman who was very much her own person and who summoned the strength of mind and character to leave fame behind and build her own life, far from the lights of Hollywood; who left an almost singularly successful thirteen-year career without ever offering an official explanation, to live out the last six decades of her life in contented obscurity.

But just as much, this is the story of the people who made Deanna Durbin a star, as well as those whose lives were touched by her stardom: Deanna's overworked mother, rescued from a life of struggle; her frail father, likely saved from an early death; the fans Deanna inspired through the Great Depression and the worst war the world had ever seen; the many actors, producers, and directors who built careers as a result of Deanna's success.

All of this, on the shoulders of one talented Canadian girl.

And so, the crowd gathers for the ball and the first waltz begins. All that is needed is for Cinderella to enter, shining with youth as she joyfully sings, trailing magic and music in her wake.

CHAPTER 1

Deanna's Early Life

1921 WAS AN EVENTFUL YEAR. MOVIE STUDIOS WERE STILL LARGELY producing silent films, and *Camille*, *The Kid*, and *Ocean of the Storms* toured nickelodeons across the country. "America's Sweetheart," Canadian Mary Pickford, starred in the silent hit *Little Lord Fauntleroy*, playing the titular role as well as Fauntleroy's mother. At just three years old, "Baby Peggy" appeared in fifty movies in a year and received over a million fan letters. After the highly publicized murder trial of silent film actor Roscoe "Fatty" Arbuckle for the slaying of actress Virginia Rappe, morality clauses were introduced into movie contracts and the Hollywood star system became popular at all the major studios.

In 1921, vaudevillian Eddie Cantor recorded the hit tune "Margie" at Columbia Records and was a year away from his first radio appearance. Future Hollywood producer, Joe Pasternak, had just arrived in America from Hungary and was determined to find success in his new land. Carl Laemmle, head of Universal Pictures, was taking advantage of the recently lifted foreign film ban in Germany by exporting dozens of movies overseas and planning a production unit in Berlin. Future director Henry Koster had just published his first short story in Germany. Leopold Stokowski, already a noted conductor, led the Philadelphia Orchestra in Chausson's Symphony in B-flat major to great critical acclaim.

Hollywood—and all America—was buzzing with opportunity, and many industrious young men and women were on the cusp of great success. And half a continent away in the Canadian prairie city of Winnipeg, a child was born who would change their lives, and the movie industry, forever.

CPR Town was an unlikely birthplace for a star.

Deanna's parents, James Allen Durbin and Ada Tomlinson Read, had been raised 3,800 miles from Winnipeg in industrial communities near Manchester, England. As a boy, James had a ringing soprano voice, but he was discouraged by his practical, middle-class parents from pursuing a professional music career. Instead, he apprenticed as an ironworker in the railway town of Newton Heath, physically taxing work for even the most robust men. James, quiet and slight, was unsuited by both build and temperament to the manual labor of his trade. Ada came from a Welsh family and grew up in the textile town of Oldham, one of twelve siblings who worked from a young age to help the family survive.

James and Ada married in 1908 and a year later Ada gave birth to their first child, Edith. In 1910, when Edith was old enough to travel, the Durbins immigrated to Canada, first settling in Peterborough, Ontario, before eventually moving west.

At the start of the twentieth century, Winnipeg, the capital of Canada's fifth-established province, was at the pinnacle of its economic power. In just forty years, it had grown from a village on the banks of the Red River to become the third-largest city in Canada. The grain trade was booming, cargo was shipped to America and to the West, and land speculators became millionaires overnight. Canada's most cosmopolitan and ethnically diverse center, Winnipeg was considered the country's liveliest city, full of bustle and optimism. It was also a major train hub, and four different railway companies were located there. With over three thousand workers, the Canadian Pacific Railway was Winnipeg's largest employer, and it offered the sort of trade labor James had been trained for in England.

In 1912, James, Ada, and Edith traveled to Winnipeg. They settled into a small house on Blake Street, directly across from the Canadian Pacific Railway's Weston shops, where James found steady work. In the early twentieth century, the neighborhood was called CPR Town and it was filled with immigrant laborers who came to work in the railyards.

The suburbs of Winnipeg remained quiet and clean, with tree-lined boulevards, birdsong, and air so pure that tuberculosis patients would travel halfway across the country for the "prairie cure." However, CPR

Town was a different world: loud and smelly, with coal smoke darkening the air and metallic clanging ringing out from the repair shops near the tracks. Around the clock, dozens of trains screeched and wheezed as they passed through the station on adjacent lines leading to and from the prairie frontier. A smelter from the Manitoba Rolling Mills steel plant belched out smoke, noise, and putrid steam over Edith and the other young children as they played on the nearby streets.

The Durbins soon moved to a larger house on Gallagher Avenue and settled into the community, but James Durbin wasn't satisfied with this new life. The CPR shops were known for long hours, dangerous conditions, and backbreaking labor. He had found employment as a blacksmith, and although he made enough to put food on the table, the fuel needed to warm his family during the freezing Canadian winters exhausted all his summer savings. Year after year, it was a constant struggle to survive. And then, unexpectedly, the family grew.

On December 4, 1921, Edna Mae Durbin was born at the Grace Hospital in Wolseley, a neighborhood in the west end of Winnipeg. She was a pretty baby, with curly hair and round blue eyes. The first time her voice was heard in public was at one of the many Baby Shows held annually in Winnipeg. Not only did Edna Mae take home the honor for healthiest baby, but she made more noise than any other infant present and was awarded the "Wailing Prize," a pewter plaque for the baby with the loudest voice.[1]

James Durbin had a comfortable home, steady work, and a growing family. But he struggled with his health. Never a strong man, the long, freezing months and the physical demands of his job were almost too much for James to take, and a physician advised him to find less rugged employment in a warmer climate. At that time, Los Angeles was experiencing a real estate boom that offered promising opportunities for work, and Southern California had almost no winter to speak of. To James, it seemed like the perfect choice.

The Durbins decided to move south. In May 1923, Ada and James packed their possessions in a car and drove to Los Angeles with twelve-year-old Edith and seventeen-month-old Edna Mae wedged in the rumble seat in back, bouncing toward their destiny between a large quilt and two feather pillows.

Edna's early life in California was told and retold throughout her career, the story subtly changing each time. Like so many famous performers in Hollywood's Golden Age, the unadorned truth was reworked by studio publicity departments to suit the manufactured image of their young star. However, all the accounts agree that as a child, Edna Mae was just like any other girl.

Throughout her childhood, the whole family coddled baby Edna. Edith often took care of her little sister, singing with her and fostering a love of music almost from birth. Edna was able to follow melodies and could sing before she could talk. Her first performance was the Irish ballad "Pal O' My Cradle Days," sung for her mother's friends. She repeated it again and again until Ada bribed her with a dime to make her stop. Edna Mae was a normal, healthy child. She was one of dozens of other little girls in her neighborhood; a quiet, brown-haired kid who went to school, helped at home, and explored her street with her black dog, Tippy, by her side.

The Durbin family wasn't interested in Hollywood. Ada and James— a thrifty, reticent, unassuming couple—were primarily concerned with just getting by. James worked as a machinist and at any other manual job he could find. Ada cleaned and cooked and worried about her husband's health, because even in this new climate James wasn't strong. Edith much preferred "legitimate" theater to films and Edna Mae had no acting ambitions. At the movies, she focused more on the popcorn in her lap than the story on-screen.

Edna began to grow up. Her mother taught her how to keep a home fresh and aired and how to make muffins for tea. Her father taught her about loyalty and the value of hard work. Edna had good friends and a loving family. She also had a voice, already growing rich beyond her years, as well as an aptitude and love for singing.

One night, left at home with her sister, Edna Mae began to sing the old ballad, "Drink to Me Only with Thine Eyes." The song ended and Edith asked her to sing it again. And again. When their parents returned home Edith excitedly announced, "I think Edna has a great future as an opera singer." Her enthusiasm flagged when she saw her father's dismayed expression. Such a career was impossibly out of reach. Money was scarce and lessons were expensive. Edith knew that if Edna Mae was to have a chance, it was up to her to provide it.

Meanwhile, Edith had met a young man. Clarence Heckman had a good job in a Los Angeles bank and was planning to propose any day. Edith was ready to begin her own life, but she also felt that Edna's voice had the potential to be truly special. She knew that once she got married, her focus would be on Clarence and his needs and her income would go to support her new family.

So Edith put her marriage plans aside. She began full-time work as a teacher, keeping five dollars of her weekly salary to pay for Edna's singing lessons at the Ralph Thomas Voice Academy. Edith went without a new coat; she went without new shoes. She would have liked to look pretty for Clarence, who was being so patient and understanding. But first of all, Edna must have her lessons.

As Edna Mae often recounted, as a child she would protest that it wasn't fair for her family to make sacrifices for her vocal training. But Edith and her parents would answer, with a laugh, "Well, when you're famous, you can make it up to us."

Edna finished grammar school and entered Bret Harte Junior High on the "UnHollywood" side of town. She was captain of the baseball team and worked as a cashier in the student cafeteria. When she was ten, Edna Mae made her singing debut at an Easter Star meeting and was paid five-dollars: her first paycheck for performing. As one of the leading talents at her voice academy, Edna started to perform regularly around the city. She sang for Los Angeles clubs and church groups as well as in concerts that Thomas staged to recruit pupils for his school.

At one afternoon recital, Rita Warner heard Edna Mae sing. Warner was a talent scout for Jack Sherrill and Frederick Falkin, two Hollywood agents. After the concert ended, Warner rushed to the agents to tell them all about the little girl she had seen "with the happy face and the marvelous voice."

Intrigued by Warner's description of Edna Mae, Sherrill dropped in to hear the next recital. When Edna, clad in a simple white dress, came onstage and started to sing, he was immediately impressed with what he heard. But Sherrill needed more than just a pretty girl with a good voice.

He sat up in his seat and shrewdly observed the audience's reaction. People watched Edna with rapt faces. Women wept and several men noisily blew their noses. Sherrill smiled and sat back to enjoy the rest of the song. This was it. *This* was exactly the girl he had been looking for.

The next day, Jack Sherrill took his discovery to MGM.

THE OPERA SINGER

Ernestine Schumann-Heink was an opera singer whose life was like a Hollywood movie. She was born Ernestine Rössler in Liben, Bohemia (now part of the Czech Republic). Her father, Hans Rössler, was a shoemaker and former Austrian cavalry officer. Her mother, Charlotte Goldman, was a Jewish-Italian singer.

Schumann-Heink grew up at an Ursuline convent school during the Austro-Prussian war. When she was thirteen, she began to study voice and had her operatic debut in 1878 at the age of seventeen in Verdi's *Il Trovatore* at the Royal Opera House in Dresden. A successful international career followed, including several performances at New York's Metropolitan Opera. In 1904, Schumann-Heink appeared on Broadway in Julian Edwards's operetta *Love's Lottery*, a piece written as a starring vehicle for her. Schumann-Heink was known for breaking character in the middle of the performance to ask audiences if her English was good enough for them to understand, a routine that delighted the theater crowds. One reviewer called Schumann-Heink "a wonder woman and great singer, not hedged about by the ordinary limitations of her sex."

During World War I, Schumann-Heink toured military training camps (just as Deanna would do a generation later), entertaining American troops and raising money for wounded veterans. She had children fighting on both sides of the war: one son had been conscripted into the German submarine service and three others served in the US Navy.

In 1929, Schumann-Heink's savings were lost in the Wall Street stock market crash and she emerged from semiretirement. In 1932, when the Metropolitan Opera fell into dire financial difficulties, Schumann-Heink offered to perform for her 1898 salary, a fraction of the fee she usually commanded. Her recordings, as well as the weekly radio show she hosted, made her a household name across America. Looking back at her success and her many adventures, Schumann-Heink's life story was indeed like a movie script.

Several studios in Hollywood thought so, too.

Ernestine Schumann-Heink's first movie performance was a small part in producer Jesse Lesky's 1935 musical comedy *Here's to Romance*, produced by Fox Film (which later that year became 20th Century-Fox). The performance was so well received that when the film was released, both Lesky and John Considine, a representative of Metro-Goldwyn-Mayer, raced cross-country to Chicago to sign Schumann-Heink exclusively to their studios. Lesky lost.

Once Schumann-Heink signed their contract, MGM announced the plan to produce a film about the great diva, titled *Gran*. Schumann-Heink would play herself, but the studio needed a young girl with a classical singing voice to play the opera star in her youth. Casting director Rufus LeMaire had interviewed, tested, auditioned, and ultimately rejected hundreds of girls with professional acting and singing backgrounds by the time he approached Jack Sherrill for assistance. At LeMaire's request, Sherrill began scouring California for a pretty, opera-singing girl. When he saw Edna Mae perform, he knew he'd found exactly what he needed.

Sherrill arranged a meeting with LeMaire and excitedly produced Edna Mae, who was invited to MGM to audition. Studio boss Louis B. Mayer was out of town and his executive secretary, Ida Koverman, was present in his place. These were busy people, and the greeting they gave Edna and her mother was perfunctory. Koverman gestured to the piano and said, in a businesslike tone, "Go ahead, sing something, please."

Edna didn't know how to act in a movie. She didn't know how to address a room containing the most important decision-makers in Hollywood. But she did know how to sing.

When Edna Mae began, the executives' eyes lit up. They pictured the upcoming movie they'd produce, a film that would undoubtedly be a roaring success. This young girl was all they needed. But remembering the cross-country race to sign Schuman-Heink and how they had almost lost her to Fox, they didn't waste any time. Koverman placed a long-distance call to Louis B. Mayer, three thousand miles away in New York. She directed Edna to sing into a studio telephone, instructing the operator to keep the line open as long as was needed.

Edna sang "Il Bacio." She sang "Two Hearts in Three-Quarter Time." She sang "One Night of Love," her clear notes skipping bell-like over the wire, ringing pure and clear above the far-off roar of Manhattan. Mayer was a man of action. The moment Edna had finished singing, he declared, "We'll take her!" Edna was immediately signed to a six-month contract at MGM at $100/week.[2]

As the phone receiver clicked, cutting off the long-distance connection, Ida Koverman turned to Edna and said, in a far warmer tone than before, "Welcome, my dear."

Edna Mae hadn't wanted to come to this audition. It was the day of her class graduation, the most important event of her young life. But Edna, who worked each day in her school cafeteria just to earn a few cents of pocket money, knew that getting a studio contract was far more important than walking across the stage in her school auditorium. She needed this job to help her family—her mother, who sighed far too often; her father, whose thin face and ebbing health was a constant worry.

She recalled, "At MGM I sang for one executive who went out and got another executive and I sang again, and I sang again. Each time I sang there was a lot of whispered consultation and someone else was sent for. I must have sung about ten times in all.

"My father started having trouble with his health. He was far from well. It was taking all of his courage to get up and go to work each morning. I remember when he came to pick up mother and me from the studio where I had gone for an audition. Dad looked pale and sick. He had fainted twice and the doctor had told him that he had to stop working for quite a while. He was desperate. 'Would it help, Dad,' I asked, 'if I brought home a hundred dollars a week? The studio wants you to come back tomorrow and sign a contract for me.' I'll never forget the look on his face, the happy tears in his eyes."

And so, thanks to a "wonder woman" opera singer, an enterprising agent, and a successful audition, in November 1935, Edna took her first step on the path to fame.

CHAPTER 2

From MGM to Universal (1935–1936)

Hollywood was trying to grow up. It had banged head-on into a tremendous change called the "talkies" when actors had to find speech. It had tried voluminous musicals that bogged down at the box office, it had experimented with "classic" singers who could sing but could not act. It had driven full-tilt into the iron gates of rigid censorship when it forgot good taste. Men had risen to heights of dizzy wealth and crashed to bankruptcies, actors had flourished and then died in poverty.
—DAPHNE McVICKER, *MODERN SCREEN*

DURING THE 1930S, MGM DOMINATED HOLLYWOOD. IT WAS ONE OF the oldest studios in the world, formed in 1924 when movie theater magnate Marcus Loew needed a steady supply of quality films to show in his chain of theaters. Loew purchased Metro Pictures in 1919, Goldwyn Pictures in 1924, and later that year he also bought Louis B. Mayer pictures, appointing Mayer as head of Metro-Goldwyn-Mayer with "boy wonder" producer Irving Thalberg as head of production.

In its first two years, MGM created more than a hundred feature films. While other studios were making small-budget monster movies or formula westerns, Metro-Goldwyn-Mayer tapped into the audience's need for glamour and sophistication, creating polished, lavish productions. In the early 1930s, MGM movies accounted for nearly one-third of the Academy nominees for Best Picture. A 1932 *Fortune* magazine profile of the studio flatly stated, "For the past five years, MGM has made the most successful motion pictures in the United States." The studio backlots, a "city within a city," were built on six separate lots and spread across 185 fenced and gated acres.

Twenty years before, most actors appeared uncredited on-screen. "Legitimate" stage actors were wary of damaging their reputation by appearing in films because, unlike theater, movies were originally intended for the uneducated working class. Also, film producers, who were aware of popular actors using their star power to command high salaries in the theater world, preferred to keep their casts unnamed and the salaries low.

However, this soon changed, partly because movie audiences wanted to know the names of the actors they were watching and partly because star power was impossible to avoid. Broadway luminaries were already known worldwide for their talent and it was even easier to adore and emulate an idol that you could actually see on-screen. And so, with a bit of help from movie producers who were beginning to realize that the actors they employed were not only useful as talent but were also marketable commodities, the star system was born. And nowhere was this more evident than at MGM.

MGM often boasted that it had "more stars than there are in heaven." Its impressive roster included Greta Garbo, John Gilbert, William Haines, Joan Crawford, Clark Gable, Jean Harlow, Jeanette MacDonald, and Nelson Eddy. From an exclusive contract with Adrian Adolph Greenburg, the foremost costume designer in Hollywood, to generous budgets, a steady stream of films being released nationwide, and the practice of having several writers independently working on the same story idea so there would never be filming delays for lack of a suitable script, MGM was rightly known as a "star factory." And for a young actress hoping to achieve Hollywood fame, it was the place to be.

Louis B. Mayer had perfected the star system at MGM. This star system (or studio system) was integrally different from movie making today, where actors are offered contracts for individual films and can work for several different studios without actually belonging to any of them. However, in 1930s Hollywood, studios essentially owned the actors they employed. Movie studios would seek out and sign promising young actors, creating new personas that included new names, ages, and even new backgrounds.

Acting, voice, and dance lessons were a common part of each actor's training. Children were educated on the backlot. Women were expected to behave like ladies, and men were expected to be gentlemen. Once under contract, actors couldn't perform anywhere else without express permission from their studio. They received a weekly salary whether or not they were making a film and both their public and private lives were strictly dictated by the studio that held their contract. Everyone—from bit players to the biggest stars of the era—was expected to unquestioningly adhere to the studio management's instructions.

At MGM, Edna was one small girl in a very large roster of actors. And it was six very long months between the contract offer and dreams of a shining future, to her unceremonious departure from the MGM backlot. Edna never forgot her treatment at the studio: "I was fourteen and ready to claim the world. They made one short of me and that's all. I walked around the studio for weeks doing nothing. I thought it was the end of the world. I didn't belong at all. I was just on the payroll. It's the most dreadful feeling in the world."

In the Golden Age of Hollywood, MGM was not so much a career as a way of life. And at first, things seemed rosy for Edna Mae. The MGM publicity department got busy, releasing glowing accounts of Mayer's reaction to Edna's unusually mature voice. A prestigious singing instructor was assigned to Edna and she received daily lessons.

The studio began to craft an image for Edna Mae, one they deemed fitting to her status as an upcoming starlet. This began with her name. Mayer decided that Durbin was all right for a singing star, but he suggested that Edna change her first name from 'plain Jane' Edna Mae to something more glamorous. And nobody turned down Louis B. Mayer.

The MGM publicity office consulted with Edna about her new name. She explained that she was called "Dee Dee" at home and she sometimes signed letters D.D. just for fun. She suggested "Diana," but the public relations man at the studio misheard it as "Deanna." Jack Sherrill and Louis B. Mayer both thought that Deanna sounded euphonious and that it gave Edna an air of glamour that matched the classical music she sang. Edna Mae liked the name. After all, she had an avid imagination and often pretended she was someone else. So why not a movie starlet named Deanna? For a while, at least, just until she grew up and became an opera singer.

The name stuck, and Deanna was born.

Deanna received a new hairstyle and posed for "casual" photographs around the backlot. She went to her first nightclub, the Trocadero, accompanied by her mother. The "Troc," a Hollywood institution on the Sunset Strip, had just opened in 1934 and was already *the* place to see and be seen.

One evening, she was invited to sing at a dinner hosted by Irving Thalberg, production manager of MGM and husband of actress Norma Shearer. Deanna was one of many performers on this star-studded evening, sharing the stage with Rosa Ponselle, Allan Jones, and Gladys Swarthout. This was Deanna's first time singing in a nightclub, her first time wearing a formal dress, and her first time standing only inches away from Rosa Ponselle, one of her favorite opera stars. Despite her nervousness Deanna sang out bravely, and to her delight and embarrassment, she received more applause than any other performer at the event.

The next day, Deanna was sent a large basket of hothouse flowers, including her first orchids. She wrote Thalberg a formal note to thank him for the floral tribute and he promptly responded with a glowing letter, thanking Deanna for sharing her talent. These were the last flowers Irving Thalberg ever sent. Just weeks later, on September 14, 1936, he died of congenital heart disease.

And then, Ernestine Schumann-Heink also fell ill. The film, *Gran*, was postponed. Deanna was still given daily voice lessons, but there were no more nightclub visits. Schumann-Heink's health didn't improve and plans for her movie were eventually abandoned.[1]

Deanna spent the rest of her time at MGM going to school, wandering the backlot, and practicing her singing. And waiting. Every day, Deanna waited to be called into Louis B. Mayer's office and told of a new movie that needed a juvenile with curly hair and a pretty voice. But that didn't ever happen. Instead, Deanna just kept waiting.

Two other important events occurred during Deanna's time at MGM. The first was a screen test she made for her first movie, a one-reel short called *Every Sunday*, and the second was the friendship she forged with another young singing actress, Frances Ethel Gumm. Although Gumm was younger than Deanna, she was already a consummate performer. Gumm was determined to be a star, and even back then she was known by the stage name that Mayer had chosen for her, "Judy Garland." She became Deanna's best friend and was considered by many to be her lifelong rival.

DEANNA AND JUDY: *EVERY SUNDAY*

They were champagne as contrasted to milk; they were an evening in a supper club as contrasted to a picnic in the country in June; they were "You're Lonely and I'm Lonely" as contrasted to "Ave Maria."
—ROSALIND WALKER, *PICTURE PLAY*

Their friendship never stood a chance.

Judy Garland and Deanna Durbin sat in adjoining desks in the schoolhouse on the MGM backlot. The classroom was an autograph hunter's dream, as Deanna's classmates included Mickey Rooney, Jackie Cooper, and Freddie Bartholomew.

Judy remembered the first time she met Deanna. "About six months after Metro signed me, another girl my age walked into the schoolroom. Nobody had ever looked so good to me. We were the only adolescent girls on the lot and we promptly formed a coalition and became fast friends."

Both Deanna and Judy were small girls with extraordinarily big singing voices and they were both under contract to the biggest studio in Hollywood. They were also close in age—just six months apart—as Edna had been born in December and Judy the following June. But even though they were similar in many ways, the early years of their lives had been very different.

Deanna had been raised in a loving family, where her parents and sister happily made sacrifices to help each other. Her mother and father were grateful for any money earned through their daughter's success, and proud that the MGM contract gave their Deanna such an exciting chance to fully develop her vocal talent, an opportunity they couldn't otherwise provide.

Judy's voice was primarily seen as a meal ticket for her family of performers. The daughter of struggling vaudevillians, she was onstage at two years old and spent her childhood as part of a trio of "Gumm Sisters," touring the vaudeville circuit around California with her two older siblings. Ethel Gumm, a controlling stage mother, had forced her ten-year-old daughter to take pills to keep her weight down and her energy up.

Like Deanna, Judy, too, had a father who was often ill. But unlike Deanna's father, whose health was saved through his daughter's movie success, Judy's dad died of spinal meningitis when she was thirteen. Booked to sing on *The Shell Chateau Hour*, Judy was informed that her father was dying just moments before she was scheduled to perform. Her father had told her again and again that performing came before anything. So she stepped up to the microphone, smiled at the bandleader, and performed "Zing! Went the Strings of My Heart!" hoping her father was listening and knowing she would never see him again.

At MGM, these two young singers were not only treated differently with Deanna as a clear favorite, but they were vocally groomed in unique ways. Deanna was sent to an operatic baritone to properly train her voice and spent two hours each day meticulously singing vocal exercises. Judy, who from the start performed in a jazzy style, received vocal training from Roger Edens, a composer of popular tunes. But Judy didn't work on scales and voice exercises; instead, she learned and practiced the song arrangements Roger gave her.

Despite—or perhaps because of—their vastly different lives, Deanna and Judy became friends in the intensely serious way that only little girls of thirteen-going-on-fourteen can be. They wandered hand-in-hand around the sunny backlot. They crept onto soundstages and spied on producers lunching in the canteen. They were invited to sing at studio birthday parties, where they stuffed their pockets with cake between songs.

And then, Deanna and Judy were finally—*finally*—given a chance to perform in a screen test. Together, of course. Someone had written a skit about a Transylvanian princess in a big castle and a little American girl who sneaked in to see her. Deanna was the princess. "Of course *she* gets chosen to be royalty," Judy remembered thinking, as the makeup woman smudged her cheeks to make them look dusty and handed her a wrinkled apple to hold. Even though both Deanna and Judy knew that a screen test could mean the difference between the starring role in an upcoming film and obscurity on the backlot, the two best friends had fun with the skit. It included what Judy called "a bone-jellifying death scene," which overwhelmed both girls in fits of giggles as they fell writhing to the floor, perishing in agony.

As part of the screen test, Deanna and Judy sang a duet where their two vocal styles were clearly contrasted. As Deanna remembered, "The test was very cute … I played a European princess and Judy was a visitor from America. Each of us sang to the other, Judy singing a typical jazz number while I was given a classical selection."

This short, titled *Opera Versus Jazz* after the song it featured, was never intended for commercial release and is no longer in existence. It was shown at the spring 1936 MGM exhibitors' convention, and the positive response from the audience prompted the studio to plan a short film for theatrical release, a film that also featured the "Opera Versus Jazz" duet.

Deanna and Judy had a marvelous time filming and recording the music for *Opera Versus Jazz*. Not only did they finally perform on camera, but they got to sing together. However, what neither girl realized at the time was that their duet had essentially been a competition to help Mayer decide which of the two juvenile singers looked best on camera and which ingénue MGM would keep. This screen test and the subsequent film, *Every Sunday*, were the only times Deanna and Judy appeared together on-screen.

Every Sunday was a one-reel movie "short." It was directed by Felix Feist, an MGM executive and lyricist for several Broadway shows. Con Conrad and Herb Magidson, who had written the hit tune "The Continental" for Fred Astaire and Ginger Rogers, composed a song, "Americana," especially for the movie. Although Deanna was no longer at MGM when *Every Sunday* went into production, a clause in her contract allowed the studio to use her in projects during the first months after her departure, and Deanna and Judy were brought together briefly to complete the film.[2]

Every Sunday was shot in July 1936 and released the following November. It featured both Judy and Deanna as themselves (they called each other "Judy" and "Edna" in the film). In the movie, Edna's grandfather is the conductor of a town orchestra that plays underattended Sunday concerts in the park gazebo. To save the orchestra, Judy and Edna try to advertise the next show by making signs and passing out leaflets. But when there is still no audience present, Judy and Edna take over. They climb onto the gazebo and begin to perform. First Edna sings Arditi's "Il Bacio." When Edna finishes singing, Judy smiles at her friend. She exclaims in what appears to be sincere admiration, "Gee, you were swell!"

Then it's her turn. Judy sings "Waltz with a Swing" and then the two girls sing "Americana," a classical/jazz duet. Crowds gather and the orchestra plays lustily amid wild applause.

What shines through in this short movie is that Deanna and Judy were two fourteen-year-old girls with tremendous potential, amazing vocal power, and clearly formed personalities. From her lacy white dress to her fluffy curls, Deanna appears slim and self-possessed with a radiance that makes her a born leading lady. Her demeanor is polite and a bit formal, more like an opera singer than an ordinary young girl. Judy is bouncier and more energetic. She appears unpolished with a changing adolescent physique and overdramatic facial expressions, but she is decidedly confident on-screen, likely from her extensive performing experience in vaudeville.

As one critic observed, "Deanna and Judy were both smart, unusually talented young women who represented youth through music in different ways. Deanna's appeal was a product of her singing talent, making high culture more accessible through a juvenile persona coupled with amazing singing ability. Judy made it all look fun. She *was* modern youth. She had an incredibly supple, mature voice, and even as a girl, her vocal tone held hints of the tragedy and heartbreak that would plague her throughout her life."

Although he had initially been enthusiastic about signing Judy to MGM, Louis B. Mayer didn't hide his preference for operatic-type singers like Jeanette McDonald and Kathryn Grayson. Whenever he passed Judy and Deanna on the backlot, he praised Deanna's voice as well as her figure. During their six months at MGM the two girls weighed about the same, but he often called Deanna "slim and lovely," and described her face and voice as "angelic." He called Judy "the fat kid."

For Judy, this constant comparison with Deanna was incredibly difficult. After all, she had been performing almost from birth. If not for Deanna, Judy was poised to be the leading girl juvenile at the biggest studio in Hollywood. And yet Deanna was clearly the favorite, and Judy's closest friend was rapidly turning into her biggest rival. What made things worse was that, for some reason she couldn't begin to fathom, Deanna didn't care that much about fame or Hollywood. She just wanted to sing. It was different for Judy; she yearned to be a movie star. But no matter how hard she tried, again and again she was firmly thrust in Deanna's shadow.

And then, in what seemed at the time a tragedy for Deanna and a wild piece of luck for Judy, talented little Edna Mae Durbin, pet of the MGM backlot, was sent away. Louis B. Mayer suddenly seemed to realize that he was paying to keep two very similar juveniles on his studio roster, and considering how unmarketable teen-aged girls were in Hollywood, he reasoned he could do just as well with only one.

There are various stories about why Deanna was dropped from MGM. The first was that Mayer took so long in deciding which girl he wanted to keep that Deanna's contract lapsed. Another version had him ordering a staff member to "drop the flat one," as he felt that Judy sang off-key, and the staffer misunderstood and fired the wrong girl. In another version of the story, Mayer was going to allow Judy's contract to lapse, but casting director Billy Grady fired Deanna instead. However, the most popular and widely accepted story about Deanna's departure was that on his way out of town, Mayer gave orders to an assistant to "dump the fat one!" and the assistant mistakenly thought he meant Deanna.

Whatever actually happened, it was left to Deanna's agent, Jack Sherrill, to break the news to his young client. "I didn't know how to go about it," he recalled. "She was so proud of that contract, so happy at being able to repay her family for what they had done. The whole thing meant so much to her . . . too much for anything to mean to a kid just starting her teens. I called for her that day and took her up to my office. She was happy and chatting away about her lesson, and then, all of a sudden, I guess her kid intuition told her something was haywire. She looked at me with those big eyes of hers and said, 'There isn't anything the matter, is there, Mr. Sherrill? I haven't said anything I shouldn't have?'

"I'd have traded places with my barber that minute. I began to talk to her about show business. I told her it was the most thrilling business in the world, but the most heartbreaking. I said that she was through with Goldwyn-Mayer. She looked at me a minute as if she couldn't quite believe it. And then it hit her and she started to cry. 'It isn't *me* I'm crying about,' she said. 'Maybe I'm no good. But my father! He'll have to go back to work now, and maybe . . . it'll be too much for him!' That kid, with that God-given voice, broken up like that over a studio mix-up. Say, it wouldn't have taken much more to have had the two of us crying there that day."

Deanna was crushed after what she felt was her ignominious dismissal from MGM. "For me this was the end. My dog Tippy and I went for a long walk. I was crying bitterly and decided that I'd kill myself. I couldn't go back to school a failure."

Judy had mixed feelings about Deanna's departure. Sure, it was a lot duller without her best friend around, but after all, Judy had been signed to the studio first. Not long before, she had overheard one studio executive discussing her and Deanna, and he had said that Judy "was a fat little butterball, but Deanna has the voice of an angel." Maybe with Deanna on the other side of the studio gates, people would stop making comparisons and Mayer would finally give her a real chance to shine.

Coming to Universal

Most child stars are born of need.
—Douglas Churchill, the *New York Times*

Although Deanna felt like her world had ended when she was dropped from MGM, her agent, Jack Sherrill, still had a few ideas. He first took her to see his friend Walt Disney to audition for the voice of Snow White in Disney's first full-length animated feature, *Snow White and the Seven Dwarves*. Deanna performed behind a screen, but as soon as she finished her song Disney turned her down, objecting that fourteen-year-old Deanna Durbin's singing was "too mature" and she sounded like she was thirty.

By this time, casting director Rufus LeMaire had also left MGM. His new studio agreement with Universal Pictures stipulated that he could put any actor he felt had potential under personal contract. This gave LeMaire carte blanche in discovering new talent. Even though he no longer worked at MGM, LeMaire had seen *Opera Versus Jazz*. And when the need came up at his new studio for a little girl with long legs, auburn curls, and the voice of a prima donna, LeMaire immediately thought of Deanna.

Deanna signed a $300/week contract with Universal Pictures on June 13, 1936. Just like at MGM, the Universal press office created a "character" for Deanna, a mix of fabricated details about her personality and her actual history, that was fed to newspapers and fan magazines. James Durbin was also given a more marketable biography by the press office. At the time Deanna was hired, James was working as a machinist. The magazines wrote that he was apprenticed in ironworks. Then they wrote he was a blacksmith. James didn't know what to tell people. He asked at Universal what he should give as his occupation and one staff member responded, "Hell, tell them you're a real estate broker. Everyone else in Los Angeles is."

Universal allowed Deanna to keep her stage name but they did change her date of birth, a common practice back then. Shirley Temple, the biggest juvenile screen draw of the time, had had a year taken off her age to extend her marketability as a child prodigy. Even her baby book was altered. Similarly, at the behest of Universal, for much of Deanna's career her year of birth was said to be 1922. This was because Universal Pictures had spent thousands of dollars advertising "Deanna Durbin, the thirteen-year-old wonder girl," and Deanna turned fourteen before the campaign got underway. To protect its investment, Universal deducted one year from Deanna's age and held to it until her true age was finally revealed with the announcement of her engagement.

When Louis B. Mayer returned to find Deanna gone and Judy still on his roster, he became livid. Mayer proceeded to put on a dramatic display that easily rivaled some of the more violent scenes from his studio's films, storming around in a rage and exclaiming, "Universal got Tiffany's and we're stuck with Woolworth's!"

MGM spent years trying to find its own Deanna Durbin, a replacement for "the one that got away." Although several talented young girls were hired, and Deanna's producer, Joe Pasternak, eventually joined MGM, there was no true replacement for Deanna.

Meanwhile at Universal, Deanna was thirteen for the second time. She was signed to her second Hollywood studio in less than a year. She was about to burst onto the screen in a feature film, and for the first time, she realized that her life was about to change forever.

TEXACO TOWN

Deanna was the most poised young lady of thirteen I had ever seen, with an unmistakable twinkle in her eye which spoke volumes about the success that was bound to be hers. She had a fine talent . . . and more, the natural ability to wear it becomingly.

—EDDIE CANTOR

Eddie Cantor was a consummate starmaker.

Born Isidore Itzkowitz in 1892 on the Lower East Side of New York City, Cantor didn't have a promising start. His parents were poor Russian Jewish immigrants, who, like thousands of others, had moved to America to seek their fortune. When they died, leaving their only child an orphan, no provisions were made for his care.

One of America's most benevolent and respected entertainers, Eddie Cantor could just as easily have ended up in jail—or dead. He spent his early years wandering the streets with an older gang, stealing from pushcarts and heckling "respectable" children. When he was twelve, he carried a gun and committed robberies. At thirteen, when a teacher ordered Cantor to joke less and to improve his grades, Cantor punched him in the jaw, knocking the teacher unconscious.

When he was sixteen, Cantor decided to take his chances in show business. At Miner's Bowery Theater, amateurs and low-level professionals competed every second Friday for five dollars prize money as well as any loose change tossed onto the stage. If a performer failed during his set, the crowd would yell out, "Give 'em the hook!" and he would be physically pulled offstage with a giant hook. When it was his turn, Eddie got up, glared at the crowd, did impersonations of several well-known local comedians, won the prize money, and never looked back.

One of Cantor's earliest paying gigs was as a singing waiter at Carey Walsh's Coney Island Saloon, where Jimmy Durante accompanied him on piano. His first major film role was in the 1913 movie *Widow at the Races*, directed by Thomas Edison. In 1917, Cantor signed a contract with Broadway producer Florenz Ziegfeld to appear in his show *Midnight Frolic*. His debut radio appearance was on Rudy Vallee's *The Fleischmann's*

Yeast Hour in 1931. Soon afterward, Cantor became the world's highest-paid radio star. With his singular mix of talent, determination, and grit, Eddie Cantor worked his way from obscurity to stardom and became the most successful radio star and vaudeville comedian who ever lived. And, through his 1936 radio show *Texaco Town*, he made Deanna Durbin a household name.

In an innovative publicity move, the Universal press office decided that the public should know and love Deanna as a singer in advance of her first movie being released. This would significantly increase the marketability of their new soprano and would likely ensure the success of the film. Rufus LeMaire, who had signed Deanna at Universal, was a friend of Eddie Cantor. LeMaire had produced one of Cantor's shows, *Broadway Brevities of 1920*, and he knew that Cantor's patronage was exactly what Deanna needed to launch her into the public spotlight.

Rufus LeMaire arranged for Deanna to perform at the Trocadero and invited Eddie along to watch. Eddie was impressed, but he didn't think a fourteen-year-old girl singing classical music would fit with the irreverent tone of his vaudeville-style show. LeMaire managed to convince Cantor to give Deanna a try, but he only successfully negotiated the deal by offering to pay Deanna's salary himself until Cantor decided if he wanted to keep her on the show.

Deanna appeared on the first episode of *Texaco Town* on September 20, 1936. Just like at her MGM audition and in *Every Sunday*, Deanna sang Arditi's "Il Bacio." And she was a hit. That first week, over four thousand people wrote letters to the radio station praising Deanna's singing. Most of the letters were addressed to "That little girl who sings with Eddie Cantor."

Deanna sang on her second *Texaco Town* episode a week later, and once again, audiences adored her. She returned, and returned again, and Cantor soon offered her a twenty-six-week contract at $1,000/week. On each show, Deanna appeared amid praise and applause. She bantered with Cantor or with fellow child star Bobby Breen, and then she sang two songs accompanied by Jacques Renard's orchestra. Once filming began on Deanna's first three movies, she would also update listeners with stories and perform songs from the upcoming films.

To Eddie Cantor, few things were sacred onstage. He ridiculed both himself and the performers around him. He joked about his sponsors, about politics, about his wife, about how he should be pitied as a long-suffering father of five daughters. However, throughout the run of *Texaco Town*, there were three things about which Eddie was deadly serious: appreciating the love of a mother, something he had never had; being a responsible citizen, and respecting others, which was very different from the devil-may-care attitude he had as a young man; and the singular talent of Deanna Durbin. Whenever Deanna sang on his show, Eddie introduced her with genuine pride ringing in his voice. He described Deanna as "sensational" and "terrific," and he was quoted as saying, without a hint of irony, "Deanna Durbin has more charm, more poise, more personality than a half dozen of the biggest stars in Hollywood . . . she has the greatest future in screen, radio, and opera of any singer today."

Judy Garland also appeared on the radio. She was a guest vocalist on several programs, including *Ben Bernie* and *Jack Oakie College* where she sang "Hold That Bulldog" and "Pennies from Heaven," and she was eventually signed as a regular on *The Pepsodent Show*, hosted by Bob Hope.

Despite the considerable time commitment, Deanna loved being on *Texaco Town*, which soon became the highest-rated program on the radio. The show rehearsed two afternoons each week and then there was an evening dress rehearsal with an audience; the next day, the show was broadcast twice on a split network for East and West coasts. On broadcast days Deanna would go without her supper, as her singing teacher would not allow her to eat before a performance. Often by the time they were finished it was too late for a meal, so she had just a small cup of hot chocolate before going to bed.

Deanna stopped performing on the show in 1938, but she and Eddie Cantor remained close. And through his patronage on *Texaco Town*, when Deanna appeared for the first time in a feature film, she already had a dedicated legion of fans.

CHAPTER 3

Two Smart Men

MGM had an army of champions who were specialists in the field. Paramount had Mae West. Twentieth Century-Fox had Shirley Temple and Warner Brothers had a gallery of gangsters and gun molls. The savior of Universal City was a brunette soprano with blue eyes, a spontaneous smile and a deft comedy touch.

—GENE RINGGOLD, SCREEN FACTS

THE MAGIC BEHIND DEANNA DURBIN'S CINDERELLA STORY BEGAN LONG before she walked through the gates of Universal, and it started with two Jewish immigrants: Joseph Pasternak and Hermann Kosterlitz. Pasternak and Kosterlitz (later known as Joe Pasternak and Harry Koster) were a producer and a director who fled Hitler's growing influence in Europe to find safety and the freedom to create art in America. It is ironic how Deanna was often considered the most 'American' of movie stars, and yet she was born in Canada, raised by English parents, and molded by newly arrived Europeans.

Koster and Pasternak were not alone in their odyssey to Hollywood. Between 1933 and 1941, over 1,500 directors, writers, producers, and other members of the German film industry were blacklisted by the National Socialist Party. Many of them immigrated to America, reviving their stolen careers in the movie studios of Hollywood. These new citizens quickly adapted to American society—learning English, anglicizing their names, and becoming integrated into their adopted culture.

Not only did Joe Pasternak and Harry Koster catapult young Deanna Durbin to stardom, but the movies they made with her were so successful that they saved Universal from financial ruin—the same film studio that decades later produced such movie classics as *Jurassic Park*, *Jaws*, and *Schindler's List*.

Joseph Herman Pasternak was born in 1901 to a Jewish family in Szilágysomlyó, Austria-Hungary (now Şimleu Silvaniei, Romania). His father was a town clerk and his mother raised Pasternak and his ten siblings in their small, overcrowded shtetl hut. Growing up, Pasternak once announced that his one goal in life was "to one day have my own bathroom."

In 1920 Pasternak immigrated to Philadelphia, where he worked in the assembly line of a factory, punching holes in leather belts. But he wanted a fuller life than that of a laborer. Whenever Pasternak had a free evening, he would visit one of the nearby nickelodeons and watch the silent screen actors live, fall in love, and die amid dramatic tremolos and rousing chords from the theater organ. He was entranced with the new worlds he discovered in the cinema, and a career as a film actor became his ultimate ambition.

When Pasternak had saved enough money, he moved to New York City. He lived in a shared tenement flat and plucked chickens to raise funds for acting lessons. Two years later, when Pasternak was twenty-one, he got a job as a busboy at the Paramount studio restaurant in Astoria, Queens. Serving shrimp cocktail and corned beef hash to the stars was a long way from actually appearing on the silver screen, but it was worlds closer than the sleepy Jewish quarter of Szilágysomlyó.

Pasternak's starting wage at Paramount was only $8 a week, barely enough to survive in New York. But this was an age of ambition, where personal industry was often directly rewarded. After just one year, Pasternak worked his way up to head waiter with a weekly salary of $120. A failed screen test in 1923 put an end to Pasternak's acting ambitions; however one of his restaurant customers, movie producer and director Allan Dwan, befriended Pasternak and hired him to work as an assistant on one of his films. Once again, Pasternak quickly rose through the ranks, this time from fourth to first assistant.

The next step in Pasternak's career was to go to California, where he worked at Universal as an assistant director on the 1925 Lon Chaney movie, *The Phantom of the Opera*. The film was a success and Pasternak was offered a long-term contract with the studio. In 1928, he was sent back overseas to Universal's Berlin subsidiary studio where he produced over a dozen German-language films for the international market.

Hermann Kosterlitz was born to Jewish parents in Berlin in 1905. His father was a lingerie salesman who abandoned the family when Kosterlitz was a child. His mother played piano in a Berlin movie theater, accompanying silent films while young Hermann sat beside her, enthralled, gazing for hours at the screen.

Kosterlitz soon became the primary supporter of his family. He worked as a short story writer and cartoonist and was hired by a Berlin movie company as a screenwriter. He met Pasternak in Berlin, they became close friends, and soon Kosterlitz was given his first chance to direct a film.

Kosterlitz's directorial debut was the 1932 comedy, *Das Abenteuer der Thea Roland* (*The Adventure of Thea Roland*). Two weeks after the movie's release, the Nazis took power in Germany. Kosterlitz saw the Germans marching in the street. He witnessed the hateful invectives directed at German Jews. He worried each day about his safety and the safety of his family, but meanwhile, he had another movie to direct.

In 1933, Hermann Kosterlitz was in the middle of filming his second picture, *Das häßliche Mädchen* (*The Ugly Girl*), when he had a run-in with a Nazi officer at a bank near the studio. The officer insulted him, and without pausing to think, he punched the Nazi so hard he knocked him out. Before the police could arrive, Kosterlitz calmly walked out of the bank. He went directly to the train station and, with nothing but the clothes on his back, caught the next train to France.

Das häßliche Mädchen was completed without him and Kosterlitz's "Jewish" name was removed from the credits and replaced by an Aryan pseudonym, Hasse Preis. Despite this effort to "Aryanize" the film, there was a Nazi-led riot at the movie's premiere where rotten eggs were thrown at the screen. When half-Jewish leading actor Max Hansen came out to take a bow after the screening, members of the audience pelted him with tomatoes, crying out, "We want German movies! We want German actors!"

Pasternak heard of Kosterlitz's escape from the *Reich* and of the violent reception to his movie. His American papers protected him from harassment, but with Kosterlitz in Paris and dozens of other Jewish film workers escaping Germany, Pasternak didn't want to stay in Berlin. As he wrote, "I saw Hitler turn up in his Nazi uniform, full of arrogance and hate, and full of contempt for us because he took kindness as a sign of weakness and stupidity. I saw the bullies in the streets, standing over ancient, gentle men, kicking them when they did not scrub the gutters to their tormentors' satisfaction."

With the permission of Carl Laemmle, head of Universal Pictures, Pasternak moved Universal's European production operations to Budapest and Austria where he continued to create German-language films. Kosterlitz soon joined him and they collaborated on the 1935 movie, *Kleine Mutti* (*Little Mother*), a comedy about a girl in a boarding school who discovers an abandoned baby.

Both Pasternak and Kosterlitz were beginning to establish new lives in Austria, and their films were well-received across Europe. However, in 1936, two full years before the Anschluss,[1] Austrian film producers signed a film convention with the Third Reich and instituted a Jewish blacklist. Austria was no longer safe. It was time to leave.

Joe Pasternak traveled to the spa town of Karlovy Vary, Czechoslovakia, to meet with Laemmle, who was there on vacation. During the visit Pasternak negotiated his return to California, signing a two-year contract effective upon his arrival at Universal. Kosterlitz was not offered a contract; however he possessed a letter of agreement signed by Ernst Wisenberg, an overseas representative from Universal. The letter would be enough to get him to safety and would at least gain him entry through Universal's gates. Laemmle assured Pasternak that once Kosterlitz arrived at the studio there would be work for him in Hollywood.

Pasternak was sent first-class boat tickets for him and his wife, Margaret Flader, and he converted them to four second-class tickets, bringing Kosterlitz and his wife, Kató Király, across the ocean to safety.

Joe Pasternak, Hermann Kosterlitz (who immediately started calling himself Henry Koster), and their wives landed at Ellis Island on February 19, 1936. Without even taking the time to show his friends his old

New York City haunts, Pasternak bought four Pullman tickets and they caught the first train heading west to California. There would be time for sightseeing later; but for now, it was time to start building a life in America.

The morning after they arrived in California, Pasternak and Koster presented themselves at Universal Pictures, confident of an enthusiastic reception. But when they arrived at the studio, they were shocked to find that Carl Laemmle was gone, nobody knew who they were, and Universal had fallen into a state of utter upheaval.

Carl Laemmle was the head and founder of Universal Pictures. He was born Karl Lämmle on January 17, 1867, to Jewish parents in Lupenheim, Germany. Laemmle was the tenth of thirteen children and one of only three who survived past childhood. His father was a cattle merchant and his mother a housewife who took charge of Laemmle's education, teaching him reading and arithmetic as well as respect for his culture and the value of family.

When Laemmle was seventeen he set out to seek his fortune, immigrating to Chicago with just fifty dollars in his pocket. He worked his way through an assortment of jobs, from drugstore errand boy to farmhand to bookkeeper. "One rainy night I dropped into one of those holes-in-the-wall five-cent motion picture theaters," Laemmle recalled. "The pictures made me laugh, though they were very short and the projection jumpy. I liked them, and so did everybody else. I knew right away that I wanted to go into the motion picture business."

In 1906, Laemmle opened one of the first movie theaters in Chicago. The nickelodeon was called the White Front Theater, and it was a roaring success.

At that time, Thomas Edison held a monopoly on almost every aspect of filmmaking, including the distribution of completed films and the sale of raw stock, films, and equipment. Carl Laemmle didn't want his theaters to be forced to play only the movies provided to him by Edison's company. Film reels were often not delivered on time and occasionally they didn't arrive at all. And even when the distribution went smoothly, films could be withdrawn if another theater owner bid a higher price for the reels.

In response to these frustrations, Laemmle decided to start his own distribution company, Laemmle Film Service, renting movies to theaters across America. Later, when Laemmle decided that the moving pictures being filmed were not up to the standard he expected, he formed the Independent Motion Picture Company to create his own films.

Edison maintained control over the early film industry by simply suing any potential competitors for intellectual property infringement. It didn't matter to him whether he won or lost, as the steep legal costs of the lawsuits drove most competitors out of business. However, Edison had not come up against anyone as stubborn as Carl Laemmle. Edison sued Laemmle over 289 times, but Laemmle won each lawsuit and eventually successfully sued the Edison Trust for remaining a monopoly through exclusionary and predatory acts.

Laemmle then joined with other independent producers to found Universal Film Manufacturing Company. Universal was an immediate success, largely because the company poached several of the most famous actresses of the day for their roster, including Florence Lawrence and Mary Pickford. This was achieved by promising the movie stars that Laemmle would list their names in his films and not just use them as uncredited actors.

The original Universal Film Manufacturing Company studios were located in Fort Lee, New Jersey. Laemmle then moved the studios to the San Fernando Valley in California and renamed his company Universal Pictures. At Universal Pictures, Laemmle produced several highly successful films, including *The Hunchback of Notre Dame* (1923) and *The Phantom of the Opera* (1925).

Universal was the first major movie production studio to be established in the Los Angeles area, and it was run in Laemmle's unique way. In an industry that was at the time primarily male, Laemmle had on staff thirty female directors and forty-five female screenwriters. Competitors often called Universal "The Female Shangri-La" or "The Manless Eden."

Most of the Hollywood studio heads were Jewish and had emigrated from Europe. However, Laemmle alone among the Hollywood chieftains—a group that included Adolph Zukor of Paramount, William Fox of the Fox Film Corporation, Louis B. Mayer of MGM, Harry Cohn of

Columbia, and the Warner brothers—made no secret of his Jewish heritage. Most successful Jewish immigrants in the early twentieth century made a point of ignoring their roots, but Laemmle embraced his past and his culture. He led Passover Seders at his house, spoke proudly of his family back in Europe, and, once he realized the dangers facing Jews under Hitler's new regime, committed himself to the task of bringing German-Jewish filmmakers and other artists to the United States. Laemmle personally assured the admission of over a thousand Jews by signing affidavits of support and paying for their immigration fees and passage to America.

Carl Laemmle first realized the danger facing German Jews in December 1930, when news reports reached him about the infamous Berlin screening of Universal's Academy Award–winning film *All Quiet on the Western Front*. The movie was an adaptation of a novel written by German author Erich Maria Remarque about the German military experience during World War I. At the screening of the movie, Joseph Goebbels led 150 Nazi Brownshirts into the theater. They repeatedly shouted "*Judenfilm!*" (Jewish Film!) at the screen, as they tossed stink bombs from the balcony, threw sneezing powder in the air, and released white mice into the theater.

Later that night, Universal's German representative, who happened to be married to Laemmle's niece, was dragged out of bed and held for questioning. His family also reported that a street named in his honor, *LaemmleStrasse*, had been changed to *HitlerStrasse*.

Laemmle was a strong man, firm in his convictions. However, he had one notable weakness: his family. As poet Ogden Nash once wrote, "Uncle Carl Laemmle / Has a very large fammelee." Laemmle was well known for nepotism at Universal, and over seventy of his relatives were given jobs at the studio. And then there was Carl Junior. In 1928, in a move that clearly stemmed from love and not from the keen business acumen that had brought Carl Laemmle such success, he made the decision to appoint his twenty-year-old son and heir, Carl Laemmle Junior, production manager of Universal Pictures.

For a few years things appeared to be going well, However, in 1936, Laemmle Junior ignored the precarious financial situation at Universal and instead staked the entire studio budget on a film version of the stage musical *Show Boat*. He hired the iconic performer Paul Robeson as well as much of the original Broadway stage cast, and he constructed elaborate sets and created lavish costumes.

Convinced he had a future hit, Laemmle Junior continued expanding the movie's budget. It eventually reached $1.275 million, nearly ten times the cost of any other Universal film produced that year. To keep the studio running, Carl Laemmle took out a $750,000 loan from the Standard Capital Corporation, using his family's controlling interest in Universal as collateral. When the costs for *Show Boat* far surpassed the available capital, the loan was called in and Laemmle couldn't pay. Standard Capital foreclosed, and on March 14, 1936, they took control of Universal. Laemmle and his family—as well as almost everyone associated with the old regime—were out.

Even with its new owners, Universal remained on the brink of financial ruin. The studio couldn't risk taking any more chances, and unless it managed to produce a big hit, Universal Pictures would likely need to close down production.

On March 3, 1936, Joe Pasternak and Harry Koster reached Los Angeles. By the time they settled in and reported to the movie lot, Laemmle was gone and the new management was busy firing anyone who had ever been connected with Carl Laemmle or his son. From the moment they arrived, it was clear to Pasternak and Koster that they were not welcome at the studio.

But Joe Pasternak and Henry Koster were survivors. At Paramount, Pasternak had worked his way from busboy to head waiter in less than a year. He had traveled across Eastern Europe and interrupted Carl Laemmle's vacation to negotiate a contract and passage to America. Koster had punched a Nazi thug in the Third Reich, had left his home and his work to wander stateless in Paris, and had crossed the ocean with a wife to support and only a letter of agreement as proof of future employment. These were not the sort of men who gave up easily.

Each day, Pasternak and Koster put on their suits and ties and reported to Universal. Pasternak knew that the new management was looking for a way to get rid of them and he didn't want anyone claiming that by not coming to work, he was in breach of his already-precarious contract. So, each morning the two men met at the studio entrance and each morning they were stopped by the gateman, who said, "You can't get on the lot without a pass."

Pasternak would respond, "My name is Joe Pasternak. I'm a producer here. This is my director, Henry Koster."

The gateman would check the staff directory. "We got nobody by that name here."

Pasternak stayed patient and firmly replied, "Just call the front office and ask them."

Eventually, Pasternak and Koster were allowed to enter. As Pasternak described, "We didn't have any place to work, no office, so we sat under a tree all day and read the newspaper. It always happened that we were no sooner settled than a gardener would turn on the sprinklers all around us."

After almost two months, Pasternak and Koster finally threatened to sue Universal for breach of contract and the studio capitulated. The men were given a tiny office in an unused horse stable and assigned a secretary, Eleanor Lewis. Pasternak and Koster were still largely ignored by the executives at Universal. They sat each day in their dim "office," listening to the stamping of the horses on the other side of the wall and trying to convince each other that coming to Universal hadn't been a mistake.

Finally, on April 30, 1936, production head Charles Rogers unexpectedly summoned Pasternak and Koster for a meeting. This was their one chance. As the men put on their hats, Eleanor Lewis warned them, "He'll ask you for a story. You'd better be prepared with something."

Pasternak and Koster had been too busy fighting for their right to stay at Universal to decide on an ideal movie plot to pitch. On the way to the meeting, the two men scrambled to come up with something compelling, something that Charles Rogers might like. Pasternak turned to his friend. "What are we going to do?"

Koster, who was still learning English, responded in German, "Tell him we want to do a story about a girl."

"A girl. That's good. People always like a story about a girl. Maybe two girls. Maybe that's better?"

Koster paused on the pathway. "What about *three* girls? Not just any girls, but smart girls. Three smart girls."

They were at Rogers's door. Pasternak nodded. "Three smart girls. I like it. That's fine."

At the meeting, after trying unsuccessfully to buy out Pasternak's contract, Charles Rogers offered him the chance to make one film for the studio. It would be a B-picture, a film distributed as the bottom half of a double feature. The men had twelve days to cast and shoot the picture.

Rogers fully intended for Koster and Pasternak to make a terrible film, and Pasternak knew they were expected to fail. "We were not regarded as pros in a business where there is no time or inclination for amateurs. We were holdovers from the old management. It was widely bruited about that after the flop which was sure to take place we would be given our walking papers, contract or no contract."

Pasternak and Koster got to work. They enlisted the help of screenwriter Adele Commandini and penned a rough script. They first called it *Three Sisters* and then changed the title to *Three Smart Girls*. It was a specific kind of light comedy with musical interludes that had been their trademark in Europe.

The script was approved and the film was assigned a modest budget of $100,000, typical for a B-movie. Pasternak and Koster were given twelve days to shoot the picture. They were also given several actors from Universal's roster, including character actor Charles Winninger, who had previously starred in Laemmle's *Show Boat*. Nan Grey and Barbara Read were cast as two of the daughters. The only thing missing was a third smart girl, a small juvenile role to complete the trio.

This is where the stories diverge. In one account, Pasternak was unable to borrow Judy Garland for the role, as his shooting schedule was limited and MGM had already loaned Judy to 20th Century-Fox. Since Deanna Durbin was already under contract at Universal, he used her instead.

In a more dramatic—and generally accepted—version of the story, Deanna had not yet signed her Universal contract. Joe Pasternak approached casting director Rufus LeMaire and asked if he knew of "a Mary Pickford-type of juvenile, a twelve-year-old girl with the indefinable charm of the girl who was once called 'America's Sweetheart.'"

LeMaire responded, "I think I know just where to find such a girl. In fact, you can have your choice of two."

"Choice?" Pasternak thought he was asking for the impossible and this casting director claimed there was more than one.

"Over at Metro they've got two kids under contract. They both have tremendous possibilities, I think. I'll get the film and run it for you. I'm pretty sure they're dropping one of them."

The next day, Pasternak watched Judy and Deanna's screen tests. He started with Judy. She was warm, lovable, natural, charming. She sang in a way that instantly won his heart. "That's the girl!" Pasternak shouted when the lights went up in the projection room. "What do you say, Henry?"

Koster agreed. They turned, beaming huge smiles at LeMaire. But he wasn't smiling.

"What's the matter, Rufus?" Pasternak asked. "Don't you understand? We like her, she's terrific. You can sign her."

"Remember I told you they had two girls and were dropping one? This is the one they decided to keep."

Pasternak fell into a chair and covered his face with the palms of both hands. LeMaire went on, "She's pretty good, this kid, huh, Joe? Her name's Garland, Judy Garland. I knew you'd like her."

Pasternak moaned, "Rufus, will you stop? What do I care if her name's Fifi LaFlamme? I can't have her for my picture, what difference does it make?"

LeMaire responded, "I think this other kid's great, too, Joe. You're here. You might as well look."

Pasternak held his breath as LeMaire gave the signal to the booth. It was a singing test, and the moment Deanna's face flashed on the screen, the two men sat up. Koster didn't say a word, just leaned forward and put his hand on his friend's shoulder. The girl had a sweetness without being arch or cloying. She was natural; she was pretty; she was wholesome; and she sang beautifully, with poise and ability far beyond her years. When the lights went up again, Pasternak took a deep breath before speaking.

"Before I say anything, is this girl free, can we sign her?" Pasternak demanded. LeMaire nodded.

"Can she act?" Koster asked. "All we've seen here is singing ... oh, never mind. I don't care. I'll teach her to act. She's wonderful."

On June 13, 1936, Deanna Durbin signed a contract with Universal for $300/week. She was cast in the juvenile role in *Three Smart Girls* and billed ninth in the cast list.

Koster went to work. Filming was postponed for two weeks, and in that time he taught Deanna to walk and move gracefully. Screen tests were made and Koster knew he had a star. "I went over to her house in the evenings and rehearsed the scenes with her. She was a complete beginner in that. I told her how to smile, and how to react, and how to suddenly turn around, and how gestures and movements become sudden when somebody is upset or startled and become soft when somebody is impressed and gentle. So these things I taught her. I went as far as telling her that the mouth goes up in the corners when you smile and goes down when you cry. Every gesture that she does was taught to her by me, with great precision."

Production of *Three Smart Girls* began on September 10, 1936. After the first few days of filming, the rushes—the raw footage from the day's shooting—were shown to Joseph Breen, director of the Motion Picture Producers and Distributors of America. Breen loved what he saw. He felt that Deanna had the sort of naturalness that transcended acting ability. He praised the script to Charles Rogers who raised the budget to $260,000 and then again to $326,000. The film was put on the A-list and was assigned an advertisement and promotion budget.

When the budget was $100,000, Deanna's name was ninth on the cast list. When it was increased, her name moved up to eighth. More scenes were shot with Deanna, and she moved up to seventh. This continued until the budget was nearing $400,000 and Deanna Durbin had become the top-billed star of the picture.

CHAPTER 4

Three Smart Girls

The world was sad, disordered, insane. . . . I thought I could help by making people laugh, by giving a moment of lightness and delight, of sweetness and charm, in a world that has always been wrong.
—JOE PASTERNAK

DEANNA DURBIN'S FIRST FULL-LENGTH MOVIE, *THREE SMART GIRLS*, changed both her life and Hollywood moviemaking in the 1930s. Although it doesn't seem especially innovative when watched today, *Three Smart Girls* was, in several ways, a groundbreaking film. For the first time since the age of silent movies, it showed that adolescent actors were employable. The movie proved that classical songs could be enjoyed by a younger audience, it partially altered the negative attitude toward European filmmakers in Hollywood, and decades later it inspired *The Parent Trap* with Hayley Mills. And, of course, *Three Smart Girls* was such a box-office success that it was directly credited with saving the foundering Universal Pictures from bankruptcy.

Three Smart Girls features teen-aged sisters Penny, Kay, and Joan Craig (played by Durbin, Barbara Read, and Nan Grey). The sisters live in Switzerland with their mother, Dorothy Craig (Nella Walker). Near the start of the film, Dorothy tearfully informs her daughters that their estranged father, wealthy New York banker Judson Craig (Charles Winninger), is planning to marry again. The sisters realize that their mother is still in love with their father, and they borrow money from the housekeeper and run away to America to stop the wedding.

For most of the movie, the sisters devote themselves to sabotaging their father's new relationship, even hiring penniless aristocrat Count Arisztid (Mischa Auer) to lure Judson's fiancée away. In the end they are successful, the two older sisters find sweethearts, and the family is reunited.

Three Smart Girls was released in December 1936 and was a smash hit, with Deanna as its shining star. The *New York Times* called Pasternak and Koster "geniuses of the month" and praised: "Miss Durbin carols most sweetly in an immature, but surprisingly well-trained voice. Her notes are rounded, velvety and bell-like; the manner of her rendition is agreeably artless." The *New York Evening Journal* described Deanna as "a little girl with pink cheeks and schoolbooks under her arm and a candy bar in her pocket. She is Jenny Lind in short socks. She likes vanilla ice cream, but she can sing a Puccini aria as well—or better—than any soprano on the screen."

Not only was *Three Smart Girls* one of the first "talkies" to feature adolescent girls in leading roles, but it also introduced a variety of European movie conventions still employed to this day. One example featured producer Joe Pasternak directing a scene where Deanna's singing was accompanied by orchestral music. This was an old, proven European film device, used countless times at his studios in Germany and Austria.

However, Hollywood was not Europe. A member of the production staff objected, "Where does the music come from?"

Pasternak responded that it was just there. The staffer suggested, "But couldn't we have a band passing under a window?"

The producer explained that the music did not come from a physical band coincidentally passing under a window. "The music comes from the heart, so everyone will hear it."

Pasternak was right. Nobody ever questioned the orchestral music and it became a convention used to this day.

At about the same time, Judy Garland was loaned to 20th Century-Fox for a small part in the B-movie *Pigskin Parade*, a role that wasn't deemed important enough for her name or image to appear on the show poster. Since *Every Sunday* was not released until November 1936, *Pigskin Parade* and *Three Smart Girls* were the first times Deanna and Judy appeared on-screen.

In *Three Smart Girls*, Deanna is presented as wealthy and educated, dressed in a crisp sailor suit that flatters her figure. She appears at the start of the movie and opens with a song, her voice echoing over a pristine lake in glamorous Switzerland.

Judy isn't seen until forty-two minutes into *Pigskin Parade*. She is first shown on a backwoods watermelon farm as a barefoot hillbilly with unbrushed hair and a wrinkled sack of a dress. Judy later described herself as "a fat little frightening pig with pigtails."

The first time Deanna's voice is heard is in the soaring melody of a song. Judy's screen premiere is merely the line, delivered in a heavy "country bumpkin" accent, "Y'all stop for melons?"

In *Three Smart Girls*, Koster's coaching of Deanna produced a polished, natural performance. Judy was clearly not given the same attention, as in one scene she fidgets with the fringe on her skirt, and when she sings, she plants her feet apart and almost confronts the audience, a technique that was effective on the vaudeville stage but didn't translate to more nuanced screen acting.

Both Deanna and Judy started out as ninth in their respective cast lists, and although Judy remained in her minor role, she made such a striking impression that she was mentioned in the *New York Times*: "Cute, not too pretty, but a pleasingly fetching personality who certainly knows how to sell a song." Usually this would be considered a noteworthy mention for a novice film actress. But at about the same time, Deanna became a star overnight.

Three Smart Girls made money for everybody involved with the film. The movie cost $326,000 and earned Universal $1,635,800 at the box office. Deanna was paid $20,000 and by May 1937, her weekly salary at the studio jumped from $300 to $1,500. The film was nominated for three Academy Awards: Best Picture, Best Sound and Best Original Story. The *Los Angeles Examiner* named Deanna Durbin one of the ten greatest discoveries of the year. Pasternak and Koster were given generous contracts and a proper office, and Pasternak went on to produce nine more movies starring Deanna.

The movie also established a clear "Durbin Formula" that was used in all Deanna's successful movies. This formula essentially featured hapless adults faced with problems they were unable to solve or recognize and Deanna as a wholesome girl, a plucky "Miss Fix-it" who used a combination of wit and ingenuity to save the day. In addition, each film contained a retinue of hired help, from butlers to cooks to valets, who embraced Deanna's cause and often risked their own livelihood to assist her.

Another key component to this formula was Deanna's significant singing talent. Several times during each movie, Deanna would lift her lilting soprano voice in song, mixing classical selections with popular refrains. As *Photoplay*, a popular entertainment magazine, stated, "People who were getting ready to throw her out helped her. People who hated her suddenly loved her. Handsome and rich men who had ignored her fell in love with her. The vocalizing of Deanna Durbin was the most effective *deus ex machina* the movies ever had." This formula was repeated with only minor variations for the first several years of Deanna's career and met with success every time.

Deanna had very much enjoyed working on *Three Smart Girls*. From the start, her days at Universal were significantly different than at MGM. She was out of bed by 6:00 a.m., then after a hurried commute through the city she arrived at the Universal backlot just in time for school. Three hours of classes were followed by a two-hour voice lesson and then a thirty-minute lunch break at the studio. Deanna was a minor and could only work for a few hours each day, so after lunch she was taken to makeup and wardrobe and then spent about three hours on camera. By 5:00 p.m., Ada arrived to pick her up. On the days when she wasn't filming, Deanna recorded music for her upcoming movies.

When *Three Smart Girls* was released, Deanna was in New York broadcasting on-location episodes of *Texaco Town* with Eddie Cantor. There was no movie premiere and she wasn't aware of the film's success until she returned to Hollywood and saw her picture on billboards all over town.

Three Smart Girls had been made in such a rush that Deanna had not even considered what would happen if the film became a hit. She had left for New York a popular young radio singer whose private life was largely her own. She arrived back in California just a few weeks later with legions of fans clamoring to know—and copy—everything about her. And the Universal press office, equally unprepared for this onslaught, worked tirelessly to broadcast every detail (with varying degrees of truth) about their ingénue.

Frank Morriss was one of the top newspapermen in Manitoba. Born in England, he moved to Canada as a young man, and in 1928, he began a lifelong career in journalism with the *Winnipeg Free Press*. Morriss wrote about the arts for forty-three years and was the city's best-known entertainment journalist. From the outset, Morriss followed Deanna's career with interest. After all, he was the lead arts writer for Winnipeg's largest newspaper, and Deanna was certainly the most famous actor ever to come from Winnipeg. Over the years, Morriss traveled to California to visit Deanna on her movie sets and was photographed with her twice.

When Deanna signed her contract with MGM, Morriss wrote an article titled "14-Year-Old Girl from St. Vital is Signed for Movies." He described her as having a "mature and golden voice" and wrote, "If fate is kind, Deanna will have her name up in lights."

Less than a year later, Deanna was under contract to Universal and her name *was* up in lights. And on January 10, 1937, three weeks after the movie's American release, *Three Smart Girls* opened in Winnipeg for a week's run.

The advertising campaign for the Winnipeg release of *Three Smart Girls* worked the entire city into a frenzy of excitement. Advertisements read, "Winnipeg's own singing sensation: Hock your diamonds! Pawn your pearls! Buy a seat for Three Smart Girls!" The Garrick, a 1,500-seat theater, expected to sell out the entire run.

Morriss wrote a glowing early review of the film, praising the "wonder singer on the threshold of a brilliant career." When the movie was held over for a second week, he released another article, boasting that the "Winnipeg-born singer has charmed thousands of fans." But even before the release of *Three Smart Girls*, Morriss had wanted to present a more compelling story than the ones appearing in other major newspapers. It was difficult being original when much of the information about movie stars came out of studio press offices, and the same releases were sent to dozens of papers and wire services.

But Frank Morriss was resourceful. He realized that in Winnipeg, two thousand miles from the lights of Hollywood, he was at a distinct advantage. The *Winnipeg Free Press* had access to the only direct press source for information about Deanna that was not being effectively censored by Universal. And this source, which provided detailed and truthful information throughout Deanna's career, was her grandmother, Sophia Read.

Morriss decided to create his own "scoop" for the *Winnipeg Free Press*, using Deanna's seventy-six-year-old grandmother as the central figure in his story. After all, the opening of a hit film starring a Winnipeg-born actress was good enough for a column of copy. But a feature article about Deanna's only grandmother seeing her famous granddaughter on the silver screen for the first time—well, that would cover almost an entire page.

He arranged for an advance screening of *Three Smart Girls* just before midnight on January 8, 1937. He invited Deanna's entire Winnipeg family, arranging taxis to bring cousins, uncles, and aunts to the theater. Morriss personally accompanied Sophia Read as his own special guest of honor, giving her an evening of "star treatment" on behalf of the *Winnipeg Free Press*.

Convincing Read to come to the screening had, at first, been a challenge. Read didn't usually venture out at night and she had recently been ill. But Morriss was insistent. Didn't Read want to see her own granddaughter on the big screen? Wouldn't she love to hear Deanna's voice again, the voice that was thrilling millions around the world?

Sophia Read remembered how Deanna had come to see her just a year before. Read had been sick in bed when her granddaughter arrived, but she wanted to hear the voice Ada had raved about in her letters, the voice that had made Deanna's sister Edith choose to delay her own wedding. Deanna tiptoed into her gran's bedroom and started to sing. Arditi's "Il Bacio," of course.

Sophia decided to go.

At 11:00 p.m. sharp, Deanna's family was led into the Garrick Theatre. The lights dimmed, the movie began, and Read stared, enthralled, at the large screen. When the first song ended she burst out, "It was just like Deanna. Wasn't she lovely!"

Frank Morriss had his scoop. Other papers were larger and more important, but the *Winnipeg Free Press* was the only newspaper with a firsthand account of how, according to the headlines, "Granny Sheds Tears of Joy as Deanna Sings Her First Movie."

When *Three Smart Girls* became an instant hit, Louis B. Mayer was incensed. Before the movie, there had been a chance that Universal would sell Deanna back to him. But not now. While audiences all across America were flocking to see Deanna, the only film MGM had to compete was their newest release, *Born to Dance*. And although *Born to Dance* was initially supposed to include Judy in the cast, Mayer had dropped her for another actress, Frances Langford, right before filming began.

Deanna Durbin had been catapulted into the hearts of millions of moviegoers around the world and into the sort of stardom no teen-aged girl had experienced before. She had left the frustrating world of MGM behind her and was now the toast of Universal. But there was one girl at MGM who had not been allowed to forget that she wasn't the one MGM had wanted to keep, one girl who desired fame more than anything in the world, and who saw Deanna's success as her own personal failure.

Judy sat in the dark and watched her best friend illuminate the screen in *Three Smart Girls*. She heard the people in the theater lobby calling the movie "a miracle," and Deanna "the most talented girl I've ever seen." She felt the silent censure from her mother, sitting in the seat beside her.

In Judy Garland's words, after seeing *Three Smart Girls* at the RKO Pantages Theater in Los Angeles, "I couldn't believe that it was Deanna. She was so much more beautiful and more poised than she had ever been before. Mother and I were really thrilled about it, but it made me awfully envious! I couldn't help thinking—why couldn't I get a break like that, too? Anyway, I called her up right away from the candy shop next door and told her how wonderful the picture was and congratulated her, and she was awfully thrilled that I called. Only, well, she was important and I wasn't, and I don't think she thought about it very much, but I did. I really felt awful."

That night, Judy went home, locked herself in her small bedroom, and cried. It was one thing when she and Deanna were at the same studio, both waiting and hoping for fame. It was another to find herself overlooked while newspapers proclaimed Deanna as important to Universal as Garbo was to MGM. Deanna! Compared to Greta Garbo! *The greatest actress who ever lived!*

"I've been in show business ten years," Judy sobbed. "Almost my whole life. And Deanna's starred in a picture and I'm nothing."

CHAPTER 5

Jenny Lind in Short Socks (1937)

The public had fallen head over heels in love with Deana Durbin. Didn't know who she was, hadn't been notified of her advent by any high-pressure publicity campaign, but they fell in love with her gay voice, her impudent smile, her pretty, funny little face. So are all real stars made.

—ADELA ST. JOHNS, *PHOTOPLAY*

WHEN *THREE SMART GIRLS* WAS RELEASED, DEANNA FLEW TO STARDOM on the wings of her first feature role. The public went wild. Box-office records were smashed, *Radio Guide* named her the most promising network discovery of the year, and Universal immediately gave her a seven-year contract.

In late 1936, Cesar Sturani, the general music secretary of the Metropolitan Opera, offered Deanna an audition. She turned it down, explaining that she needed more vocal training before embarking on an opera career. Met Opera officials responded by publicly announcing that Deanna would be ready for her opera debut within three years.

Universal executives commissioned a top vocal instructor for Deanna. Andrés de Seguróla was a former opera star and had taught Marion Talley, who at the age of nineteen was the youngest prima donna to make a New York operatic debut. To protect her voice, Deanna's contract guaranteed no more than three pictures a year, and de Seguróla sent the Metropolitan Opera regular reports on the young star's progress.

Until Deanna, there was no one to inherit Canadian-born silent screen star Mary Pickford's title of "America's Sweetheart." But within weeks of the release of *Three Smart Girls*, that and other honors started raining down. In March 1937, Deanna was made an honorary colonel of the Canadian Legion Los Angeles branch, a title last awarded to Mary Pickford in 1928. During the ceremony Commander Edgar Butler declared, "You'll never lead a regiment into battle, but you'll lead a nation into song and that's a greater step toward peace!"

Deanna was made a captain of the 116th California Infantry. She was named an official "Texanita," a citizen of Texas, by former state governor James Burr Allred. The Greater Miami Boys Drum Corps made her their mascot. Boy Scout Troop 42 of San Diego appointed Deanna an honorary Boy Scout, at that time the only female Boy Scout in the world. They presented her with an engraved certificate of membership and a rendition of "March Deanna," a piece they composed just for her. Fan letters began pouring in for Deanna, some from as far away as Paris. These included marriage proposals for the fourteen-year-old actress from men of all ages.

An American businessman in China attended *Three Smart Girls* at one of the Shanghai theaters. After the movie, he was invited to a reception at the home of T. V. Soong, a prominent Chinese businessman. At Soong's house, he recognized the man who had sat beside him in the cinema that afternoon. It was Chiang Kai-shek, former warlord and leader of the Republic of China.

Everyone, it seemed, was smitten with Deanna. Wherever she went, she was mobbed. Reporters vied with each other to fill their columns with superlatives describing Deanna and her voice. Adela St. Johns, a writer with *Photoplay*, described her experience seeing *Three Smart Girls*:

> *I saw the little Durbin girl's first picture in a movie house in Omaha during a blizzard that had grounded the plane on which I was flying to New York. The other passengers and I had been through some storms upstairs and we were exhausted; a little frightened, very cold, and far from home. There was a woman who was flying to her mother's deathbed; a boy on leave from Annapolis who might be chucked out for being AWOL since the Navy doesn't take weather as an excuse; there were several men in real distress about business appointments. Frankly, we were a tough audience that terrible winter day as we waited to know*

when we might take our journey, as we speculated on what kind of a
journey it might be.

Well, we decided to go to the cinema while we waited. And when
Three Smart Girls *began playing, we forgot everything. We laughed*
and cried, our troubles stood off from us and we naturally fell in love
with the little girl who had been able to help us, who had warmed us
and made us laugh.

Deanna was singlehandedly credited with the sudden popularity of teen-aged Hollywood actors. Before *Three Smart Girls*, juveniles were considered passé once they stopped being children. After the film's release, newspapers reported a "new breed of film stars ... no longer banished from the studios for their growing-up pains." These actors, many of whom had been in show business almost since infancy, included Mickey Rooney, Bonita Granville, Edith Fellows, Jackie Cooper, and, of course, Judy Garland.

In addition to appearing weekly on *Texaco Town* and shooting films at Universal, Deanna also began a commercially successful recording career. Not long after she came to Universal, Decca Records signed Deanna to a multi-album contract. This was unusual for a film star, as many old Hollywood studios did not allow their actors to sign recording contracts, inexplicably fearing that record sales would lead to diminished box-office profits. Universal encouraged Deanna's Decca offer, realizing that her recordings would serve to promote her movies. However other studios, such as Fox, forbade their roster of singing actresses—including Shirley Temple and Alice Faye—from pursuing recording careers.

Deanna also worked in the studio to record music for her movies. She would film scenes during the week and on Saturdays would add the vocals for her songs. The sessions would often be supervised by Pasternak and studio chief Charles Rogers as well as a small army of technicians. Deanna would stand before one microphone and the orchestra would be placed before another. Between them there was a "sound baffle" which helped to isolate the two recordings.

Music director Charles Previn would stand in front of the baffle, conducting both singer and orchestra. The song lyrics were written on a large blackboard hung high up in front of the microphone, so Deanna could see the words clearly without changing her position. Previn would often puff cigarettes while Deanna sang. He said he knew the smoke bothered her voice, but he wished to teach her to sing under any circumstances and to grow up without any "prima donna fussiness."

Through her appearances on *Texaco Town*, the Decca albums, and the songs in her films, Deanna became *the* source of music inspiration for aspiring singers. She made it seem like high art was within everyone's reach. Many girls who had never aspired to carry a tune soon clamored for an operatic career, and sheet music for "Il Bacio" flew off the shelves.

Deanna also became a juvenile fashion icon. A salesman named Mitchell Hamilburg became interested in Deanna Durbin when he saw *Three Smart Girls*. Hamilburg was the Los Angeles representative for the Touraine Company, a major New York sportswear house, and he had the idea for a line of trademarked "Deanna Durbin" children's dresses. When Touraine rejected the idea, Hamilburg signed a personal agreement with Deanna's father and licensed the Deanna Durbin trademark to eleven different manufacturers. From a knitted College Day ensemble to a ging-ham bathing suit to a "snappy turban," Deanna's outfits set fashion trends across the country. During the height of the Depression, sales of Deanna Durbin clothing made over a million dollars a year.

Fashion was just the beginning. There were Deanna Durbin collect-ible dolls, paper dolls, coloring books, toys, school supplies, recordings. Deanna's name was used to sell food, housewares, and appliances. In Lowell, Massachusetts, two newspaper ads appeared on the movie listings page: "Smart Girls demonstrate their smartness by going to Dana's Fruit Store" and below: "Smart Girls choose Lee's Chop Suey!"

In Winnipeg, an intrepid shopper could get a Deanna-inspired per-manent wave for $3.50 at Scientific Beauty College on Portage Avenue. Eaton's department store carried licensed sport pullovers, with an adver-tisement that read: "Deanna Durbin wore them, and now you will wear them. It's a 'smart girl' who shops early at this low price of 95 cents!" Another ad insisted, "You will thrill to the singing and charm of Deanna Durbin, as you will to General Electric Appliances." Almost overnight, a merchandising empire was built around the star.

With the release of *Three Smart Girls*, Deanna's world completely changed. Edith had married her sweetheart Clarence the year before, and Deanna moved with her parents from their modest rented bungalow into a sprawling Spanish-style hillside house with a large rooftop garden. The house had a special room for Deanna to practice singing as well as a bedroom made of glass bricks built specially by the studio to give the growing actress a daily shot of "health-giving" ultraviolet rays. Ada and James went from a hand-to-mouth existence to a life of means. Ada hired staff to run the house and James stopped the menial work he wasn't at all suited to do, instead taking time to rest and heal.

Despite her fame, Universal marketed Deanna as being "a normal, healthy fourteen-year-old child." They decided that her favorite movie heroes were Mickey Mouse and Oswald Rabbit (another popular Disney cartoon character). Her favorite books were *Little Women* and *Winnie the Pooh*. She loved spaghetti but wouldn't eat mushrooms.

Universal Pictures became Deanna's home and the crew her second family. Just like the characters she played, Deanna found friends and allies in the workers: lighting technicians, gaffers, even errand boys who were always rewarded with a smile as they hurried past. Her studio buddies called her "Durbish," a much more familiar nickname than they dared use to address most stars.

Deanna was neither a diva nor a brat. The most trouble she ever made during a shoot involved a movie camera and a piece of candy. Henry Koster told the story about one day on the set when he suddenly paused in the middle of a shoot. He had noticed that Deanna's jaw was moving in what was supposed to be a close-up shot and he immediately stopped the cameras and hurried over to her.

"You're supposed to look dreamy, Deanna," Koster said. "So how about parking the gum?"

"It isn't gum," was Deanna's answer. "It's a caramel, and I intend to finish this."

And so she did, Koster explained, while forty coworkers stood by and $2,000 worth of production costs soared merrily up.

Whether the story is true or not, it was printed in newspapers around the country, delighting Deanna's Depression-era fans, many of whom could barely afford a two-cent caramel and couldn't in their wildest dreams imagine seeing—or wasting—$2,000.

Deanna had the almost-impossible task of being both a working professional and dependable financial support to her parents, as well as being a natural, wholesome young girl. She studied second-year high school Latin, algebra, and Shakespeare. She played with her dog Tippy and Henry, a white rabbit Koster gave her as an Easter gift. Although Deanna was too young to drive, she owned a car, a sedan given to her by Charles Rogers after the success of her first picture.

Magazines described Deanna as physically perfect, from her weight (110 pounds) to her height (5'3"). Columnists wrote that Deanna's only flaw was that her skin was *too* healthy, and that with a complexion so smooth, with pores so fine and skin so taut, the greasepaint actors were required to wear on-screen just slid off her porcelain forehead and cheeks.

As a special-but-regular girl, Deanna was held up as an example to other girls her age. One article in *Photoplay* described Deanna's diet as "confined entirely to wholesome, healthful foods. She does not lunch on ice cream sodas and pie, which is the usual fare of many city girls her age. For breakfast she usually takes a glass of orange juice and perhaps some chocolate. She has a good appetite at noon and eats a hearty luncheon, although she is not allowed to eat between meals. Her favorite vegetable is carrots."

The magazine writers clearly lacked firsthand knowledge of Deanna's diet, as the actress regularly ate French fries for breakfast and often stopped at the Universal commissary for an ice cream soda between takes.

When she first arrived at Universal, Deanna attended school each morning in the tiny schoolhouse on the backlot. The school was described as "a dilapidated little frame building which could easily have used a fresh coat of paint." In truth, the unassuming building was one of the most exclusive schools in America, with a singular entry requirement that was almost impossible to obtain: the possession of a Universal Pictures contract.

The schoolhouse contained eight cream-colored desks in graduated sizes, a well-stocked library, a phonograph for music appreciation study, and a large desk for the instructor with a globe and a vase of flowers. There was also a canvas-backed director's chair with teacher Mary West's name lettered on the back. Classroom decorations consisted of a studio production schedule posted on the blackboard and files of daily movie trade papers. The walls of the class were hung with autographed photographs of the studio's child stars, signed: "To Mrs. West, a swell teacher," and "With love to my favorite teacher."

A decade earlier, vaudeville and stage children received limited schooling. If they couldn't spell very well, at least they knew the geography of the towns on their touring circuits. But by the 1930s, things were different. Juvenile actors worked under the watchful eyes of both their studio and the Los Angeles Board of Education. They studied with state-accredited teachers using the same books as regular schools and were graded under the same system. However, the stakes were a lot higher for these elite students: if they failed in their studies, they also lost their movie contracts.

California State law required children under eighteen to have three hours of schooling and to work for fewer than four hours each day. When juvenile actors were between films, they attended regular classes in the schoolhouse. If they were filming a small role, classes moved to a quiet corner of the soundstage or to an on-location supply truck. A movie child starring in a film often had tutors following her throughout the day, carrying elaborate charts to check off each brief interlude of learning. At Universal, temporary instructors came and went. But one teacher was always present: Mary West.

West was born in 1887 in Illinois. She moved to California in 1924 with her husband Hy West, a pitcher for the Cleveland Indians. West was hired by the Los Angeles Board of Education for the 1925 MGM silent film *Ben Hur*, where several children were present on set. During her early career, West advocated for laws requiring humane working conditions for child actors. She went on to become the resident teacher at Universal Pictures for over twenty years, instructing Nan Grey, Billy Birrud, Edith Fellows, Jean Dante, and even RKO's Shirley Temple when she was lent to Universal for the film *Baby Burlesk*.

West's official mandate was to "oversee the welfare and schooling of children on the set." And she took her job very seriously. Although Nan Grey (Joan in *Three Smart Girls*) had recently become engaged, she was not yet eighteen. Once, Nan was filming a scene where she was supposed to smoke a cigarette. West forced the director to stop the scene and throw the cigarette away.

From the start, Mary West took Deanna under her wing. She understood the pressures facing a child in Hollywood and she personally concerned herself with Deanna's well-being. One day, when Deanna was in the middle of filming, West interrupted the scene to take her for a walk. The crew objected, but West was firm. "Can't you see the child is nervous and needs fresh air? We'll be back in an hour or so." This was another delay that cost over $2,000; however, Mary West's word was law.

West described Deanna as "a conscientious student and very cooperative, though she occasionally needs to be reminded about neatness. She has an inquisitive mind, always on the alert for bits of information. She's not a genius, just a normal little girl, rather shy, though she has a great deal of poise—and we try to keep her her age. Her naturalness is one of her greatest assets."

In addition to her formal education, voice instruction, and movie commitments, Deanna was often scheduled for several interviews each day. The questions posed were usually the same: what was her favorite song? Her favorite food? Her favorite boy? The press office had prompted Deanna with approved responses and she followed their instructions about what to say. Most of the time.

One day, Deanna was speaking to reporters about the casting for her second film. One reporter told Deanna the story of how Judy Garland had recently sung the song "Dear Mr. Gable," at Clark Gable's birthday party. The reporter added that Gable had given Judy a charm bracelet in appreciation, that she cherished the bracelet and wore it every day, and that one of the charms contained the inscription, *"To My Best Girl Judy— from Clark Gable."*

The reporter then asked Deanna if she would like Clark Gable to be cast as her leading man. Deanna replied, with what one reporter described as "almost preternatural" self-countenance, "Why, I admire Mr. Gable's acting very much, but I believe the choice of a leading man depends on whether or not he is suitable for the role."

A stunned silence followed. At the time, Clark Gable was the toast of Hollywood and every young girl's dream. One reporter timidly asked Deanna if she fancied anyone else around town as a future husband. Deanna paused. She then said that she had thought about it and she had decided to devote herself to her music and would "probably never marry."

The next day, a feature article about Deanna appeared in the *New York Times*. Its dramatic headline proclaimed: "Deanna Durbin, Spinster."

CHAPTER 6

One Hundred Men and a Girl (1937)

Deanna Durbin has won her fame right smack in the middle of that awkward age which crippled the careers of every screen prodigy on record before her. The age which hangs today like a threatening thundercloud over the brilliant tops of Shirley Temple, Jane Withers, Freddie Bartholomew and every youngster in the business. The studios frantically make movies before the storm descends, but Deanna is singing in the rain.

—JENNIFER WRIGHT, REPORTER

IN HIS AUTOBIOGRAPHY, PRODUCER JOE PASTERNAK WROTE, "PRODUCE A flop, star in an epic that the public stays away from in droves—the problem of your next effort is simple. Comparatively, I mean. But come up with a smash hit and you're in trouble. The bigger the hit, the bigger the trouble."

Three Smart Girls had been a success beyond Universal executives' wildest dreams. One journalist claimed the film "had the singular effect that it actually made people better for having seen it." However, there were still grumblings around the studio. Charles Rogers thought *Three Smart Girls* was "just a flash in the pan." One staffer was even overheard muttering that if a million monkeys typing for a million years on a million typewriters could produce *Hamlet*, it wasn't inconceivable that even Joe Pasternak and Henry Koster could create a hit.

Pasternak and Koster realized that despite generous new contracts, their futures at Universal weren't secure and their careers would stand or fall on their next movie. This second film needed a strong cast, a well-written script, and good music. But most vital of all, it needed to be an original and compelling idea. Pasternak and Koster seriously considered several options, including *A Queen at Fourteen*, a film script based on the early years of Marie Antoinette. The final choice, however, was *One Hundred Men and a Girl*.

According to Hollywood lore, the film idea came when a fiddle player Koster knew from Vienna approached him about a job and he called up a music director friend to see if he needed another musician.

"There are hundreds of musicians in Hollywood who are out of work," replied the friend.

Koster was appalled. "Something should be done about a situation like that," he exclaimed.

"Of course," agreed the music director. "But what can I do? I have all the musicians I need."

Suddenly Koster had a brilliant idea: the next movie he made with Pasternak would be about a large group of musicians and would employ scores of professionals—including his fiddle-playing friend.

When Pasternak and Koster pitched the idea of a heartwarming Depression-themed script about a plucky young girl who saves her father's livelihood by forming a symphony orchestra of unemployed musicians, the studio immediately objected. Hollywood shouldn't tell stories about the unemployed; that was the hard reality most of America was currently living, and audiences didn't want to pay to watch their hardships reflected on-screen. And who would want to see a symphony orchestra play, anyway? Certainly not the younger moviegoing audience. Perhaps things were different in old-fashioned Europe, but in America, classical music was considered box-office murder.

During the production meeting where Koster outlined his idea for *One Hundred Men and a Girl*, an assistant producer objected, "People in America don't want to hear symphonic music."

Koster responded dryly, "That's funny, because I was at the Hollywood Bowl last night and there were eighteen thousand people listening to Beethoven's Fifth Symphony."

Charles Rogers interrupted, "If you use bandleaders Benny Goodman or Tommy Dorsey, we might consider doing the picture."

Koster shook his head. "No. I want a big symphony orchestra with a big conductor. There are too many pictures made with dance bands. I want to try to get Leopold Stokowski."

Pasternak and Koster once again convinced the studio management to trust them. They promised their second film would do as well as *Three Smart Girls* and that famed conductor Leopold Stokowski (whom neither of them had actually met) would appear in the movie. They were finally granted provisional approval, a generous budget, and a lot of doubtful looks.

One Hundred Men and a Girl was a unique movie for a variety of reasons. It starred a teen-aged girl at a time when adolescents were almost never cast in leading roles. Instead of building a few songs into the movie's plot, classical music was used dramatically as an integral part of the story. But the most unique aspect of the film, apart from what one reviewer called "the magical sound of Deanna's bell-like coloratura soaring over a full orchestra," was her co-star, Leopold Stokowski.

Stokowski had never aspired to be a movie star. Born in London in 1882, he was an English child prodigy of Polish descent who began his studies at the Royal College of Music in London at the age of thirteen, one of their youngest-ever students. By sixteen, he was working as a professional musician and had been given a coveted membership in the Royal College of Organists.

He worked at St. Mary's Church in Charing Cross and St. James Church in Piccadilly before moving to America to become choir director of St. Bartholomew's Church in New York City. Stokowski soon changed his focus to orchestral conducting and led the Cincinnati Symphony Orchestra and then the Philadelphia Symphony Orchestra. By the 1930s, Stokowski had reinvented the Philadelphia Symphony and had turned "his" orchestra into what composer Sergei Rachmaninoff called "the greatest in the world."

Stokowski's free-hand conducting technique became his trademark, and he was the first conductor to adopt the seating plan used by most orchestras today, with first and second violins together on the conductor's left and violas and cellos positioned to the right. He made his Hollywood premiere in the motion picture *The Big Broadcast of 1937*, conducting two of his Bach transcriptions. Stokowski was a classical icon, at the top of his field.

The casting of Leopold Stokowski in *One Hundred Men and a Girl* had initially been fourteen-year-old Deanna's idea. When Koster and Pasternak had discussed possibilities for a second film, they mentioned the unemployed orchestra idea to Deanna, who thought the idea was "swell" and immediately suggested Stokowski, one of her musical idols.

At first, Pasternak was nervous about approaching Stokowski. A representative at the Philadelphia Symphony Orchestra told Pasternak that conducting on-screen was one thing, but a respected music legend wouldn't want to "demean himself" by acting in a Hollywood movie. Pasternak was firmly reminded that most classical musicians considered movies as "less than dust beneath a true artist's chariot wheels."

Leopold Stokowski had a reputation for being difficult and intransigent. However, he also had an innovative spirit and was often eager to try new things. To Stokowski, an orchestra was a living, breathing entity, and the idea of presenting it in dramatic terms intrigued him. When Pasternak arranged to meet this formidable music legend to discuss the possible movie role, he found Stokowski surprisingly friendly. Pasternak hesitantly mentioned the movie and was relieved when he wasn't immediately rejected.

"What kind of music would you want in the movie?" Stokowski asked.

Nervous, Pasternak stumbled. This was the moment of truth. "I don't know, that is, I hope, or rather maybe you have . . . or should have . . . seen a picture I did called *Three Smart Girls?*"

"Oh!" Stokowski exclaimed. "*Three Smart Girls!* Did *you* do that? I loved it. Those charming, sweet girls."

Pasternak nodded. "And this movie, it will be that kind of story."

Stokowski walked across the room and looked Pasternak straight in the eyes, as if truly seeing him for the first time. "Why do you want to make a picture with such music at all?"

"A personal reason," Pasternak confessed. He explained that back in Europe, his friends thought of America as a land of installment plans, canned soup, and used car lots. Pasternak wanted to prove to European filmmakers that American people also appreciated quality of the highest sort.

At that, Stokowski agreed. "I'll do it."

Joe Pasternak was very aware of Stokowski's legendary status in the world of classical music. He was careful to treat the conductor with respect, to call him "Maestro," and to approach him with a certain amount of timidity. Deanna, however, viewed Stokowski as an equal, a fellow artist. When Deanna first met Leopold Stokowski, a man who was feared and respected by musicians twice her age, she merely smiled and greeted him with a cheerful, "Hello!"

Pasternak recalled a scene he rehearsed featuring Deanna and Stokowski:

> *You can imagine my consternation at rehearsal one day when I heard Deanna break off her singing sharply and announce to the great conductor in firm, unshaken tones: "You're not doing it right, Mister Stokowski!"*
>
> *The conductor waved his hands for the orchestra to stop. A terrible hush descended on the players, as well as everybody else on the recording stage. I moved up discreetly to be handy when the full weight of the maestro's anger fell on the child.*
>
> *Stokowski descended from the platform and walked toward Deanna. "How am I not doing it right?" He demanded coolly.*
>
> *"It's just not right," Deanna said.*
>
> *"Oh, it isn't, is it?" Stokowski asked, lifting his brows.*
>
> *"No."*
>
> *Just "No." Not sir, not maestro. Just "no." I had dizzying visions of the whole picture falling apart, of Stokowski walking off, refusing to have anything to do with a fourteen-year-old child who dared to tell him about music.*
>
> *But Stokowski smiled suddenly. "Tell me how you would like it done, my dear," he said simply.*
>
> *He was big enough so he didn't have to fear losing face by accommodating himself to Deanna and wasn't afraid to listen to a young girl. Deanna already knew what was musically right for her and intended on doing it that way even if it meant taking on the conductor of the Philadelphia Orchestra.*

Years later, Henry Koster called Stokowski "the world's worst actor, but as good a conductor as he was a showman." He recalled a day when Stokowski was scheduled for a close-up shot conducting the orchestra. Koster checked lights and sound and prepared the scene with the stand-in. When the camera was ready he said, "Call Mr. Stokowski."

Koster's assistant Frank Shaw sheepishly responded, "Mr. Stokowski can't come. He's having his shoes shined."

The director stared at Shaw. "Tell Mr. Stokowski his shoes are not in the picture. It's from the waistline up, arms and head only."

Stokowski still refused. Koster, aware of the mounting costs and the impatient crew, went to Stokowski's dressing room. He pleaded, "Please come. You don't need your shoes polished. It's only a close-up. For all I care you can wear slippers." Stokowski gravely responded, "I want to be prepared for anything. Suppose you pan the camera down on my feet while I'm conducting?"

"I won't," Koster assured.

"But suppose you did?"

Several minutes later, Stokowski briskly walked back to the set and filmed the close-up. With his polished shoes shining off camera.

In another scene, Stokowski was directed to walk down a corridor after conducting a concert. He was followed by a rolling camera on a dolly.

Partway down the hall, Stokowski stopped at a door that said "Orchestra." There was nothing behind that door but the studio wall. He opened the door, leaned inside, and called, "Gentlemen, you were superb tonight and I want to thank you." Then he closed the door and went on.

Koster called, "Cut!" He explained, "Mr. Stokowski, there is nobody there and there is no actual room there. The rolling camera will film the studio wall if you open that door. All you have to do is walk straight through the hall, past the door to your office."

Stokowski responded, in all seriousness, "I never finish a concert and go home before I have thanked my musicians."

There was no arguing with Stokowski. The next day they shot the scene again with an "Orchestra" room built behind the door.

Koster told another story about visiting Stokowski's dressing room to discuss an upcoming scene. Koster knocked at the closed dressing room door and the conductor called out, "Come in."

When Koster entered the room he found Stokowski lying completely naked, a masseur rubbing his glistening body with alcohol. Koster turned away, embarrassed.

Stokowski repeated, "Come in, come in. I have nothing to be ashamed of."

As Koster later told his friends, "So, I saw the naked Stokowski there."

One Hundred Men and a Girl was based on an original story by German actor and screenwriter Hans Kräly. The movie was originally titled "120 Men and a Girl," but Stokowski's $80,000 fee didn't leave enough money in the budget to hire twenty more extras.

In the movie, Deanna plays a girl named Patsy. Her father, John Cardwell (Adolphe Menjou), is an unemployed trombone player. Cardwell tries to arrange an audition with Leopold Stokowski (who plays himself), but is thrown out of the theater by the guard.

Patsy, seeing that her father is desperately in need of work, convinces a wealthy patron to sponsor an orchestra featuring Cardwell and ninety-nine other unemployed musicians. She then sets out to recruit Stokowski as the orchestra's conductor. After several failed efforts, Patsy and the hundred-man orchestra sneak into Stokowski's mansion. The orchestra begins to play Liszt's Hungarian Rhapsody No. 2 and Stokowski, from the balcony in his foyer, starts to conduct the piece. Afterward he agrees to lead Patsy's orchestra in a gala concert that ends with Patsy breaking into impromptu song, the "Brindisi" from Verdi's *La Traviata*.

The music for *One Hundred Men and Girl* was recorded in multi-channel stereophonic "stereo" sound, the first time this 1930s cutting-edge technology was ever used to record music in a film. Most theaters could not play stereophonic sound, so the film was released in monaural. The first movie actually released in stereo was Stokowski's next screen hit, Disney's *Fantasia*.

The orchestra members in the film were Los Angeles–based musicians miming to a prerecorded soundtrack played by Stokowski's own orchestra. Deanna's stand-in for the movie was ballerina Jane Barlow. Some of the sets used in the movie, such as the opera boxes in the concert hall, were left over from Universal's 1925 production of *The Phantom of the Opera*. Deanna recalled, "I had to run as hard as I could to get from one opera box to the next. The set had a tin roof and the weather was broiling. It was a hundred and twenty-five degrees under that roof one afternoon. That night, I was in bed by six."

One Hundred Men and a Girl was released on September 5, 1937, and it took the world by storm, receiving dozens of glowing reviews. The *New York Times* stated that the movie "reveals the cinema at its sunny-sided best ... a film which has already covered itself and its makers with distinction." It called Deanna "a joyous sprite with an astonishingly mature soprano, whose abiding faith in mankind makes the impossible seem only moderately improbable."

The review pointed out that just down the street from New York's Roxy Theater where the film was playing, pickets from actual unemployed musicians were marching in front of theaters to protest their use of "canned music." *One Hundred Men* not only "shed a commiserate tear over these unemployed artists, but it suggested a creative—if fanciful—solution to their plight."

In Winnipeg, Frank Morriss published an article with the headline, "Winnipeg's Wonder Child: Deanna Sings Her Way to New Heights." It stated, "As clear as the air on a crisp winter night in the city that gave her birth, the crystal voice of Deanna Durbin rang out to let listeners know that Deanna had done it again ... a golden voice in the slim throat of a little girl. The dancing heart of a child in everything she does."

One Hundred Men and a Girl was immensely popular in Russia. According to Koster, "I won a prize in Moscow for it. They liked it, maybe less for the quality of the picture than for the fact that it was about unemployed people. The Russians like to show that Americans are unemployed."

In Australia, Deanna's new film was equally a hit. The *Adelaide Advertiser* described the movie as "that strange mixture of music and pure comedy, with the inevitable dash of pathos, which produces an astounding bestseller." In Southern Australia there was a rigid rule that no film, however successful, could remain in a cinema for more than a week. *One Hundred Men and a Girl* was allowed to run indefinitely.

The budget for the movie was $733,000, almost double the cost of *Three Smart Girls*, and it made over $2,270,200 at the box office. The movie received an Academy Award for Best Music Score, which was composed by Charles Previn. It also received nominations for Best Picture as well as Best Film Editing, Best Sound Mixing, and Best Original Story.

The same month *One Hundred Men and Girl* was released, Judy Garland appeared in *Broadway Melody of 1938*, a star-studded movie extravaganza featuring Robert Taylor, Eleanor Powell, Sophie Tucker, and Binnie Barnes. Although Judy didn't have a leading role, was only on-screen briefly, and was seventh in the cast list, many critics felt she stole the show. Sophie Tucker even called Judy "the next Red Hot Mama," the highest-possible compliment from the performing legend. However to Judy, her success in a small movie role was nothing compared to the adulation being heaped on Deanna. And although she worked regularly for the next decade, Judy's dream of stardom was still a long way off.

The opening of *One Hundred Men and a Girl* was Deanna's first Hollywood premiere. There hadn't been a lot of fuss when *Three Smart Girls* was released, but this was different. This time Deanna was a star, the movie was eagerly anticipated by both moviegoers and the press, and it was Deanna's big night. On the evening of the screening, Deanna was too excited to eat dinner. She carefully brushed her fluffy curls and put on her first long party dress: aquamarine taffeta with pink and red roses pinned to the shoulder.

The premiere took place at the Pantages Theater in Los Angeles, with a full house and a premium ticket price of $2. When Deanna arrived at the theater, she calmly observed the reporters who lined the path leading into the building. She declared she wasn't nervous—much—but her eyes sparkled as she stepped from her car into the calm but eager throng that crowded the street for over a block and jammed the lobby of the theater.

When Deanna first saw the crowds, so thick that a team of police officers was dispatched to clear a path, she almost couldn't believe that all this fuss was for her, that it was her picture everyone was lining up to see. Deanna was ushered from the car as flashbulbs went off and dozens of photographers cried out, "Look this way, Deanna!" She tried to shine for them, smiling as she had been taught by Pasternak and Koster.

With her parents and Edith by her side, Deanna took her seat in the fifteenth row of the theater. The picture began and after her first song the audience burst into enthusiastic applause. Deanna applauded, too, as her mother reached over and squeezed her hand.

When the film was over, Deanna couldn't leave the theater. The entrance was blocked by hundreds of people, no longer calm. They cheered as she edged past, calls of "Bravo! Bravo!" echoing through the lobby.

Deanna thought back to when they were shooting the film, how one day Henry Koster had taken her up to the projection room to watch the daily rushes. "How do you like yourself?" he asked, as the screen flickered to life.

Deanna hadn't known what to say. Because although the figure on the projection room screen had looked like her and sounded like her, *she* still felt like Edna Mae—a regular girl—and that precocious, plucky young actress in the feathered beanie hat was someone else entirely.

It was the same at this movie premiere. "I can hardly believe this is happening to me," she mused to one of the reporters. "It seems more like something I have read somewhere than something happening to me. I couldn't believe the girl on the screen was me. It seemed like someone I knew, telling me a story I already knew by heart. Even the voice didn't sound like my own. Menjou was Menjou, Stokowski was Stokowski. But the girl who sang wasn't me, it seemed."

Even if Deanna didn't feel a personal connection to that young starlet shining on the screen, everyone else in the theater certainly did. The world was in love with her. As Pat Galaway, the reviewer for the *New Statesman* wrote, "Useless to pretend that I am tough enough to resist the blandishments of Miss Deanna Durbin. The candid eyes, the parted lips, the electric energy, the astonishing voice; surely a critic may be pardoned for wobbling a little on his professional base."

Following the release of *One Hundred Men and a Girl*, Deanna became the darling of Hollywood. She seemed to be the luckiest girl in the world. Perhaps she was. But the night of the movie premiere, as thousands of fans cheered and yelled her name, Deanna remembered a day in Philadelphia several months before. She had been working with Stokowski, recording music for the film. In her hotel room, after a day of work, Deanna declared that she wanted an ice cream soda.

Koster offered to send out for the drink, but Deanna explained that if the soda were delivered the fizz would go out. Besides, she wanted to sit at the drugstore counter and drink her fizzy soda, like any other kid.

Deanna looked so wistful that Koster quickly took her down for the soda. But in the drugstore, she was immediately recognized as *Smart Girl* Penny Craig. People crowded around Deanna, talking and squealing, asking her to sign books, ribbons, napkins, scraps of paper. She gave a dozen fans an afternoon to remember, but she didn't even get to taste her ice cream before it melted.

And now, on this fairytale night, Deanna thought back to that melted ice cream soda. She was glad the movie was so well received; that her parents were happy and that Stokowski, Pasternak, and Koster were beaming. But she also wondered if she would ever be able to just sit in a drugstore with a fizzy soda and a cold scoop of ice cream, like a regular girl.

CHAPTER 7

Durbin-Daffy (1937)

Out of 45,000 extras registered with the Central Casting Bureau in Hollywood since 1926, only five have achieved stardom. The sensation of 1937 has been fourteen-year-old Deanna Durbin, whose clear soprano and provocative personality skyrocketed her to stardom with her first screen effort.

—ANGUS MCSTAY, *MACLEANS*

IN 1937, A WRITER FOR THE AMERICAN PAPER *LIBERTY* DECLARED, "THE whole Dominion of Canada is Durbin-Daffy." And indeed, it seemed that it was.

After a year filled with film shoots, radio broadcasts, and recording sessions, the closest Deanna got to a break was the one-day trip to her hometown in April 1937. Deanna's brief stay was received with as much excitement as visiting royalty. The *Winnipeg Tribune* excitedly announced her arrival: "Idol of millions, 14-year-old Winnipeg singer who has gained worldwide fame with her golden voice, returns to her hometown today."

Shortly before visiting Winnipeg—a banner day that would go down in the annals of the city's history—Deanna had recorded an album in Philadelphia under the baton of her *One Hundred Men and a Girl* co-star, Leopold Stokowski. The press office at Universal Pictures had initially announced that Deanna was planning a ten-day stay in Winnipeg with a possible concert appearance and had added, "Deanna's visit in Winnipeg will probably do her more good than a year's vacation anywhere else." In the end, Deanna spent just one day in the city of her birth, on the way, somewhat indirectly, back to California after completing the recording. But that day made a lasting impression upon a city that had already claimed Deanna as its own.

After arriving at the crowded Canadian Pacific Railway station, Deanna, her mother, and agent Jack Sherrill were taken to the Royal Alexandra Hotel. Ada and Sherrill took time to rest while Deanna breakfasted with the mayor and other dignitaries, signing autograph albums and photographs for their families.

When the brief meal ended, Deanna, Ada, and Sherrill visited the office of Mayor Frederick Warriner, where the mayor presented them with small silver Winnipeg coats-of-arms depicting a buffalo, a train, and three sheaves of wheat. He then escorted Deanna to CJRC, the local radio station. Mayor Warriner introduced her on the air, saying that he was happy and proud to welcome Deanna back to Winnipeg. Deanna had also prepared a speech, "My dear friends of Winnipeg, I'm sorry time makes it impossible to greet each and every one of you personally, but I do want to take this opportunity to express to you my sincere thanks for the loyal support you have given me in my work in pictures and on the radio. It is quite a thrill to return to the city of my birth, Winnipeg. Again, may I thank you from the bottom of my heart for your kindness and generous reception."

Next came a brief appearance at the Shriner's Circus between the boxing teddy bears and the elephant clowns. Then, finally, Deanna was free to see her grandmother. According to the *Winnipeg Free Press*, "The bright spotlight of public acclaim that rested on the slim, fourteen-year-old shoulders of Deanna Durbin for many a month faded to the warm glow of the family fireside Friday evening, as her uncles, her aunts and her cousins gathered at a St. Vital cottage and staged an affectionate private reunion."

It wasn't entirely private. Crowds gathered on the street outside Sophia Read's cottage, and this one private family evening was interrupted twice. The first visit was by members of the St. Vital Board of Trade who presented a bouquet of roses to the star, and then reporter Frank Morriss came by with a press photographer, staying only long enough to greet Deanna and take an exclusive photograph of Sophia, Deanna, and Ada.

That night, the *Winnipeg Free Press* reported, "A bed in one of the Royal Alexandra Hotel's largest suites went unslept-in while Deanna said her prayers beside Granny's bedside." The hotel suite had been prepared for Deanna, but she was tired of the crowds and the fuss and didn't want to sign any more autographs. And Sophia was thrilled to see her. So Deanna's manager slept at the Royal Alexandra without his famous client, while Deanna remained ensconced inside Sophia's small house with her family.

Deanna departed Winnipeg early the next morning. She wore the same spray of orchids she'd put on for her arrival, still fresh after the short visit. Once again, Deanna smiled at her fans and signed the autograph books pushed in her direction. She waved to the cheering crowd as the train pulled away from the station and headed for the open prairie. Then Deanna finally lay back in the Pullman car for the only true rest of her "vacation."

After Deanna's departure, Frank Morriss wrote several articles about her visit. In Morriss's characteristic style, one article featured Sophia Read and the other focused on Jack Sherrill. According to Morriss, "Sherrill, an enterprising Hollywood actors' agent, has put his hand into the mass of unknown talent that waits at the doors of studios and has pulled out a plum. Deanna has the bloom of youth and is full of the sap of talent and charm. Oh, what a lucky boy is Mr. Sherrill!"

The article discussed how Sherrill had made it clear to reporters that neither Deanna nor her mother was allowed to speak to the press without his express permission. Morriss had been planning an article about Sophia Read's reunion with her granddaughter, with a personal interview from Deanna. Sherrill refused. He informed Morriss that it was customary for journalists to talk to a star's agent, who would provide any relevant information and then give the article final approval before publication.

Jack Sherrill may have been a figure of authority in the movie world, but this was Winnipeg. Frank Morriss was a respected community leader and had no intention of kowtowing to an imperious agent. When Sherrill learned that Morriss had visited Sophia's cottage, he was incensed. He made it clear to Morriss that the penalty for printing the picture of Deanna with her grandmother would be "dynamite."

When Frank Morriss refused to back down, Sherrill called the mayor of Winnipeg to complain. Mayor Warriner assured Sherrill that he would handle the situation, but in the end, Sherrill's bluster was ignored and the exclusive article and photograph appeared the next morning in the *Winnipeg Free Press*.

By the end of 1937, the income from Deanna's first two movies accounted for 17 percent of Universal's annual revenue. Executives credited her for saving their studio and publicly demonstrated their gratitude to their young star.

One gesture of appreciation was an "elegant studio dressing room" built for Deanna on the studio grounds. This was not a mere trailer, like the type typically given to bigger stars, but a Colonial-style bungalow the size of a small family home. Located on a quiet corner of the lot directly beside the false front of a brick mansion, it was Universal's second-ever actor bungalow and the first actually occupied by a star.[1] The house cost $3,000 to build and contained a living room in "Eleanor Blue" with all-white furniture and a piano, boudoir, dinette, kitchen, and bath. The entrance was surrounded by a garden filled with nasturtiums, phlox, and rambler roses, and the yard was circled by a white, waist-high picket fence. Deanna stopped attending classes with the other actor children and instead received schooling and voice lessons in her bungalow.

Both Deanna and her "studio dressing room" were featured in several articles, including a Betty Crocker cooking column: "In the kitchen of her gay little bungalow on the Universal lot, Deanna Durbin likes to whip up quick meals for callers."

Although Deanna was kept so busy that her dainty kitchen remained largely unused, she had decided tastes about food. Despite what some articles called her "tendency to plumpness," Universal did not attempt to starve Deanna or put her on dangerous medications. This is in direct contrast to Judy Garland, who was not only prescribed pills to control her weight, but she also was forced by Mayer to eat only chicken soup at the MGM commissary, a meal that Judy later bitterly referred to as the "prisoner's menu." She was even discouraged from sitting with the other teenagers, in case one of them slipped her some of their more hearty meals.

The grateful management at Universal didn't ever consider interfering with Deanna's food. From the start she decided what she would eat, and that was that. Meals varied, but for breakfast each morning Deanna insisted on French-fried potatoes liberally doused with ketchup.

Joe Pasternak was aghast when he learned of this. "If she'd insisted on having Algerian strawberries flown in by chartered airplane, it would have been something I could appreciate. But French fries and ketchup! It was—well, it was un-starlike. I absolutely put my foot down. Besides, I insisted, it was bad for her digestion and her figure. Deanna was equally firm: 'No French fries and ketchup for breakfast, no work.' There was a movie to finish, and so Deanna got her fries. On schedule, every morning."

Deanna's fame was never more apparent than the night in October 1937 when she, along with hundreds of other Hollywood luminaries, attended the party Eddie Cantor threw to celebrate his twenty-fifth anniversary in show business. Newspapers reported, "Six hundred celebrities arrived at the Ambassador Hotel arrayed in their whitest shirts, longest broadcloth tails and barest backs." There was vintage 1928 champagne, music, dancing, and speeches.

Eddie Cantor was the most well-loved vaudeville performer in America, and this special night was devoted to honoring his achievements. However, instead of focusing on Cantor, the Associated Press headline, printed in newspapers across the nation, proclaimed: "Deanna Drinks Nothing but Water at Cantor's Anniversary Party!"

Meanwhile, the Durbin Empire was expanding. Two mystery adventure books written by Kathryn Heisenfelt were published with Deanna as the plucky (and musical) heroine. She was featured in ads for everything from Simplicity sewing patters to Wrigley's Doublemint gum. Lux soap ran a magazine ad containing a quote from Deanna's mother Ada: "Deanna is as finicky about her clothes as I am myself; with Lux it's easy to keep dresses always spick and span!"

And then there were the letters. As one Hollywood reporter declared, "Deanna Durbin seems to get the most remarkable fan mail. And nobody quite knows why."

Kathleen Ehlen was in charge of fan mail at Universal, and each week, her office received thousands of letters for Deanna. There were the regular letters, usually something similar to: "Dear Deanna, I saw your last picture and thought you were swell. Please send me your photograph." And there were letters asking for money: "Please send me $500 at once so I can pay my bills and won't need to mortgage the old homestead."

Original poetry dedicated to Deanna poured into the studio. One verse, from Robert Robertson of Belmont, Massachusetts, read:

Last night as I lay dreaming, / I heard a voice so grand;
A voice with haunting reverence, / A voice from another land.
Through the air came "Ave Maria," / In accents soft and low;
I thought an angel was calling, / From the past of long ago.
But now my dream is over, / My eyes still wet with tears;
For standing there beside me, / The Deanna of my dreams.

There were also gifts. Some of the more unusual tributes included a fifty-pound, five-pointed star from an Appalachian miner. It was fashioned from a gilded wooden frame filled with concrete and set with ore samples grouped around a picture of Deanna. A Hungarian boy sent her a calfskin canteen decorated with handcrafted beadwork. An ancient lace wedding gown arrived at the studio, sent by a woman who, in Confederacy days, had been a noted belle. Her letter authorized Deanna to copy the gown for her own wedding dress someday and then to return the original.

A moviegoer in Manila sent a tiny skull, a trophy from an Igorot headhunter collected over a century before. An admirer in Los Angeles mailed her a "Cecile Brunner Sweetheart" rose every day for almost five months. It arrived in an envelope each morning, crushed and wilted amid the piles of mail. Deanna also received hundreds of pictures of herself: drawn, painted, and etched. One likeness was created from thousands of typewriter symbols. Another came from a man who had lost his hand and had drawn a large pencil portrait of Deanna using only his left foot. One fan sent a picture of a fully rigged ship, complete with waves and blended sky tones. But instead of being sketched with lines, the ship was drawn with almost microscopic printing of the name "Deanna Durbin" repeated over twelve thousand times.

Deanna was overwhelmed at the largesse of her fans. "At first I was stunned. Now I'm trying hard to take such things for granted. They're so flattering that they almost frighten me." But Deanna's fans didn't just stop at letters and gifts. Mildred Parsons, a young Boston girl, managed to track down Deanna by telephone. She talked with Deanna for twenty-five minutes—a $55 call—urging her to come to Boston as her houseguest.

Mildred Price, director of the China Aid Council, described how during a recent visit to China she was taken to a "typical" Buddhist home: the furniture was typical and the living room contained a coffin with the body of the head of the household who had died two years earlier. This, too, was typical. Then Mildred was taken into the bedroom, and there, under an old piece of glass on the dresser, she found—typically enough— a photo of Deanna Durbin.

Deanna was compared to the great opera divas of the world: Adelina Patti who sang her first concert at eleven and Lucrezia Bori who sang publicly at fourteen. Vocal specialists examined her throat and claimed that she possessed a vocal rarity: a woman's voice in a child's body. During an interview, Deanna's personal physician assured her fans, "Miss Durbin's blood pressure and nerves are absolutely normal. Her temperament is directed into its proper course and finds its full expression in her acting and singing ... she is no more nervous than the average normal child. She becomes frightened at frightening events; she cries when she is sad and laughs with abandon when she is happy. We find no evidence of a fidgety, nervous, spoiled child."

Back at MGM, Louis B. Mayer had decided to push ahead with what he called the "Garland Agenda." He was still livid that his staff had dropped Deanna, who had become the toast of America and made millions for a rival studio. He was determined that Judy Garland would be equally as big. Mayer started announcing to his investors, to studio executives, to anyone who would listen, "I'll make the fat kid an even bigger star than Deanna." When guests visited the studio, Mayer would bring them within earshot of Judy and proudly point her out. "Do you see that girl?

She used to be a hunchback, but now she's the greatest musical comedy star on our lot."

Deanna Durbin was the toast of Universal and Judy was starting to do well, too. But the MGM process for making a star differed considerably from Universal. MGM was a much bigger studio and could afford to take its slow and sure way with potential talent. Universal, fighting for its existence, had to quickly cash in on any glamorous finds. So the bright star of Deanna Durbin rose higher and higher while Judy languished, getting only promises from the MGM office that they "had big things in mind for her."

Judy later recalled, "The MGM bosses were just dreadful. They had a theory that they were all-powerful and they ruled by fear. What better way to make a young person behave than to scare the hell out of them every day?"

It was common practice at the time for movie studios to name foods in their commissaries after their stars. For example, at MGM there was the Joan Crawford casserole. At Universal, a fresh, crisp Deanna Durbin salad graced the commissary menu. The Judy Garland was a common sandwich.

In December of 1937, Deanna Durbin celebrated her fifteenth birthday, which was fêted by newspapers worldwide. According to her actual birth date she was sixteen, a young woman; however, to the world and to her studio, Deanna remained a child with the modest and sensible tastes of a girl. When Ada was asked by a reporter if she planned to give Deanna a mink, the customary accessory for a movie star, Ada responded, "Deanna likes little things, lots of packages to open. She asked for perfume and books and phonograph records. Her wristwatch has stopped running and we should get her a new one, I suppose."

Keeping Deanna looking like a child became more difficult. Her makeup artist had to minimize her full lips to suit the youthful roles she played. Universal's head costume designer, Vera West, dressed Deanna in high-waisted frocks and full skirts, using bolero jackets to cover her growing bust.

By her "fifteenth" birthday, Deanna was earning $3,000 weekly at Universal with a $30,000 annual bonus, as well as $2,000 a week on Eddie

Cantor's radio program. A party was thrown for her by Joe Pasternak and director Norman Taurog on a "Swiss private school" soundstage used in her third movie. Universal gifted Deanna another car, a 1938 DeSoto Convertible Sport.

Despite being a movie star and one of the richest fifteen-year-olds in America, Deanna lived a life of strict rules. She stayed home most evenings with her parents and was in bed by ten-thirty. No boyfriends were allowed. Her wardrobe was overseen by both her mother and staff at the studio.

When interviewed about her future plans Deanna responded, "I started voice training in earnest four years ago. I would like to sing opera, but I haven't time—I'm under contract to Universal for the next seven years. It doesn't give me time for anything. I'd like to go to college, but I won't be able to sandwich it in. I'd like to go to Europe—but, again, I haven't time. I work eight hours every day for pictures, schooling, posing for pictures and singing lessons. Doesn't leave me much time for fun, but I love it."

Although Deanna assured the reporters that she enjoyed her work, she couldn't help sounding wistful. She was starting to realize that training for an opera career would take a lot more time than she currently had. She couldn't go to college, and an overseas vacation wouldn't fit in with her shooting and promotion schedule. Although the money Deanna earned represented a certain freedom to her and her family, it also bound her to constantly play a public role.

Right after she turned fifteen Deanna's family moved again, this time to a fourteen-room house in the Los Feliz district of Los Angeles, east of Hollywood. The property was French Norman style, with a swimming pool in the terraced backyard and gardens that ambled up the hillside toward the Griffith Park Planetarium.

The house had a large living room that contained an organ and a combination radio-phonograph, all Christmas gifts from the studio. Deanna's bedroom was "a symphony in blue." It had blue draperies, blue bedspreads, and blue furnishings. The room contained walnut twin beds, a large glass-topped perfume table, and a tan rug. Adjacent to her bedroom was a small study for Deanna to practice piano and do her voice exercises.

Everyone, it seemed, loved Deanna Durbin, with one notable exception: actor and notorious child hater W. C. Fields, who was a close neighbor. Each day when Deanna vocalized, Fields would throw open his window and shout insults, such as, "Go buy yourself an electric chair!" Sometimes he imitated her singing in his own harsh voice, trying to drown her out. Fields once wrote Deanna a letter, claiming she sounded like "a squeak through a plugged nostril." A friend claimed that Fields even shot at Deanna's conservatory while she practiced her scales.

One day, W. C. Fields discovered a dying bush and a dead mockingbird on his property. He stormed around raving, "Her voice is destroying all flora and fauna in the community. Call the Audubon Society. Call some botany club. If there isn't any, organize one. The woman is a dangerous menace!"

CHAPTER 8

Prints at the Chinese Theatre (1938)

Less than two years ago Deanna was an unknown schoolgirl, not even dreaming of a screen career. Her first picture established her as a child of promise; her second confirmed that promise. Her third, Mad about Music, *proves beyond a shadow of a doubt that little Miss Durbin is a genuine star, firmly established in her niche of screen fame.*

—New York Commercial Advisor

Sid Grauman was an American showman. Son of a failed Klondike prospector, as a boy Grauman supported his family by selling newspapers in the Yukon during the Gold Rush. From childhood, he was obsessed with movies. When he grew up, Grauman partnered with his father to open vaudeville theaters along the West Coast, venues that included the Million Dollar Theatre, the Egyptian Theatre, and one of Hollywood's greatest landmarks, the Chinese Theatre.

Grauman spent $2 million to create what *Motion Picture News* called, "a theatrical palace." He brought in artisans from China to create "authentic" fittings and sculptures, and secured permission from the US government to import temple bells, pagodas, stone Heaven Dogs, and other artifacts from China. He also started the tradition of inviting Hollywood's greatest celebrities to create a permanent record of their stardom by leaving their signatures, handprints, and footprints in cement.

Two versions of how the "footprint" tradition began have been published, one with theater co-owner Mary Pickford and the other featuring Norma Talmadge. But whichever woman was actually involved, an actress

75

accidentally stepped into wet cement and left her prints outside the theater, Grauman was delighted with the result, and an iconic tradition was born.

Tourists from all over the world traveled to Hollywood to see these famous impressions. One woman claimed that she spotted the ghost of Marie Dressler searching for her cement block, which had been covered by the theater's new box office. Another tourist said she could feel the ghost of young Jean Harlow, who had recently died, staring wistfully at her prints—the silent record of her brief triumph on earth. One reporter observed people wandering among the footprints after dark at two in the morning and before sunrise at seven. He noted how the prints, which felt like living things, were almost never alone.

The cement blocks that immortalized the stars' impressions cost a hundred dollars a square and were mixed with a secret formula. Grauman himself chose the stars who ranked posterity in his forecourt. Although Judy Garland was not chosen until October 1939, in early 1938 Deanna was asked to record her prints. The ceremony took place at the premiere of Deanna's third film, *Mad about Music*, on February 7, 1938. In addition to the movie attendees, almost two thousand people crowded in front of the Chinese Theatre to witness the event.

Cheered on by her fans, Deanna stood at the edge of a wet cement block. She was dressed in a wool coat with a Peter-Pan collar and fur sleeves and a matching woolen hat with a half-upturned brim. She was flanked by Sid Grauman and Joe Pasternak. Around Deanna shone the bright glare of studio arc lights, and the cool February air was punctuated by clicking shutters from press photographers.

Sid Grauman began the ceremony with a speech: "I predict that by the time she is twenty-one, Deanna Durbin will be recognized as the greatest singing star the screen has known. Seldom does the theater discover such a personality. Words fail to describe my enthusiasm for her talent and ability. Millions of theater patrons have approved her right to be represented in this Hollywood Hall of Fame!"

The crowd shouted its agreement as Deanna signed her name in the wet cement block. Above the signature she wrote, "To Sid, with all my love." She then carefully left prints of her hands and her high-heeled footprints, pushing a penny into the reddish cement as a memento of "Penny" Craig, her first starring role.[1]

High above, on a platform constructed for the occasion, a slight, middle-aged man stood looking down on the scene. A cameraman standing nearby glanced at the man several times. Finally he leaned in and said, "Some kid, eh?"

Just then, Deanna raised her eyes and blew a kiss to the platform above. The cameraman looked startled. "Hey, was that for me or for you?" he asked.

"I think," the man responded quietly, "it was for me. You see, I'm her father."

The cameraman's mouth fell open. "Well, I'm darned. That's the first movie star I ever knew that had a father around!"

Several new films were being planned for Deanna, and Hollywood gossip columnist Louella Parsons, who had already made a special pet of Deanna and who described her as having "the screen presence of a Garbo, the glorious voice of a Grace Moore," got the scoop on them all. First, Louella announced that Pasternak had taken the movie option on *Unfinished Symphony*, an original story by Nicholas Laszio. Deanna would play a young girl on New York's East Side being raised by three good friends: a policeman, a priest, and a cantor. She would sing Catholic hymns and Jewish chants and the movie would end with a love story. In the end, *Unfinished Symphony* was never made.

Another "scoop" that Parsons announced was Pasternak's "inspirational" idea of starring Deanna in a film about Swedish soprano Jenny Lind. Parsons reported that Pasternak had bought a script, a Hans Rameau original story. In the end, this movie wasn't made either.

However, soon Louella Parsons had the biggest news of all: after years in Hollywood building theaters and promoting stars, Sid Grauman himself was going to make a movie appearance in *Mad about Music*. As Parsons wrote, "I thought when I was persuaded to turn actress in *Hollywood Hotel* (1937) the millennium had come. But it's just as surprising that Sid Grauman, who has seen the parade of screen favorites come and go, should be in a Hollywood motion picture."

Mad about Music, originally titled *Father Meet Mother*, was produced by Joe Pasternak and directed by Norman Taurog. By this time, the Universal executives no longer questioned Pasternak's decisions, and he was given free rein with casting and scripts. The movie was appointed a generous marketing budget and a nationwide campaign was launched to promote the film. However, although the studio granted almost all of Pasternak's requests, they refused to give him Henry Koster.

Koster, the quiet German immigrant who had, without a thought, punched a Nazi back in Europe, had once again shown his resilience and drive by building a name for himself in Hollywood. In just two years, he had gone from being Joe Pasternak's shadow, unable to speak more than a few words in English, to being a respected director and even a starmaker. He had discovered Abbott and Costello working in a nightclub in New York and convinced Universal to hire the comedy duo. He also met and fell in love with actress Peggy Moran, and through her he entered the Hollywood social scene.

Just before *Mad about Music* was scheduled to begin filming, executives at Universal asked Koster to direct *The Rage of Paris*. The film was a comedy, written by Bruce Manning and an old friend of Koster's from the Universal Berlin studios, Felix Jackson. This was a great opportunity for Koster and he immediately signed on for the project.

Norman Taurog, the director assigned to *Mad about Music*, was accomplished and respected throughout Hollywood. He had even won an Academy Award in 1931 for his work on the movie *Skippy*. In a way, this pairing of Taurog with Pasternak was a vote of confidence from Universal and showed that the studio believed Pasternak would once again produce a hit.

But Pasternak felt dismayed by the separation from Koster. "Working with a great star, making a succession of successful pictures, it was inevitable that someone, some bookkeeping executive, would try to separate the elements that went into the team's pictures. Koster and I never gave it a thought, but some business genius in a front office conceived the idea that if they separated us they might be able to get twice as much for their money. They assigned Henry to do another picture for another producer, and, to tell the truth, I could not help feeling that I was being cut off from my support, my team; yet I knew Henry was too splendid a talent to limit himself to one genre of filmmaking and one producer."

Despite his feelings, Pasternak was a professional with a strong team. The music was scored by Charles Previn and Frank Skinner and costumes were designed by Academy Award–winning designer Edith Head and Universal's head costumer Vera West. And of course there was Deanna herself, now a polished movie actor.

Even without Koster, the movie surpassed all expectations. When *Mad about Music* opened, excited fans jammed the theaters and critics raved that Pasternak had achieved the impossible by turning out a third straight hit. The film was nominated for four Academy Awards: Best Art Direction, Best Cinematography, Best Music Scoring, and Best Original Story.

The plot was another variation on the themes of pluckiness and devotion to family that were featured in Deanna's earlier films. Gloria Harkinson (Durbin) is the secret daughter of Gwyn Taylor, a famous Hollywood actress (Gail Patrick, a popular femme fatale). Gloria has been tucked away in a boarding school in Switzerland, and although she doesn't reveal her mother's identity, she regales her classmates with tales of her imaginary explorer father.

A classmate, Félice (Helen Parrish), accuses Gloria of fabricating the stories. When Gloria insists her father is coming for a visit and is confronted by schoolmates at the train station, she claims an arriving passenger, Richard Todd (Herbert Marshall), is her father. Confusion ensues, and after several adventures Gloria and her mother are reunited and the movie ends with Gloria performing the song "Serenade to the Stars" while Gwyn Taylor and Richard Todd sit cozily together, watching her sing.

Mad about Music received widespread critical praise. In his syndicated column, Paul Harrison wrote that he had "never heard such enthusiasm from hard-boiled preview customers as greeted the first showing. They were acclaiming a bright and nearly flawless picture, of course, but mostly they were applauding the Canadian kid and the mild little ex-busboy from Hungary who together have saved the life of a major studio, and are going on to contribute importantly to the well-being of this whole industry." *Motion Picture Herald* called the film "the best picture of the season" with "a swell story and cast." *Screenland* wrote, "Little Miss Durbin is almost too good to be true."

Sid Grauman's brief appearance as himself in *Mad about Music* also garnered a fair amount of press attention. The *Indianapolis Jewish Post* declared, "After forty-five years in the movie business, Grauman is still no camera actor." It appeared they were right. When Grauman first arrived on the set, he realized he'd forgotten his costume. As he admitted, "I'd have fired any actor who forgot his costume for any one of my shows!"

A suitable costume was found and Grauman's brief shoot began. Director Taurog shouted, "Ready, roll 'em!" Lights blazed, cameras turned, and Grauman, the great Hollywood showman, froze. He appeared petrified with fright. It required thirty-eight takes to get one successful, brief shot of Grauman playing himself.

At the time *Mad about Music* was released, Judy Garland starred as the leading juvenile in the movie *Listen Darling*, MGM's version of a "Durbin Formula" film, with a plot uncannily similar to *Mad about Music*. The *New York Times* gave Judy's movie a noncommittal review, calling it, "A natural, pleasant and sensible little film." *Listen Darling* lost $17,000, while *Mad about Music* made well over a million dollars.

In late February, Deanna returned to New York with Eddie Cantor to broadcast *Texaco Town* from New York's Capitol Theatre and to attend the East Coast premiere of *Mad about Music*. Deanna, her mother, and a tutor stayed at the Essex House, a forty-four-story hotel just south of Central Park.

Deanna received star treatment from the moment she stepped from the "Century" train onto the plush red carpet Grand Central Station kept for traveling celebrities. Mayor Fiorello LaGuardia met Deanna and presented her with the key to the city. He asked if there was anything he could do for her and Deanna responded by thanking him and requesting an ice cream soda.

Accompanied by photographers from *Life* magazine, Eddie Cantor showed Deanna all around the city of his birth. They visited Central Park Zoo on the coldest day in winter. They visited the Empire State Building and experienced the world's tallest skyscraper swaying on its base in a seventy-five-mile-an-hour gale. And, of course, Deanna and Cantor stopped for sodas at Park & Tilford, the famed Fifth Avenue drugstore.

Deanna performed on several episodes of *Texaco Town*, attended the premiere of her movie, and was featured at a press party following the film. She gave almost every waking hour to her public without a thought for herself. And yet, it wasn't enough. Delight Evans, the editor of *Screenland*, a popular entertainment magazine, published an open letter of complaint not long after Deanna left Manhattan.

> *I wanted to meet you. As I'd want to meet any grand person who had given me much pleasure and whom I wanted to thank. But Deanna Durbin—I mean the girl in New York—was not to be met. Of course I was disappointed. I still don't believe it. I persist in hoping that Deanna Durbin of the three-smash-hits-in-a-row is the real girl.*
>
> *Unless—unless somewhere along the way she forgets all about us. Us? Just the fans, Deanna. We really are too important to overlook. There are so many of us, and we are sincere about you. We can take our illusions or leave them alone, as a rule. But we certainly don't want to believe that Deanna Durbin, of all people, is any different than she is on the screen. She just can't be "difficult" or spoiled, or indifferent.*
>
> *If not, and even though she is getting to be a big girl now, I wish someone would give her a big spanking.*

Although some New York reporters may have resented their limited contact with the star, in Winnipeg, Deanna's third movie was met with excitement and adulation, and the two local newspapers competed in their praise. The *Winnipeg Tribune* proclaimed, "Screen Homecoming Triumph for Deanna." The *Winnipeg Free Press* gushed, "The girl with a tear in her voice comes home again, by way of pictures, to her own folk. To say that Deanna is good would be nothing more than attempting to paint the lily or gild refined gold to exult that glorious voice."

In March 1938, Deanna's *Texaco Town* contract expired and Universal decided that although Deanna was a hit on the radio, she shouldn't continue regular broadcasts. Deanna was replaced by Janice Chambers, "a twelve-year-old combination of Judy Garland and Deanna Durbin" who had recently been signed to MGM and was described as "a singer of jazz, swing and opera, and as cute as a bug."

A month later, three of Deanna's "discoverers" sued agents Jack Sherrill and Frederick Falkin for royalties from Deanna's salary. Rita Warner requested 35 percent, claiming she set up Deanna's first audition. Music teacher Olive White asked for 33 percent for calling Rita Warner's attention to Deanna. Agent Milo Marchetti demanded 50 percent, insisting he made a verbal agreement with Sherrill and had arranged the audition that led to Deanna's Universal contract. Added together, these three "discoverers" sued for 108 percent of Sherrill and Falkin's earnings.

The cases were sent to trial in the Superior Court. After several months, Judge Carl Stutzman ruled that Sherrill and Falkin had to pay out a large sum of money, including over $7,000 to Olive White and $41,391.86 to Rita Warner. Not long after this, on August 30, 1938, Universal Pictures and James Durbin bought Deanna's contract from Jack Sherrill. James worked as Deanna's agent until her first marriage, handling all her business deals with close guidance from executives at Universal.

Deanna was a skilled actor, a talented singer, and the world's sweetheart. But she was also very much a girl who yearned for the pleasures of other girls her age. Earlier that spring, Deanna had been staying in a hotel with Ada and Jack Sherrill when a message arrived explaining that a party for a society debutante was being thrown in the hotel ballroom. The debutante was a fan of Deanna and the host humbly asked, would she please come and let the partygoers have just a glimpse of their idol?

Deanna, Ada, and Sherrill had a discussion. The evening was already getting late. Deanna had to sing the next day and she always went to bed early before performances. But the party was in the hotel and a brief appearance would mean so much to the young guests. It was decided that Deanna would appear at the party just long enough to say "hello" and to sign some autographs.

Below, the ballroom was filled with joyous young people in fancy dress. Deanna's arrival was hailed as the pièce de résistance of the evening as she stood on a platform and made a short speech. She then laughed and threw a kiss, departing amid a thunder of applause.

But when Deanna returned upstairs, she sat quietly on her bed. Two tears trickled down her cheeks. She quietly said, "They're having lots of fun, aren't they?" Then, mindful of her upcoming performance, Deanna wiped her face, undressed, and went to sleep.

CHAPTER 9

Deanna Durbin Devotees

Then there were the fan clubs.

The *Associated Collegiate Press* circulated an article from the *Harvard Crimson* with the headline, "Soph sees Deanna Durbin Movie 141 Times." The article described how Theodore Held, Harvard class of 1941, was obsessed with Deanna's movies. Held's roommate, Barclay Feather, explained how six times in four days he had trailed Held to the Square, a neighborhood theater, where Theodore sat through three movie showings at once. After *Mad about Music* left the Square, Head started going to the Exeter in Boston, then the Tremont, and then even farther afield to theaters in Brookline. Feather explained, "He confided to me that he was pretty fond of the girl."

"Pretty fond" seemed like an understatement. However, Held didn't let the bemusement of his roommate or his fellow college students dampen his ardor. Instead, he found an outlet for his obsession. And this outlet was the Deanna Durbin Devotees.

Founded in 1937 by Jay Gordon, a twenty-three-year-old fingerprint expert with the United States Department of Justice, the Deanna Durbin Devotees quickly became Deanna Durbin's primary fan club. This wasn't the largest Hollywood fan club in the world, but it publicly claimed to be the most devoted. The Devotees' mission statement described them as "a group of sincere admirers, in order to provide for Miss Durbin's followers the world over a closer contact than is possible through ordinary channels." The Devotees claimed that their ultimate goal was to have Deanna "constitutionally" declared Queen of the United States.

The Devotees grew out of an earlier fan club, founded in Winnipeg just after the release of *Three Smart Girls*. It was headed by four teenagers: Marguerite Slaney, Mary Blockwell, Ann Inman, and Marian Jentz. With Deanna's official approval from Hollywood, they published a mimeographed newsletter, *Deanna's Journal*, and recruited members from around the world. By 1938, the membership had grown to three hundred, with only about ten members actually residing in Winnipeg. Dues were fifty cents a year, and upon joining members were sent an 8"×10" signed photograph of Deanna.

The Deanna Durbin Devotees, a larger and more organized group, was formed after *Life* published an article and photo spread featuring Deanna. In response to the article, the magazine received several letters, including one from Jay Gordon. His letter read, "Thanks a million for the liveliest picture ever printed in *Life*—the full-page photograph of Deanna Durbin. I'm framing it and redecorating my room around that picture."

After Gordon's note was published in a subsequent issue, he received hundreds of letters from fellow fans. He decided to start his own club, which became so successful that soon Gordon himself was featured in a *Life* pictorial spread. According to club records, members of the Devotees received a personally autographed photo of Deanna, a year's subscription to the club's newspaper, a "handsomely-printed membership card," and "the privilege of wearing a Durbin pin," which could be purchased by mail-order. Some branches had matching jackets. Others held Deanna look-alike contests. Gordon, as president, oversaw the publication of a glossy magazine, *Deanna's Diary*.

Each issue of *Deanna's Diary* followed a similar format, with a studio photo on the cover and contributions from club officers, branch club news, a personal letter from Deanna, fan letters, and a Devotee Correspondence Club (essentially a pen-pal service). There was also fan poetry and a profile of Deanna's latest film or biographical notes about the star.

One fan letter in *Deanna's Diary* came from a teen-aged girl named Hedwig Federowicz: "Like millions of girls I have grown to love Deanna more than just a child star. I have attended operas, balls, visited an emperor, worn beautiful clothes . . . not in reality, but living through each and every

Durbin picture." Another Devotee fan letter came from Arthur Barrett of Norfolk, Virginia:

> *I want to say something about my very special favorite, Deanna Durbin. I am a young fellow, eighteen years old, and am simply, uncontrollably nuts, foggy, goofy, and else-what over this nightingale of the "fillums." I recently became a member of the Deanna Durbin Devotees and have been doing nip-ups ever since I received my card of membership, which I carry with me always.*
>
> *Why shouldn't I like her? When a guy depends upon the movies for entertainment, he wants the movies to give it to him. Deanna Durbin gives it to me—right smack-dab between the eyes and the surrounding territory of my heart. Her freshness, vitality, youthful loveliness and extreme beauty are unsurpassed.*

Personal scrapbooks were another central element of 1930s movie fandom. They became status symbols based on the book size and the memorabilia they contained. Making scrapbooks was a distinctly individualized activity, and the books ranged from leatherbound store-bought albums to newspapers glued to a cardboard spine. Scrapbooks usually contained photographs and articles clipped from papers or magazines as well as film programs from premieres and other personal keepsakes. Teenager Loraine McGrath attained prominence among Devotees because she had the largest collection of "Durbiniana" in the world, with four scrapbooks of clippings and an additional fifteen hundred photos of Deanna.

The Deanna Durbin Devotees had over three hundred chapters worldwide and operated with the full support of Universal, which supplied mementos, funded publication of the club's journal, and even gave stipends to club officers. The studio also granted officers special privileges, such as access to movie sets during filming. Kathleen Ehlen at the Universal Fan Mail Department provided the Devotees with names of fans who might be interested in club membership.

British chapters of the Devotees published a fan magazine titled *Universal Outlook: The Magazine for All Interested in Deanna Durbin*, edited by James Robert Stannage. A branch of the Devotees was started even further afield in Western Australia by eighteen-year-old Alice Walker. An article in the *Freemantle Mail* informed fans that in exchange for membership dues, they would receive an autographed photo of Deanna, a quarterly magazine, a list of American members, and a membership card.[1] Several independent Deanna Durbin fan clubs also existed, including The Durbinites in Canada and The Deanna Durbin Club in Stockholm, Sweden.

In 1938, the Deanna Durbin Devotees became embroiled in a bitter dispute with a rival fan group, the We-Love-Deanna-Durbin-Club (WLDDC) at Harvard University. The WLDDC was founded by a group of students as an "association of admirers and lovers of Deanna Durbin at Harvard." There was no membership fee, but members were required to view each of the star's films at least three times and dream of her at least four nights in succession. According to John Otvos, 1939 WLDDC president, "Love her? Why we are thrilled every time we see her; she is the greatest little girl in the world!"

The feud began when Nelson Blair, National Secretary of the Devotees, was informed of the Harvard club's stiff admission requirements. He replied that anyone could dream, and that a dream about Deanna did not mean a thing. Blair also boasted that the Devotees were much more loyal to "the most beautiful girl in the world," noting that he had seen *One Hundred Men and a Girl* twenty-four times.

WLDDC President Otvos countered, "Anyone can see movies. The Devotees are not serious enough for us."

A later incarnation of the Deanna Durbin Devotees was based in England, which already had a queen, so the club dropped the earlier demand of making Deanna royalty. This new Devotees club published a quarterly newsletter, held an annual convention and, later, hosted a comprehensive internet site. The modern club had its first meeting in London in 1982 and operated with the full support of Deanna. Several club members began personal correspondence with the star, exchanging letters for almost two decades.

THAT CERTAIN AGE (1938)

Deanna Durbin seems to be the one star in Hollywood who can always "play herself." In That Certain Age, *she is still the unspoiled spontaneous youngster she has always been. And while a good script, appropriate dialogue, sensible teen-age clothes and wise direction have something to do with its success, the chief credit must go once more to Deanna herself.*

—ANN ROSS, MACLEANS

Deanna's fourth movie, *That Certain Age*, was released on October 7, 1938. It was produced by Joe Pasternak, but although Pasternak had again requested Koster to direct, he was instead assigned Russian Edward Ludwig. The screenplay was originally written by Bruce Manning and based on an original story by F. Hugh Herbert. However, just before shooting, Pasternak secretly hired his friend Billy Wilder and his partner Charles Brackett, who were working at Paramount, to provide uncredited rewrites. As Wilder later admitted, "I don't know if we helped the picture or not."

That Certain Age wasn't just a simple "sub-deb" film like MGM's popular *Andy Hardy* series with Judy Garland and Mickey Rooney. Deanna's fourth movie represented a compromise between Pasternak, Universal, and Deanna's fans. And the subject of this conflict, which would continue throughout Deanna's career, was how much the ingénue should be allowed to grow up.

From the start, Pasternak took a firm hand in Deanna's career and personally curated her on-screen persona. He was determined that Deanna would never be seen as arch or romantically precocious and that her screen adolescence would progress naturally, with nothing more serious than puppy love to mar her innocence. In his words, "It was my idea that Deanna would be an example for every girl to look up to. She would be dressed as a girl of her years should dress. Her growth would not be forced. I knew that some of our greatest actresses were playing adult roles by the time they were sixteen, but I didn't want this for Deanna. When she was sixteen, she would play parts suitable for a girl of that age."

Universal executives disagreed.

The *New York Times* reported that the initial script for *That Certain Age* involved significantly more romance, including a scene where Deanna runs away with her love. The article stated that when word got out about the elopement scene, Universal was deluged with protests from parents who feared their offspring would follow suit. The studio capitulated and the scene was eliminated from the script.

That Certain Age also originally included a kissing scene, but after the public outcry over Deanna's possible on-screen elopement, the studio solicited advice about the kiss from fans, including a "Kissing Ballot" in movie magazine *Screen Guide*. The results were clear: Deanna was not yet allowed a movie romance. As Pasternak explained, "Deanna has been kept exactly her own age in the picture. Deanna is fifteen, nearly sixteen. There'll be plenty of time in future pictures for her to have serious romantic roles."

The movie features Ken Warren (Jackie Cooper), a Boy Scout who is putting on a show to raise money to help underprivileged boys. Alice Fullerton (Durbin), the star of his show, offers him the family guesthouse to rehearse. Meanwhile, Alice's father has loaned the guesthouse to his star reporter Vincent Bullit (Melvyn Douglas). Alice begins to develop feelings for Bullit and Ken, becomes jealous. By the end of the film, Alice gives up her crush, makes up with Ken and performs in the fundraiser. The movie ends with a chorus of young actors all singing the song, "That Certain Age."

That Certain Age was met with glowing reviews. *Photoplay* wrote, "Chalk up another triumph for Deanna Durbin's singing." *Silver Screen* called Deanna "starry-eyed and golden-voiced." The movie was nominated for two Academy Awards: Best Original Song and Best Sound Recording. Two song recordings from the movie, "You're as Pretty as a Picture" and "My Own," immediately became hits.

After the movie was released, Pasternak assured moviegoers *That Certain Age* had been made, in part, to prepare the public for more mature films to follow. He also stressed that future pictures would contain nothing controversial and that Deanna would not be ready for grown-up roles for at least three years. He firmly declared, "There'll be no 'necking' or 'petting' in Deanna's pictures for some time to come—if ever."

THE WIZARD OF OZ

Another important Hollywood event occurred in 1938. At MGM, Louis B. Mayer was assembling a cast for his new film, *The Wizard of Oz*, a remake of their 1925 and 1910 silent films *The Wizard of Oz* and *The Wonderful Wizard of Oz*. Although MGM had no idea the film would achieve such lasting popularity, the studio took special care in casting the character of the young lead, Dorothy.

With each film she made, Judy Garland had become more and more popular. She was MGM's lead juvenile and a solid box-office draw. However, she was not necessarily Mayer or producer Mervyn LeRoy's first choice to play Dorothy. She was still being cast in "freckled and frumpish" roles as a "girl next door." And LeRoy wanted someone wide-eyed and innocent, someone to inspire the imagination. Someone like curly-haired Shirley Temple. Or Deanna Durbin.

At the time *The Wizard of Oz* was cast, Shirley Temple was ten years old. She was closer to the actual age of Dorothy in L. Frank Baum's series and the most popular child actor in Hollywood. However, Temple was under contract with 20th Century-Fox and MGM couldn't work out a deal with their rival. When her studio refused to lend out Shirley Temple for the role, MGM claimed that Temple was not a strong enough singer for Dorothy. This was unlikely, as Temple sang regularly in her pictures and was known for her voice.

Other juvenile actors considered for Dorothy included Jane Withers, Bonita Granville, and of course, Deanna. Deanna was already a fan of the Baum books, and one novel in the series, *Rinkitink in Oz*, had a prominent place on her bookshelf. Some sources said that Deanna was turned down because she looked too mature for the part. Some hinted that Universal wouldn't consider lending out their biggest moneymaker. Another source said that MGM executives decided they were "not in the business of furthering the career of someone under contract to another studio." Others claimed that Universal didn't want to risk Deanna's popularity by allowing her to appear in a fantasy film.

Several months before, Universal had planned to star Deanna in *Cinderella*, the studio's first-ever Technicolor film. However, movie exhibitors protested that casting Deanna in a fantasy would significantly injure her drawing power. At the same time, Disney claimed he owned the rights to the movie title and the film was abandoned.

The casting of Judy as Dorothy, announced by columnist Louella Parsons, was not universally well received by reporters or by fans of the Oz books, who pictured Dorothy as blonde and considerably younger. *Silver Screen* wrote, "Judy isn't as strong on looks as many of our Hollywood girls." However, according to *Oz* screenwriter Noel Langley, Mayer didn't ever seriously consider anyone aside from Judy, "if for no other reason than reprisal. He was determined to make Judy Garland a bigger star than Deanna Durbin, just to prove he was right."

During the production of *The Wizard of Oz*, Judy was paid $500 a week, while her co-stars were each paid $3,000. The only lead actor in the film that was paid less was Terry, the dog that played Toto. Judy was treated like an acting machine, forced to wear a corset to flatten her figure and to smoke cigarettes to suppress her appetite. At this time, Deanna was making around $3,000 a week with a $10,000 bonus for each film she shot, and she was a treasured star at Universal.

When *The Wizard of Oz* was released, 20th Century-Fox regretted their mistake in not lending out Shirley Temple for the role of Dorothy almost as much as Mayer had regretted letting Deanna get away. In response to the film, Shirley Temple's studio produced its own *Wizard*-type of movie, *The Blue Bird*, which was such a flop that it effectively ended Temple's career.

According to Judy, it was only after the success of *The Wizard of Oz* that "people at MGM stopped referring to me as 'the kid they were stuck with when they let Deanna Durbin go.'"

SIXTEEN YEARS OLD

Deanna belongs to the public. She is their child as much as mine and their wishes must be considered before my own.

—ADA DURBAN, *ADELAIDE ADVERTISER*

In December of 1938, seventeen-year-old Deanna publicly turned "sweet sixteen." She said, "I think a girl is growing into a young lady when she becomes sixteen." In truth, Deanna had already been a young lady for a full year, and more and more she was feeling the vast divide between the Deanna Durbin character she played on-screen and in public and Edna Mae, her true self.

As if to further solidify the divide between the two, on December 24, 1938, Deanna legally changed her name from Edna Mae to Deanna through court petition. The petition claimed the actress was known almost exclusively as Deanna, that sometimes the confusion in ages embarrassed her, and that the possession of one legal name would facilitate the contracts and agreements she entered into as an artist. It also stated that legally becoming "Deanna" would protect her from infringement and exploitation.

Deanna wasn't confused. But she also didn't mind changing her name, because, as she saw it, this made the division official: Deanna was the star, just "sweet sixteen." Her clothes and hair and food and even her age were mandated by her studio and open to public scrutiny—for now. But Edna Mae, well, that was someone else; someone independent, someone the studios couldn't ever possess. And someday—somehow—Edna Mae would come into her own.

CHAPTER 10

Academy Award (1939)

THE NEWSPAPER HEADLINES PROCLAIMED: "DEANNA DURBIN ADOPTED by Her Own Parents!" Of course, this wasn't exactly true. But in 1939, under the newly enacted Coogan Act, Ada was officially appointed Deanna's social guardian and James became her court-appointed business guardian.

The California Child Actor's Bill, also known as the Coogan Act, was a law passed in 1939 designed to safeguard a portion of the earnings of child performers. It was named after Jackie Coogan, a child movie star whose millions were squandered by his mother and stepfather. Under this new law, courts assumed a commercial guardianship of millionaire minors to ensure their earnings were protected until they reached the age of majority.

Before the Act was enacted, parents and guardians of child stars were managing their children's earnings with varying degrees of responsibility. *Texaco Town* co-star Bobby Breen's sister carefully managed his salary. Judy Garland endorsed her paychecks to her mother, incorrectly assuming the money was being safeguarded for her. Deanna Durbin had a $50,000 house held in trust for her, and her savings were regularly invested in ten-year annuities.

With this new law, Deanna's Universal contract had to be approved by the California Superior Court. It went before Judge Emmett Wilson on July 1, 1939. In addition to approving the contract, the court worked out a schedule for Deanna's care and training and ruled that $15,000 a year could be used for living expenses and education, that 5 percent (instead of the usual 10 percent) of Deanna's earnings could go to her father as agent, and that $4,200 a year could be paid to her attorney. After annual taxes, at least $50,000 a year would be placed in trust for her.

Knowing that a large sum of her earnings was being saved, Deanna began thinking about her future. After all, she would legally be eighteen in less than a year. Judy Garland and Helen Parrish, over a full year younger, were frequently seen enjoying the Hollywood nightlife. Mickey Rooney was photographed at the Coconut Grove nightclub every Saturday and nobody batted an eye. Deanna wondered how long she would need to keep pretending to be a child. And once she could finally make her own decisions, well, what would she do then?

JUVENILE OSCAR (1939)

Although most of Deanna's movies received at least one Oscar nomination, the only Academy Award Deanna received was on February 23, 1939, at the eleventh annual ceremony. This special award was for "significant contributions in bringing to the screen the spirit and personification of youth, and as a juvenile player, setting a high standard of ability and achievement." The ceremony in 1939 was the second time a Juvenile Oscar had been awarded, and it was only given nine times more. The first went to Shirley Temple in 1934, and future winners included Judy Garland in 1940, Margaret O'Brien in 1944, and Peggy Ann Garner in 1945.

The host was ventriloquist Edgar Bergen, who was scheduled to present special Juvenile Oscars to both Deanna and Mickey Rooney at the Academy dinner at the Los Angeles Biltmore Hotel. However, Mickey Rooney was out of town and his award was accepted by Bergen's ventriloquism dummy, "hayseed" Mortimer Snerd.

In the 1930s, the Academy Awards were not attended by the public. Radio coverage was actually banned at the 1939 ceremony. A reporter from the KNX in Los Angeles locked himself in a hotel phone booth and was able to broadcast for just a few minutes before security guards broke down the door and threw him out. However, although live coverage was inexplicably forbidden, reporters and photographers were present to capture every detail of the evening.

Deanna attended the ceremony dinner with her parents. She was dressed in a long blue taffeta gown with a matching ribbon fastened in her curls. Her only accessories were a spray of orchids, a small gold ring, and a thin gold chain and watch. This was a noted contrast to Judy Garland's outfit when she received her Juvenile Academy Award a year later: Judy wore a silk dress paired with a jeweled necklace, long white gloves, lipstick, and a short white fur coat. She brought Mickey Rooney as her escort.

Although the Best Actor and Actress awards in 1939 went to Spencer Tracy and Bette Davis, and the Best Picture was *You Can't Take It with You*, Deanna was the toast of the evening. When she received her award, Deanna appeared humble and self-assured. Her acceptance speech was short, "Two-and-a-half years ago when I came into this business, I had one desire. That was to be as good as I could be. Tonight you have made me very, very happy. My aspirations had not reached such a peak. I am extremely grateful."

CANOE RIDE TO HOLLYWOOD

By midway through 1939, Deanna had fans worldwide, and she had received over fifty marriage proposals by mail. In America, Deanna's popularity had no equal, and Universal was so deluged with fan letters that one staff member worked full-time opening Deanna's mail. However, not all of Deanna's admirers were satisfied with merely writing letters or belonging to an organized club like the Devotees. Some were willing to go to far more dramatic lengths to meet their heroine.

In the summer of 1939, the *Louisville Kentucky Courier-Journal* reported the story of nineteen-year-old Jack Miller and his eighteen-year-old cousin, Wally Miller, who announced their intention to travel from Louisville to Hollywood. In a canoe. Their goal was simple: to meet their favorite Hollywood star, Deanna Durbin.

The boys spent weeks preparing. They made their own tents from unbleached waterproof cotton, sewed cases for their shotgun and rifle, and prepared a notarized affidavit proving their identity. They also packed two hundred postcards to send along the way, as well as a photograph of Deanna for inspiration. The canoe was named "The Miss Deanna Durbin." It was eighteen feet long, weighed about 100 pounds, and was painted bright red. On the side was written, "California, Here We Come!"

Over four months later, on December 26, 1939, a follow-up article appeared in the *Courier-Journal* along with a photograph of Deanna and two beaming young men. The cousins had paddled down the Ohio and Mississippi Rivers to the Gulf of Mexico, then across treacherous Corpus Christi Bay. They traded their canoe for a 1925 flivver and drove until it broke down. Then they "thumbed" the rest of the way. Meanwhile, Universal press agents had heard about the journey, and a meeting with Deanna was arranged. According to Jack Miller, "The charm and beauty of the young star exceeded our greatest expectations."

GLORIA JEAN

Even as Deanna's star rose higher and higher, Hollywood was already searching for the next Deanna Durbin. From Jean Harlow to Jane Powell to Kathryn Grayson, girls with classical voices were signed to studios and starred in films. Joe Pasternak also joined the search. Yes, he was still producing Deanna's movies and he hoped to keep guiding her career for some time. However, with each film, Deanna was becoming less of a child. And with the world so enamored with juveniles who could sing classical music, well, it wouldn't hurt to start promoting a second, younger girl.

That girl was Gloria Jean Schoonover. Gloria Jean was born in 1926. Her family lived in Scranton, Pennsylvania. She loved movies and singing and had just one goal: to be Deanna Durbin.

As Gloria would often recall, whenever she had enough pocket money, she and her little sister Bonnie would see Deanna's latest movie. "If I had a fairy godmother," sighed Gloria one afternoon, stepping out of the cinema into the bright sunshine, "I'd make a wish that I could go to Hollywood and meet Deanna and sing a duet with her."

"Well," Bonnie declared, "you can sing just as good as she can. When she was your age, I'll bet she wasn't any prettier than you are. Anyway, she couldn't be nicer."

That evening, a neighbor came over to inform Gloria's parents that Joe Pasternak was in New York, searching for a little-girl singer to replace Deanna Durbin. "Well, not replace exactly," he explained. The neighbor had heard Gloria Jean sing and was a good friend of Mr. Pasternak's secretary. He said that if Gloria Jean was interested, he could arrange an audition for her.

Interested? Gloria Jean couldn't believe her luck. This was her big chance. She knew Mr. Pasternak would pick her. He just *had* to!

But the next day, when Gloria arrived at the audition, hot and rumpled from the train ride to New York, she wasn't so sure. "There were hundreds of beautiful little girls there. They already looked like movie stars, and I didn't look so nice. I had pigtails and my teeth were a little crooked."

Pasternak asked Gloria Jean to sing, and after handing the music to the pianist, she began. But the piano didn't sound right. It wasn't *fair*. An old piano couldn't be allowed to ruin her chance of becoming Deanna Durbin! Gloria stopped mid-verse. She told Pasternak she couldn't continue because the piano was out of tune. Pasternak laughed. He said, "I like this kid. Let's get the piano tuned and bring her back tomorrow."

As Gloria later put it, "On the long ride home my mother almost shot me." But the next day she auditioned again, won the starring role in Pasternak's movie *The Underpup* (1939), and was soon on her way to Hollywood. Gloria Jean appeared in twenty-six movies, including her best-known film, *Never Give a Sucker an Even Break* (1941), where she co-starred with Deanna's old musical nemesis W. C. Fields.

Although many successful careers were launched while searching for the next Deanna, it was soon clear that no other girl could bring the same magic to the screen. Meanwhile, the question of how much longer Deanna could remain a little girl was once again under debate.

THREE SMART GIRLS GROW UP (1939)

After *That Certain Age*, Universal's press department announced that Deanna was ready for an on-screen romance. Once again her fans objected, and for months the debate raged on.

Eleanore Green from Brookline, Massachusetts, wrote:

> *Will Universal jeopardize her career by casting her in far-fetched pictures? Her winning smile has captured millions of fans here in the East, and she is a great favorite among the younger generation. Miss Durbin's fate lies in the hands of Hollywood who either makes stars*

or breaks them. We trust the producers will do their part in keeping Deanna the sweet little girl she really is.

Joe Pasternak was also getting worried. He could see Deanna struggling against the "little-girl" character that her fans demanded, both on- and off-screen. He had also heard whispers about Deanna and Vaughn Paul, a second assistant director on several of Pasternak's films. Perhaps it was best to move ahead and let Deanna become a young woman. Pasternak had several ideas for films, all of which would allow Deanna to mature gradually and naturally.

However, after thousands of letters poured into the studio demanding that Deanna stay a child, Pasternak decided to compromise, to mix Deanna's childhood innocence with the glamour of a debutante. And for his next movie, he decided on *Three Smart Girls Grow Up*, a sequel to his first Hollywood hit.

In *Three Smart Girls*, Deanna's character Penny had played cupid for her estranged parents. This time, she reprised the "cupid" role to solve the romantic woes of her two older sisters. Barbara Read and Nan Grey had played Penny's sisters in the original film; however Barbara was considered too adult to reprise her role in the sequel, so it was recast with Helen Parrish, one of Deanna's closest friends. Bruce Manning and Felix Jackson wrote the screenplay, and Pasternak was delighted to finally be paired again with Henry Koster.

As the movie was specifically written to show that Deanna was "growing up naturally," it opens at the coming-out party for Penny Craig (Durbin), where several guests clearly remark how Penny is now a young lady. During the party, Richard Watkins (Richard Lundigan) proposes to Penny's sister Joan (Nan Grey). When Penny sees that her other sister, Kay (Helen Parrish) is in love with Richard, she devises a plan to find another man for Kay, recruiting pianist Harry Loren (Robert Cummings), who falls for Joan instead. After several romantic misunderstandings, Joan's wedding day arrives. At the ceremony, all is resolved as Joan is delivered into the arms of Harry, Kay joins Richard at the altar, and Penny smiles happily as she sings.

Three Smart Girls Grow Up was released on March 24, 1939. It was the fifth hit in a row for Deanna, and the reviews once again exploded with a seemingly endless string of superlatives. Reviewer Rose Pelswick raved about "the wealth of incident, the expertly-rounded characterizations and the naturalness of the players." *Box Office* magazine called the movie, "A masterpiece . . . definitely a hit. Deanna Durbin is more golden-voiced and charming than ever."

In Winnipeg, Frank Morriss once again got creative. Instead of penning a review of the film or writing about the acting or the cast, he published his feature article . . . about ham. The headline read, "Ham off Deanna's Menu," and the article described a scene in the movie where Deanna had to talk, cry, and eat huge mouthfuls at the same time. Because of how the scene was filmed, she had to actually eat in every take.

Before the filming began, Henry Koster asked Deanna what she wanted to eat in the scene and she responded, "Roast ham, and more roast ham."

The scene didn't go as well as Koster had planned. In the end, it took twenty-two takes to get it right. And poor Deanna talked and ate until she was so full, she didn't want to see another meal for a week. To celebrate the completion of the scene and to reward Deanna for being such a good sport, Koster offered to take her for dinner to celebrate. "But only," he added with a smile, "if you promise to order the ham." Deanna firmly refused.

At the behest of Universal, newspaper advertisements announced, "Deanna appears in her first glamorous role!" But even this tagline was controversial. *Variety* magazine noted, "It is with some wonderment that one observes that Miss Durbin is being trained for the 'glamour' market." The *New York Times* went even further and published a scathing rebuke to the advertising campaign. "To suggest that this teenish Miss is glamorous, with a leer ringing the word, is not simply stupid but obscene. If we had any authority over the matter, we'd wash the culprit's mouth with soap."

But Deanna *was* growing up. In the spring of 1939, whispered rumors began to circulate that she was about to get, or perhaps already was, secretly married to Vaughn Paul. In the blunt prose of gossip columnist Louella Parsons, "The rumored elopement plans of Deanna Durbin caused more excitement at Universal than Hitler's march into Vienna."

Six months before, Deanna was considered a "grave, innocent-eyed child, with no thoughts beyond her books and music, her home and work." She had only ever attended a nightclub accompanied by her mother and was in bed every night before ten. And now *this*.

The Universal publicity department, at a loss about how to handle this potential disaster, turned to Deanna's mother. Ada was quoted in newspapers worldwide: "Why shouldn't Deanna, who is seventeen, go out dancing if she wants to?[1] She is a normal girl and entitled to a little fun. Deanna studies music two hours a day. She is still in school and I never permit her to go out on school nights. I know Vaughn and I consider him a nice boy. If Deanna wants to go dancing with him it is all right with me, and I think it's a shame for such a nice friendship between two young people to be exaggerated."

Fans appeared satisfied; however Pasternak knew that his earlier timeline must be abandoned. Deanna would need to start growing up on-screen—and soon. However, Universal executives suddenly changed their minds and decided to keep Deanna a young girl for as long as they could. As the Associated Press reported, "By now the masterminds at Universal Pictures had been holding conferences for weeks, making decisions, changing their minds and spoiling their digestions—worrying about a most important kiss. One faction pointed out that as the movie studio's greatest child singer, Deanna had earned Universal over $10,000,000, largely by steering away from kisses. The other, led by Joe Pasternak, insisted that Deanna was growing up and that there wasn't much anybody could do about it. She was already almost seventeen years old, and so why not let romance gently, delicately, and casually enter her life on-screen?"

Pasternak won. There would be a kiss. The only question was: who would give it?

Judy Garland and Mickey Rooney in *Love Finds Andy Hardy*, 1938

Judy Garland as Dorothy in *The Wizard of Oz*, 1939

Judy Garland and Mickey Rooney at the 1940 Academy Awards

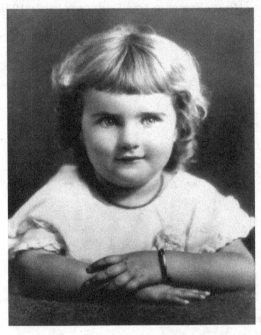

Three-year-old Edna Mae Durbin (Edna May Durbin)

Edna Mae at seven, with her parents and sister Edith

Deanna and Judy at MGM, 1936

Deanna and Judy in a publicity photo during the filming of *Every Sunday*, 1936

Deanna and Judy in a scene from *Every Sunday*, 1936

Deanna Durbin and Eddie Cantor in *Texaco Town*

Sudden stardom after the release of *Three Smart Girls*, 1936

Deanna with her voice teacher, opera singer Andrés de Seguróla

Publicity still with Leopold Stokowski for *One Hundred Men and a Girl*, *1937*

Deanna performing for her parents in their new Hollywood Hills home

Deanna leaving imprints of her hands and footprints at Grauman's Chinese Theatre, 1938

Henry Koster directing Deanna in *Three Smart Girls*, 1936

Deanna and Edgar Bergen at the 1938 Academy Awards

Just before Deanna's first onscreen kiss with Robert Stack in *First Love*, 1939

From one of Deanna's last portrait sessions in 1948

Engaged to be married: Deanna and Vaughn
Paul, 1941

Deanna with Henry Koster and Joe Pasternak during *Spring Parade*, 1940

Publicity glamour shot from *Spring Parade*, 1940

Promo shot for *Can't Help Singing*, 1944

Deanna, Robert Cummings, and Charles Laughton filming *It Started With Eve*, 1941

Wedding portrait with Gene Kelly for W. Someret Maugham's *Christmas Holiday*, 1944

Deanna in a publicity still for *Hers To Hold*, 1943

Deanna with Joseph Cotton during a break filming *Hers To Hold*, 1943

Deanna christens a Pullman car, 1945

Deanna with her husband Charles David and son
Peter

Deanna and Charles David

Deanna in the 1980s

CHAPTER 11

The Kiss (1939)

While I was kissing Deanna Durbin, Adolf Hitler was starting a war.
—ROBERT STACK

MOST PEOPLE KNOW ROBERT STACK AS AN AMERICAN ACTOR, SPORTS-man, and television host. He appeared in over forty feature films, starred in the TV series *The Untouchables*, and hosted the true crime series *Unsolved Mysteries*. He was also nominated for an Academy Award for the 1956 film, *Written on the Wind*. However, what people don't know is that Stack didn't break into Hollywood because of his stage presence and dramatic ability or his deep, commanding voice. No, Stack became famous as the first boy to publicly kiss Deanna Durbin.

Fair-haired, blue-eyed "Bobby" Stack came from an influential and wealthy family. His great-grandfather owned the Orpheum, the first the-ater in Los Angeles. His grandmother, Modini Wood, was a star soprano at La Scala in Milan. Stack started as a character actor in Duffy's Califor-nia Stock, a touring theater company. He planned to eventually move to "legit" Broadway shows, but these plans changed when he was spotted by a Universal scout who arranged for a screen test.

At that time, Henry Koster was having difficulty finding the ideal young man to be Deanna's first Romeo in her next film. But when he ran into twenty-year-old Robert Stack at the studio, he immediately thought, "This is the handsomest man who ever was."

Never mind that Stack was just a college student, that he had never acted in a movie, and that the whole world had its eye on this film. After all, according to Koster, "All my life I have worked with people who have never made a picture before." Koster had made Deanna a star overnight; he was confident he could do the same with this young Adonis. He walked up to Stack, introduced himself, and almost immediately signed Stack for the part.

The kiss generated more publicity than the wedding of Elizabeth Taylor to Richard Burton and was reported in *Variety* as "the most important kiss in Hollywood history." According to Pasternak, "The occasion of Deanna's first kiss was as significant to us, and as it happened, to her audience, as must be the first kiss of any girl." According to Koster, "Her first kiss was quite sensational for the press and the publicity department. And maybe for Deanna, too, although I doubt that. She probably knew already."

On the day the scene was filmed, Stack was understandably nervous. As he later admitted, "Who wouldn't have been nervous? Getting ready to play a scene that all America had its eye on?"

A staff member present on the set described the historic event:

> *The big moment had arrived. The doors to the set were locked from the inside. All doors were guarded against outsiders. Two brawny guards were stationed outside. Their instructions were: "No one is to get in— not even the president of the company." Director Henry Koster wanted all the privacy possible for Deanna Durbin's first screen kiss. He had visions of her being nervous enough, without spectators.*
>
> *However, Koster didn't have to fret about Deanna. She took the scene in stride. Not so, Robert Stack. During the first take, Robert flushed pink and his hands were so sweaty that he had to dry them. When the camera stopped, he blurted: "I feel terrible." Deanna giggled.*
>
> *They tried again. Robert was crimson during the second take, and red photographs black. The makeup man paled him with powder. Four more takes, nervous perspiration bubbled through that. The seventh take would have been all right if Deanna hadn't giggled. The eighth struck Bob as funny. On the ninth, he finally relaxed.*

This brief on-screen kiss made international news. It was given more coverage than the war in Europe and replaced front-page stories of the rising Nazi power. For Deanna, it was merely one more on-screen landmark, aired to the world. For Robert Stack, it was the kiss that launched a long and successful film career.

First Love, originally titled *After Schooldays*, was a clear reworking of the Cinderella theme. In the movie, Constance Harding (Durbin) is an orphan sent to live with her wealthy relatives, including snobbish cousins Barbara (Helen Parrish) and Walter Clinton (Lewis Howard).

Connie is overjoyed when handsome Ted Drake (Robert Stack) invites the entire family to his ball. Connie is ordered to stay behind but the servants secretly arrange for her to attend the fête, delaying the rest of the family so they don't arrive at the ball until midnight. That night, Drake and Connie share a memorable first kiss, but when the clock strikes twelve she runs off, leaving a slipper behind.

After Barbara tells Connie that Ted didn't actually have feelings for her, Connie is heartbroken and runs away to become a music teacher at the boarding school where she grew up. But as she auditions for the position by performing Puccini's "Un bel di" to a roomful of spinster teachers, Drake arrives with the missing shoe. The music swells as Connie rushes into his arms.

The film received three Academy Award nominations: Best Cinematography, Best Art Direction, and Best Music Scoring. The tagline for *First Love* read, "Deanna's in love! The most exciting event in her life! The most enjoyable experience in years!" Reviews were positive. The *New York Times* felt the movie would "gratify and delight ... practically everybody capable of appreciating any form of entertainment above the aesthetic level of a six-day bicycle race." *Photoplay* called the film "gay, with climactic moments of charm and pathos that will make you say 'Aaaaah' quietly and wipe away a pleasurable tear."

And so, kissed in front of the world, Deanna officially became a young woman.

ENTER VAUGHN PAUL

Vaughn Austin Paul was an ambitious young man.

Son of Val Paul, a longtime "big shot" in Hollywood, Vaughn, too, wanted to make it big. From public speaking at Hollywood High School to basketball games at the local Y, he had always found success. Growing up, he spent summer vacations working at Universal where he had a variety of jobs that ranged from delivering messages to arranging props.

Vaughn wanted to succeed in Hollywood, but he didn't want to start at the bottom. After three years in law school, Vaughn dropped out and asked his father, Universal's general production manager, to arrange a more permanent job for him at the studio. The best position Val Paul could get for his son was second assistant director on a film, but Vaughn was certain he would soon be making movies of his own.

Vaughn and Deanna first met while filming *Three Smart Girls*. At the time, Deanna was fourteen and he was nineteen. Two years later, during a pool party Deanna threw for her film crew, she and Vaughn started to chat and they quickly became friends.

Not long after, Deanna invited Vaughn for a private swim in her pool. Afterward, he took her to dinner at Lucey's, a hangout for movie stars. They attended a movie preview of *Boys Town* at the Filmart Theatre before heading to the Colonial Drive-In on Sunset Boulevard for hot fudge sundaes. By eleven, they were back at Deanna's door.

Vaughn didn't seem awed by Deanna's superstar status. In fact, he often jokingly criticized her movies. Deanna felt this showed an honesty and frankness she found refreshing. Vaughn had a way of looking right at her as if he actually *saw* her. He even called her Edna Mae.

And Deanna was lonely. She had few friends her own age and no boyfriends. Over at MGM, Judy regularly went out with a gang of young male actors. Mickey Rooney, Freddie Bartholomew, and Jackie Cooper would sneak off to neck with girls on the backlot and were photographed drinking in nightclubs. Even during the filming of *First Love*, Robert Stack kissed Deanna on camera but escorted her co-star Helen Parrish to a friend's Hollywood film preview.

Soon Deanna and Vaughn began to date regularly, unchaperoned by her parents or her elder sister. This unlikely romance whipped the media into a frenzy. Determined reporters trailed Deanna and Vaughn around Los Angeles. A cameraman broke his leg trying to get an exclusive photograph of the couple. Studio executives advised Deanna against becoming too serious, but Deanna refused to let the studio dictate this one aspect of her life. She was going to grow up, and she was going to do it with Vaughn Paul at her side.

The attack on Pearl Harbor and America's entry into World War II was still over two years away, but even before her own country went to war, Deanna was an inspiration to soldiers fighting overseas. Not long after the outbreak of the war, Deanna received a letter from members of the Promotion Guynemer at the Air Force school in Salon, France, asking her to be godmother of their graduating class. In the United Kingdom, Deanna was nominated as the ranking box-office star of Britain and Ireland, displacing Shirley Temple and beating out Mickey Rooney, Jeanette MacDonald, and Spencer Tracy. Judy Garland didn't make the list.

Deanna continued to prepare for an operatic career. She had regular voice instruction and practiced singing daily. She still considered performing at the Metropolitan Opera her greatest ambition and explained to the press that she hoped to play the role of Mimi in Puccini's *La Bohème* after her Universal contract expired.

"To do the job properly—and that's the only way I would do it—I would have to spend several months in the East having intensive training. I might have to be away from pictures six months and I wouldn't want the added strain of having to worry about picture-making."

In December of 1939, Deanna officially reached adulthood. As columnist Ida Zeitlin wrote in *Screenland*, "Deanna is about to step across that imaginary line that separates girlhood from womanhood, and the possibility of romance will have to be faced." According to Zeitlin, Deanna had "the springlike freshness of a peachtree in bloom. . . . Her fans know the blossoms must fall if the fruit is to ripen, yet they can't suppress a pang when the process begins." For her birthday Universal presented Deanna with a harp, an instrument she didn't have time to play.

By the end of 1939, ten separate dress goods companies were licensed to make Deanna Durbin dresses, adding an additional $50,000 to her annual salary. Deanna had more money than most people in Depression-era America, where the average wage for common labor was forty-five cents an hour. But all that money couldn't give her freedom or the time to discover who she was and who she wanted to be.

CHAPTER 12

A Dash of Sophistication (1940)

Deanna Durbin has left childhood behind, and while Universal sym-
pathizes with her over this tragedy, the studio is being compensated for
its grief by the fact that maturity has shortened her shooting schedule.
It's a Date, which was recently completed, was finished in the record
time of 54 days.

—Douglas Churchill, *New York Times*

In 1940, Deanna became "America's most prominent high school graduate." Although she and Judy completed their high school education in their respective studios, their diplomas came from Los Angeles University High School and their names were listed in the school's 1940 yearbook.

The diploma Deanna received represented years of schooling "the hard way," with her three legally mandated hours of daily instruction squeezed in between an additional three hours of singing practice. There were also daily screen tests, recordings, still pictures, costume fittings, promotional appearances, as well as actually making movies. And, as the star of her films, Deanna had an extensive shooting schedule. For *It's a Date*, her first release of 1940, she was called for fifty-two days out of the fifty-four scheduled for filming.

With America on the brink of war and several countries already fully engaged in armed conflict, this was a year of change for Deanna as well as for the world. She spent the year fighting for her personal freedom while searching for happiness. Deanna needed time and space to discover what she wanted. But studio work filled her days, and she was under constant scrutiny both by the media and by Universal.

It's a Date (1939/1940)

During the filming of her seventh film, *It's a Date* (originally titled *It Happened in Kaloha*), Deanna turned eighteen. This meant that even though Universal still kept half-heartedly promoting the story that Deanna was still a child, she was now legally an adult. Like all of Deanna's earlier movies, *It's a Date* was produced by Joe Pasternak. He was assigned director William Seiter, borrowed from 20th Century-Fox. Seiter was an accomplished director, known for his Laurel and Hardy movies as well as for his work with the comedy duo Burt Wheeler and Robert Woolsey. Noted bandleader Harry Owens and his orchestra were also signed on for the picture.[1]

It's a Date begins with a closing-night performance by renowned Broadway actress Georgia Drake (Kay Francis). Georgia plans to travel to Hawaii for a rest and to prepare for the upcoming part of Saint Anne, which she calls "the role of a lifetime." However, director Sidney Simpson (Samuel S. Hinds) and writer Carl Ober (S. Z. Sakall) feel Georgia is too old for the part of twenty-year-old St. Anne. After observing Georgia's daughter Pamela (Durbin) onstage, they offered her the role in her mother's place.

Pamela travels to Honolulu to ask Georgia to coach her, not knowing her mother is preparing for the same role. On the ocean liner she meets John Arlen (Walter Pidgeon) and she decides Arlen has feelings for her. But after they arrive in Hawaii, Arlen falls in love with Georgia. Arlen proposes to Georgia and she accepts, giving up the role of Saint Anne. The movie ends with Pamela onstage as Anne, singing "Ave Maria."

It's a Date was released on March 22, 1940. Deanna wore twenty-eight outfits, including eight evening gowns. She also had her first period costume, a black chiffon velvet gown featuring a hoop skirt and trimmed with six hundred ermine tails. It cost $1,500 and Deanna wore it on-screen for just three minutes.

For the first time, Deanna did her own stunt work, jumping off a cruise ship into the ocean for a shot that took half a day to get right. *It's a Date* was also the first movie where Deanna was, as movie magazines put it, "soundly kissed." After this film, there was no longer any debate about Deanna growing up on-screen. Although the characters she went on to play often contained qualities of "Smart Girl" Penny Craig, the ingénue had become a young woman.

It's a Date was also an important movie for actress Kay Francis. Earlier in her career, Francis, the "Queen of Warner Brothers," was considered one of the most glamorous stars in Hollywood. However, in May 1938, an article titled "Dead Cats" in the *Independent Film Journal* named Francis one of several "poisonous stars whose box-office draw is nil." After that, no other studio would sign her to a contract. *It's a Date* was considered, as *Modern Screen* put it, "Francis's comeback de luxe."

Although the film was shot at Universal, Pasternak insisted on making everything as "authentically Hawaiian" as possible. Grass skirts were brought in from Honolulu each week by clipper plane and kept in an ice chest, wrapped in a damp towel. In one scene, poi—a Hawaiian staple made from taro—was served. The props department decided that nothing but genuine poi would do. They cabled Sidney Smith, executive chef at the Moana Hotel in Honolulu, asking him to ship some on the next clipper. A return cable from Smith reported a delay and suggested that instead of waiting, the crew order from a restaurant known for their Hawaiian poi, conveniently located just eight miles from Universal.

It's a Date received glowing reviews. *Silver Screen* called it, "the best of the Deanna Durbin pictures, and that's saying a great big mouthful, as they have all been excellent." The *New York Times* wrote, "A practically compulsory rendezvous." Frank Morriss proclaimed, "Deanna Durbin develops a dash of sophistication. While the results may prove disconcerting to those who would like to keep her in a state of dewy innocence, there is no question that she takes to her new role like a duck to water, with eminently satisfying results."

Deanna's popularity as a recording artist was also growing more and more with each film. In the spring of 1940, Universal sent five hundred recordings of Deanna's songs to London and Paris Red Cross headquarters for distribution to soldiers at the front. One movie magazine claimed she received "more invitations to college proms, June weeks, and winter carnivals than any other girl in the world." In Poland, Deanna was considered a national favorite and each month, she received a ten-page fan letter from Alexis Holmonsky, a White Russian exiled to Shanghai, China.

Holmonsky wrote that he believed Deanna was the reincarnation of a saint, and informed her that her mission was to bring peace and light to a world filled with darkness.

SPRING PARADE (1940)

For a star to have two or three hits in a row is astonishing; but to appear in eight is nothing short of a miracle.
—FRANK MORRISS, *WINNIPEG FREE PRESS*

In early fall of 1940, an article was published titled, "Extras Breathe Thanks When Deanna Durbin Production Is Started." The article described how in almost every one of Deanna's films, a thousand or more extras obtained several days' employment. It noted how the salary of each extra player, $8.25/day, represented a lot of paid-up grocery and rent bills.

Deanna's eighth movie, *Spring Parade*, used over 1,600 extras in the production of the film. Released on September 27, 1940, *Spring Parade* was Deanna's first "costume picture," a movie where the actors wore period costumes instead of contemporary clothing. The movie was another Pasternak/Koster collaboration, written by Felix Jackson. It was a remake of *Frühjahrsparade*, a movie Pasternak and Koster had made in Budapest years before. The music in *Spring Parade* was written by Robert Stolz, a Viennese composer often called "the new Johann Strauss."

In this musical, reminiscent of an Old Vienna that was about to permanently disappear under the Nazi regime, Ilonka Tolnay (Durbin), a young Hungarian peasant girl, visits a town market to sell her goat. At the market, Ilonka buys a fortune from a fortune teller. She initially scoffs at the prediction, but after mistakenly traveling to Vienna, getting a job in a bakery owned by Latislav Teschek (S. Z. Sakall, the only actual Hungarian in the film), falling in love with corporal Harry Martin (Robert Cummings), and even meeting Kaiser Franz Joseph I (Henry Stephenson, who also played the Kaiser in the 1935 film *The Night Is Young*), the prophecy is tunefully and joyously fulfilled.

Spring Parade was nominated for four Academy Awards: Best Cinematography, Best Original Song, Best Musical Score, and Best Sound Recording. The movie was both a fascinating and an interesting choice for Pasternak. First, there was the nostalgia factor: Pasternak, Koster, and Jackson were all German-speaking immigrant filmmakers who had worked in Hungary and Vienna, and this film was a romanticized view of Imperial Austria. Kaiser Franz Joseph I was presented as a benevolent, grandfatherly figure, and the citizens as happy peasants and petite bourgeois citizenry loyal to the emperor.

Then there was the political statement. In 1940, the American government still considered the Anschluss of 1938 an act of Nazi oppression and saw Austria as an occupied country, rather than a nation that actively embraced the Nazi regime. By overtly celebrating Austrian nationalism, *Spring Parade* was a clear political critique of Nazified Austria.

Although these subtleties were largely overlooked, *Modern Screen* wrote, "A few years ago, *Spring Parade* would have led the field without any possible quibbling. It is gay, happy, full of life and fun—but it is set in pre-war Vienna. Consequently, the gayer it gets, the more happiness and life it exudes, the sadder you feel, sitting there in the theater knowing that that carefree, wonderful way of life is dead and gone." The *New York Times* mused, "Never did we expect to see another musical tale of Old Vienna bouncing with any more life than a summer stock revival of *Countess Maritza*. Yet Old Vienna it is—and as fluffy and sugared an Old Vienna as certainly did not exist."

Spring Parade was the first picture where Deanna demanded to be treated like a star and one of the first times she was willful on the set. Pasternak took Deanna's occasional demands in his stride: "I am theatrical enough to appreciate temperament. Heaven save us from the day when the players of the make-believe world are as even-dispositioned as bearings inspectors on an assembly line."

Koster was less patient. "She seemed to be too stubborn sometimes and I seemed to be too stubborn to let her get away with it." He explained that although he never showed his actors the raw footage from the day's shoot, when Deanna once asked to see it, he didn't refuse. "She came back the next morning with a different hairdo to continue the same scene. I said, 'You can't do that,' because we would have to do everything over again that we had shot the last two days. She said, 'Well, then, shoot it over.' I got pretty upset, but Pasternak agreed to shoot the scenes over."

Koster also recalled one night when he was shooting a late-evening scene. He set up the scene with lighting and stand-ins and when everything was ready he instructed his assistant, "Get Miss Durbin, we're ready to shoot."

The assistant replied, "Miss Durbin left. She told her wardrobe girl that she doesn't work this late and went home."

Koster was incensed. The next day he resigned from the picture. That afternoon, a studio executive brought him and Deanna together in his office. Koster looked coldly at Deanna and said, "If this young lady wants to work with me, fine. If she doesn't want to work with me, just as fine." They made up and Koster came back, but tensions between the two continued throughout the shoot.

THE ENGAGEMENT

In late 1940, Deanna became engaged to Vaughn Paul. He proposed to her in his automobile. Instead of kneeling down or giving a flowery speech, they merely, as Deanna later put it, "came to an agreement." Vaughn suggested to Deanna that they get married, he pinned his Phi Kappa Psi pin on her, and they were engaged.

Soon after, likely under orders from the Universal press department, Vaughn presented Deanna with an engagement ring from Brock & Company, the most prestigious jewelry store in Los Angeles. And once a traditional engagement ring firmly circled Deanna's fourth finger, the studio decided to break the news to the world.

The day before her engagement was announced, Universal held a birthday party for Deanna where she was presented with a song, "I'm Nineteen Now," written for her by Walter Jurmann and Bernie Grossman. The musical tribute was arranged by Universal so Deanna would appear as less of a child bride. Deanna's actual age became official in the December 16, 1940, issue of *Life*, where it was reported that Universal had made "an error in calculations" and that Deanna was, in fact, nineteen years old.

On Deanna's birthday, to the delight of millions of starry-eyed young girls and the despair of just as many young men, Ada Durbin formally announced the engagement between nineteen-year-old Deanna Durbin and twenty-five-year-old Vaughn Paul. When Deanna's engagement was made public, a Harvard sophomore jumped fully clothed off a bridge into the Charles River in protest. He repeated the act on her wedding day.

To Pasternak, the engagement didn't come as a complete surprise. The year before, he had promoted Vaughn from second assistant director to assistant director on *The Underpup*, reasoning that if Vaughn were kept busy with his career, he wouldn't have as much time to pursue Deanna. However, once Vaughn was back on set with Deanna in *Spring Parade*, it became clear that there would soon be an engagement—or worse.

When Deanna and Vaughn were, as one executive put it, "a done deal," the Universal press office got busy. As *Modern Screen* reminded Deanna's fans, she and Vaughn were on "distinctly different planes. . . . Her success is achieved; he's still at the bottom of the ladder. Her salary is staggering; his looks like pin money beside it." After all, if the studio didn't feel that Vaughn was worthy of their golden child, surely the moviegoing public would feel the same. And that couldn't be allowed to happen.

Press releases went out calling Vaughn Paul a "studio executive." He was given his own office on the backlot with a hanging nameplate outside the door, perfect for photoshoots. Magazines were encouraged to write feature articles calling Vaughn one of "Hollywood's most eligible bachelors." One article even made the wildly inaccurate claim that Vaughn's assistant director position was "the most important job in pictures."

If Deanna's romance with Vaughn did not sit well with staff at Universal, to Joe Pasternak it felt like a betrayal. The year before, when talk of a possible engagement or elopement reached Pasternak, he had immediately summoned Ada to discuss the issue. Pasternak told her, "Of course Deanna will marry someday, but I don't think it ought to be now. To the world outside the studio, Deanna is the normal, healthy, everyday girl, the charming kid next door. But has she ever had a real childhood? She's worked hard, really hard, during the years that other girls play. You know what I think she misses? A chance to be a girl just like every other girl. Why don't you let her travel for a year? Take her around the world. All she knows is Hollywood and the way to the studio. Give her a chance to see what other people are like."

Deanna's mother had agreed. But Universal kept Deanna too busy shooting films for her to go anywhere. And the lure of romance—and freedom—with Vaughn was too strong for Deanna to resist.

When Deanna became engaged, Pasternak had to put his feelings aside and do some quick thinking. In his words, "You can't have a married woman being coy about getting kissed." Pasternak had planned for Deanna to get married in the movies when she was twenty-two or twenty-three. But when she burst into his office, flashing the Phi Kappa Psi pin and trilling, "Look, Joe!" his plans fell apart. The next movie would have to present a much different Deanna, fully mature.

After the engagement, Pasternak's relationship with Deanna changed. Before, he had been guiding a trusting girl with the full support of her parents. Now Deanna had opinions, and they weren't always her own. One day she came into Pasternak's office to ask if Vaughn's brother, a cameraman at the studio, could film her next picture. Pasternak firmly refused. He said he had made a promise to allow only top-notch cameramen to work on Deanna's pictures, and although Vaughn's brother may be great, Pasternak wasn't willing to take the chance.

Deanna accepted his decision, just as she always had. But she was clearly chafing at the bit. And although Pasternak was now a respected producer at Universal, there had been other offers coming his way, and his contract was ending soon. He, too, started considering plans for his future, plans that didn't necessarily include Deanna.

The Romances of Judy

Judy Garland's next film, *Babes in Arms*, opened to even bigger crowds than *Oz*. She was the shining star at the movie premiere, and just like Deanna at the opening of *Mad about Music*, she began the evening by recording her prints at Grauman's Chinese Theatre. Judy was suddenly a valuable asset to MGM. But unlike Deanna, whose movies were contractually limited to two each year, Judy worked at a hectic pace, often starting a new movie while still shooting the final scenes for another.

Deanna became engaged to the first boyfriend she'd ever had. But Judy had several "boy friends." These included juvenile actors Freddie Bartholomew, Billy Halop, and Mickey Rooney. There were also several older men, including thirty-two-year-old concert pianist Oscar Levant and thirty-one-year-old composer Johnny Mercer.

Then there was clarinetist Artie Shaw. Although he was almost twice Judy's age, Judy convinced herself that she was in love and that Shaw loved her in return. But in February 1940, Shaw met Lana Turner on the MGM backlot. That night, Shaw and Turner flew to Las Vegas and eloped. Like everyone else in Hollywood, Judy learned about their marriage from the newspaper headlines the next day.

Judy truly believed her heart was broken. To distract herself, she launched into the Hollywood social scene, spending her evenings at a succession of nightclubs: Ciro's, Cocoanut Grove, Trocadero, Victor Hugo, and La Conga. She also became close with married thirty-year-old songwriter David Rose. Her parents and Louis B. Mayer were clear in their disapproval of Rose, and when he gave Judy an engagement ring for her eighteenth birthday, the studio intervened.

Although Judy reluctantly agreed to postpone the engagement until Rose's divorce from actress Martha Raye became final, few people took the relationship seriously. Louella Parsons assured her readers, "If it is any comfort to MGM, I don't think there is a chance of Judy and Dave marrying." Judy was still waiting six months later when Deanna's engagement sent Hollywood—and Deanna's international fandom—into an excited frenzy.

Deanna's fans had definite opinions about her romance, and their letters expressed wildly different opinions about whether she should—or shouldn't—marry.

Hollis Smith from Vinton, Virginia, was matter-of-fact about it all:

It seems to me that about half the population of the United States is busy trying to keep Deanna Durbin from getting married. Personally, I think this is her own business and that she is entirely capable of attending to it. I know of no national catastrophe that has been caused by the marriage of a movie favorite and can see no reason why Deanna shouldn't be just as sweet after she is married as she is now.

Dorothy Fisher from Miami, Florida, felt it was past time for Deanna to mature on-screen:

Why all this controversy over keeping Deanna Durbin young? She is now a beautiful picture of blossoming womanhood. Naturally, along with maturity comes certain emotions which develop with the years. To me, the experience of watching a young girl grow into a woman of sincere, simple beauty is one which I would not readily forfeit.

Patsy Lester from Abilene, Texas, had definite opinions of how Deanna should plan her future:

Although you have your own ideas about love and happiness, are you sure marriage would be the wisest step to take now? I enjoy seeing you play the happy-go-lucky schoolgirl with your schoolgirl romances. If you should marry now, it would change the whole course of your career. So please, won't you wait at least three or four more years?

Deanna appeared deeply, if not somewhat defiantly, in love. Louella Parsons observed her "sitting in the commissary at Universal, drinking a tall glass of milk and eating chocolate cookies, young and lovely and confident, wearing happiness like a crown." Deanna *was* happy. Her movies were hits, she was in love, and she had never been more excited about the future. Finally, her life was truly beginning.

CHAPTER 13

The Greatest Love Story (1941)

There have been many great love stories in Hollywood, blazoned upon front pages for all to read. Some of them magnificent and violent, some beautiful or desperate, some tragic or happy or bitter. The greatest love story Hollywood has yet known is the one I want to tell you, for the first time: the courtship and marriage of Vaughn Paul and Deanna Durbin.

—Adela St. Johns, *Photoplay*

Nineteen forty-one was a year of vast change for Deanna. The safe world where she lived and worked turned upside down when the United States entered World War II. Her movie characters became decidedly adult. She married the only man she had ever dated. Joe Pasternak, who had guided Deanna's career and produced all her films, left Universal for MGM. And instead of remaining sweetly compliant while others made her career decisions, Deanna went on strike.

By 1941, Deanna had been in Hollywood for four years. She had become a symbol of America for millions of men risking their lives to keep their country free, as well as to the dictators who threatened this freedom. She remained in the confusing position of being seen—onscreen and in real life—as both a child and a capable young woman.

Deanna was praised for staying the same after her engagement: she practiced singing each day and regularly visited with her parents while she planned a wedding "with all the trimmings dear to every normal and nice American girl." At the same time, Deanna was regarded as a sex symbol—a pin-up girl—and columnists across the country praised her "ideal feminine measurements." (Height, 5'5"; weight, 114 lbs.; bust, 34"; waist, 24"; hips 35"; leg length, 35".)

One of Universal's most valuable actors, Deanna commanded a salary impressive even by Hollywood standards. In a nationally published list of leading US annual incomes, she was listed as earning $209,833 (as compared to Bing Crosby at $150,000 and Jeanette MacDonald at $173,333). Official Durbin merchandise sales included cotton and silk dresses, sportswear, pajamas, robes, dolls, hats, bags, records, songbooks, and sheet music.

Joe Pasternak, forced to abruptly speed up Deanna's on-screen maturity, decided to make a "transition" movie to clearly bridge Deanna's youth and adulthood. The film still presented Deanna as a plucky, charming ingénue, but the studio cautiously and deliberately permitted romance and a hint of scandal to creep into the plot. The movie contained enough innuendo to come to the attention of the "Morality Police" at the Hays Office,[1] and it was called, appropriately, *Nice Girl?*

NICE GIRL? (1940/1941)

Deanna's ninth movie was originally titled *Love at Last*, then *Nice Girl*, and then *Nice Girl?* as one studio executive deemed the unpunctuated title to be "too virginal to intrigue ticket-buyers." The movie was based on a play by Phyllis Duganne. It was produced by Pasternak and directed by William Seiter.

Nice Girl? features Professor Oliver Dana (Robert Benchley) and his three daughters. The youngest, Jane (Durbin), is dating Don Webb (Robert Stack). When Dana's business associate Richard Calvert (Franchot Tone) visits the family, Jane decides to stop being a "nice girl." She drives Calvert to New York, where she tries to seduce him. When Calvert ignores Jane's romantic advances she drives back home, still wearing a pair of borrowed red pajamas.

Jane is spotted arriving home in lingerie and rumors start to fly. To save face, she announces that she and Calvert are engaged. They eventually fake a quarrel and "officially" break their engagement, but meanwhile, Webb has been drafted into the Army. Jane finds him at his Army camp and they reconcile with a kiss. Jane then mounts a bandstand and sings,

"Thank you America."[2] In the last shot, the back of her outfit is covered with Webb's handprints, a souvenir of their recent embrace.

Nice Girl? was enjoyed by most critics. *Hollywood Magazine* called the film, "One of the season's most buoyant comedies." The *New York Times* wrote, "Hollywood and the Universal graybeards in particular have been torn asunder over the question: when and how should little Deanna be advised on what every young girl should know? Like tremulous parents approaching that crucial chat, they have finally broached the subject in *Nice Girl?* Everyone should breathe easier this morning, for the matter has been carried off with surprising finesse."

GOODWILL TOUR

After filming *Nice Girl?* Deanna went on a cross-country "Goodwill Tour." Although at the time this was a novel event, it wasn't unusual for actors to go on "roadshow" tours to promote their movies. Starting with Sarah Bernhardt in *Les amours de la reine Élizabeth* (1912), new movies often had a special limited theatrical release in major cities. There were reserved seats with higher ticket prices, souvenir memorabilia, and appearances by members of the cast.

However, this trip was different. Louella Parsons called Deanna's tour "a social get-together, with the little Durbin girl meeting the boys who sell her pictures and also the critics and press of the country." Deanna was accompanied by her mother and Universal advertising director John Joseph. Pasternak was so in favor of the tour that he delayed Deanna's filming schedule to accommodate her time away.

Wherever she went, Deanna was a sensation. In Miami, when she attended the premiere of *Back Street*, a Charles Boyer/Margaret Sullivan film, fans lined the streets for blocks. Headlines announced, "Crowds Jam Premiere to See Deanna Who's Not in Film." A reporter described the scene: "Six thousand people battered down the police lines to get a glimpse of the star. Deanna finally stepped from a limousine, dressed in a dazzling and shimmering creation of the sort of white which is used in the construction of angels' wings. Had the crowd reached their goal, there wouldn't have been enough of the creation, or of the corsage of gardenias or the white fox which topped it, to clothe Sally Rand."[3]

On February 1, 1941, Deanna appeared in Washington, D.C., at President Franklin D. Roosevelt's Birthday Ball. This was just one of hundreds of annual birthday celebrations for the president held across the nation to raise funds for Infantile Paralysis, prompted by Roosevelt's own struggle with polio.[4] Deanna attended the main ball with the president and his wife and danced with the famed general, William S. Knudsen. However, a second "Cinderella girl" was also at the ball. For the first time since the release of *Three Smart Girls*, someone had temporarily, as the *Winnipeg Free Press* stated, "literally taken the spotlight away from such movie stars as Lana Turner and Deanna Durbin."

The girl was fourteen-year-old Anna Sklepovich, daughter of a coal miner from Anawalt, West Virginia, an Appalachian mining town. Anna's birthday was the same day as Roosevelt's, and a month earlier she had written to the president to wish him happy birthday. Anna received a typed response thanking her for the letter. Written in pencil at the bottom was the message, "P.S., He says he would like you to come to his birthday party."

The penciled invitation had been written by Anna's younger brother as a joke. But Anna, assuming it came from Roosevelt's office, set out to Washington to attend the ball. The local paper alerted the Associated Press about Anna's story, the AP contacted the president, and Roosevelt decided to make the trip a special event for Anna.

When she arrived in Washington, Anna was met by a presidential aide and taken to the Mayflower Hotel, where she was presented with a pink chiffon evening dress and silver slippers. That evening, Anna attended the ball as a guest of honor. The official photograph of the event featured Anna, Lana Turner, Eleanor Roosevelt, and Deanna Durbin, grouped around a massive birthday cake. The next day, Anna explained that when the picture was taken, "Lana Turner sort of poked me in the ribs to get me out of the way," but that "Deanna Durbin was simply divine, just as sweet as could be."

Engaged to Be Wed

The sophisticated young lady wearing a smart leopard-trimmed hat with a veil and carrying a huge leopard fur muff couldn't be Deanna

Durbin. But it was, for we had a luncheon engagement and this was the girl who arrived to keep the appointment. Deanna Durbin, the sensational child songstress of the screen, has grown up.

—COLUMNIST NORMAN SIEGEL

Even if nobody else was ready for Deanna to become a woman, in her opinion it was far past time. By 1941, Deanna had filmed nine pictures. The first eight, which cost Universal about $6 million to make, had grossed over $19 million. Deanna had watched her older sister and several co-stars marry and start families. And now, in just a few months, Deanna would have a husband and a home of her own.

Deanna had an engagement party with 250 guests at the Beverley Wilshire Hotel. She had a bridal shower and also a lingerie shower, hosted by actors Anne Shirley and Helen Parrish at the Hollywood restaurant the Brown Derby. Actress Marion Nixon later said, "A girl like Deanna could have anything she wanted—just go down and buy it. But when a shower was planned for her, Deanna acted just like any other bride. I think that's sweet. And Deanna is getting such a kick out of it all."

A dress manufacturer offered Deanna $10,000 to copy her wedding gown for resale. She promptly turned them down, saying, "This is a time of sentiment, not commercialism." At the same time, Deanna's house was fairly bursting with wedding gifts. The tributes filled four large rooms and included a piano, over fifty lamps and mirrors, an entire room of linens, and a handmade sterling silver dinner set for twelve from Universal.

The wedding was scheduled for June 7, 1941, to accommodate Deanna's shooting schedule. However, when her next film was postponed, the wedding was moved to April 18, Ada and James's thirty-third anniversary. The ceremony was originally going to take place at Deanna's home, but the large number of attendees made this impossible and it was moved to Wilshire Methodist Episcopal Church.

When Deanna and Vaughn visited the Hall of Records to obtain their marriage license, a reporter asked her if she was nervous about the marriage date, since a Friday wedding was traditionally bad luck. Deanna, in a trim green gabardine tailored suit, replied, "I'm not afraid of anything.

Besides, Friday is my good luck day, and this is one marriage that isn't going to end in a hurry. I've been in love for a long time, you see."

Deanna flatly refused to reveal her honeymoon plans or any details of her wedding gown. "Not even my husband is going to see my wedding dress until I march up the aisle," she said. "As for our honeymoon, I just won't tell you a thing about it. . . I'm getting married only once, and I'm going to have everything that goes with it. All the trimmings. It's going to be old-fashioned just like my mother's and father's and it's going to stick just like their marriage, too. I am so very happy. This is my first romance and I hope to make it my last one."

JUDY AND DAVID ROSE

Deanna may have broken a million hearts and sent her bosses into temporary confinement when she brushed aside all obstacles to marry Vaughn Paul, but at least the engagement was not completely unexpected. And thanks to the foresight of Joe Pasternak, Deanna's fans already thought of her as a young woman. In a stark contrast, MGM had several years of juvenile films planned for eighteen-year-old Judy Garland when she stepped straight out of little-girl roles to marry David Rose.

Although Judy and Deanna were both making popular films and were both young women in a relatively small circle of Hollywood stars, they seemed to be living parallel yet separate lives. *Modern Screen* wrote, "I think of how Deanna Durbin and Judy Garland began together in the same studio, once made a short subject together, are so near of an age, should have so much in common, and yet never meet at all." *Photoplay* added, "These two were bosom friends before being parted by that champion partner, Fame and Fortune."

As Deanna's wedding approached, she and Judy were constantly compared, largely in Deanna's favor. Deanna was described as "truly in love," while Judy "cast mooning glances and cheek-to-temple poses with David Rose, whose divorce from Martha Raye is not quite final." The two ingénues may have had vastly different romances, but the issues their studios faced were the same. As *Photoplay* wrote, "Producers pine, 'How can these girls get married and still play sweet youngsters getting a few kisses per picture when the public knows they get dozens in real life?'"

The glamour that surrounded Deanna's wedding simply wasn't an option for Judy, who had fallen for an older, married man. At first, Louis B. Mayer absolutely forbade her to wed, warning her that it would ruin her reputation as the innocent teenager from *The Wizard of Oz*. But for once, Judy held her ground. Her marriage to David Rose was the one big act of rebellion in her young life.

When Mayer realized that Judy was going to go ahead with or without his permission, he devised a plan. After all, the Durbin romance and nuptials were being lavishly covered by the world press. Whatever the future consequences of Judy marrying someone completely unsuitable, MGM might as well benefit from some free publicity.

Not long after Deanna and Vaughn's wedding, while Judy was filming *Babes on Broadway*, Mayer informed her that she was going to have the wedding of the year, an event that would become famous in the annals of Hollywood. She would have a church, a white dress, thousands of flowers, and she would also have him, Louis B. Mayer, publicly giving the bride away. And the wedding would be conveniently scheduled so that it could be used as promotion for her upcoming film.

When Judy heard Mayer's plan, she promptly eloped. The next day, a telegram arrived on Mayer's desk:

I AM SO VERY HAPPY. STOP. DAVE AND I WERE MAR-RIED THIS MORNING. STOP. PLEASE GIVE ME A LITTLE TIME AND I WILL BE BACK TO FINISH THE PICTURE WITH ONE TAKE ON EACH SCENE. STOP. LOVE JUDY.

Louis B. Mayer immediately sent a telegram in return. It said that under no circumstances would filming for *Babes on Broadway* be held up. Judy was instructed to immediately return to the studio, and was informed that if she wasn't on set when the cameras started to roll, she'd be through at MGM and would never work in pictures again.

Even love wasn't as important to Judy as making movies, and she was back in the studio within a day.

THE WEDDING

With a thirty-second kiss which melted the heart of every spectator, Deanna Durbin, child star of the movies, tonight spotlighted her transformation into womanhood.

—FLORABEL MUIR, *DAILY NEWS*

At 5:30 p.m. on April 18, 1941, Deanna and her bridal attendants arrived at the Wilshire Methodist Church. Before their arrival, the church had been decked in seventeen thousand gardenias and searched from belfry to basement for uninvited guests. The bridesmaids, dressed in pastel blue and pink shepherdess dresses, were Deanna's cousins and friends, as well as screen stars Ann Shirley, Helen Parrish, and Ann Dwynne. Deanna's sister, Edith, was matron of honor. Vaughn's half-brother Elwood Bredell was best man, and the ushers were all associate producers at Universal.

The celebration began at 8:30 p.m. Vera West, who had costumed Deanna in all her movies, had designed her wedding dress: an old-fashioned, princess-style, ivory satin-and-lace gown with a sweeping train. The gown had long sleeves, ending with the graceful outline of a calla lily over the wrists. Deanna wore a Madonna halo of matching lace and carried a bridal bouquet of white gardenias, lilies-of-the-valley, and bouvardia, with a shower of phalaenopsis orchids.

Many of the wedding guests were friends from the studio: electricians, cameramen, carpenters, and wardrobe women. They wore tuxedos and gowns from department stores, and the customary Hollywood swank was conspicuously absent. Of course, there were also celebrities present: Eddie Cantor, Marlene Dietrich, Adolphe Menjou, Kay Francis, and Judy Garland. Deanna's singing teacher, Andrés de Seguróla, sat in the front row.

Deanna's father gave her away, escorting her down an aisle lined with lighted candles. She was called "Edna" during the ceremony—a telling choice—and she spoke her vows almost too softly to be heard. It was a double-ring ceremony, a rarity in the 1940s.

Deanna later said, "The wedding was the happiest moment of my life. As I walked down the aisle, out of the blur of the hundreds of faces turned toward me, I saw here and there the familiar faces of my studio crews, boys I've worked with ever since I went to Universal. They were smiling at me fondly, proudly—like my family. I was so glad to know that they were there."

Over ten thousand fans jammed Wilshire Boulevard, many of them lining up for hours for a chance to catch a glimpse of the bride. A dozen good-natured motorcycle police were present, hustling fans back when they crowded too close.

The reception was held at the Beverley Wilshire Hotel. Deanna and Vaughn traveled to the party behind a police escort while passing motorists stopped their cars and waved. The highlight of the reception was a five-tier wedding cake topped with a bird cage holding two candied lovebirds. Twenty reporters were allowed half an hour to take photographs in exchange for letting the guests enjoy themselves freely for the rest of the evening. Over 2,500 pictures were snapped in the brief time allotted to the press.

The newlyweds spent the night in the Wilshire bridal suite, which had once hosted an Indian rajah. The next morning, they left by automobile to a secret honeymoon vacation in Del Monte, planning to return a month later when Deanna was scheduled to begin filming her next movie.

Winnipeg fans sent a ledger of greetings to Deanna, and her grandmother, Sophia Read, made a rare trip to California to attend the celebrations. Former neighbors who had received wedding invitations showed them off around town, and one invitation was even printed by Frank Morriss in the *Winnipeg Free Press*.

Deanna's wedding was a magical event, full of love and genuine affection. Of all the tributes she received from her friends in Hollywood and from around the world, two of the sweetest came in the form of letters. The first was written by a reporter:

I am one of the nine hundred little friends who were guests at Deanna Durbin's wedding. With my best girl on my arm, I arrived in a Yellow Cab and a rented dinner jacket. I've never seen a greater mob at any Hollywood premiere, and for a moment I thought it was a little too-too. Once inside the church, that impression changed. The decorations were simple and beautiful, the music was out of this world.

We sat next to Judy Garland and David Rose. As the wedding march started, I saw Judy reach over and clasp Dave's hands. I felt the whole church brim over with affection for Deanna when she began her walk down the aisle. She was lovely. This was her great moment.

At the altar, the church now darkened, came the minister's voice saying, "Dearly beloved . . ." Vaughn's voice, firm and strong, carried to the farthest corner of the church. Deanna's was a whisper. It seemed odd to hear the minister's use of her real name, "Edna." The thought occurred to me that this must be the one time in her life that Deanna really wanted to burst into song but couldn't.

I'll never forget how these two looked as they came back down the aisle. The radiance of her face was something no makeup department could ever match. All I know is that an hour later I proposed to my best girl and she accepted me. How could she have refused?—W.D.

The second letter was tucked away and forgotten for decades in a dusty scrapbook:

I went to a neighborhood movie last night to see your latest picture. I caught the last show, and just about the time your name was flashed on the screen for the first time, you were getting married 3,000 miles away. The house was full, mainly composed of middle-aged people, but with a fair sprinkling of young couples.

Well, there was applause when your name appeared, but you should have heard those 800 suburbanites shout when you first appeared on the screen. They shouted so loud that the first few lines of dialogue couldn't be heard. You shouldn't mind that, though, because it was their wedding present to you.

I guess we didn't hear much of the dialogue all through the picture, come to think about it. Everybody was talking about you. A lady in front of me said, "Remember her in her first picture? She looked just like Helen."

Her husband whispered to her to keep quiet, and besides, Helen had black hair and her nose turned up. "Oh," said the lady. "I didn't mean she LOOKED like her. I just meant that she had the same nice, honest expression on her face."

That started somebody else off down the aisle. "She looks like my kid sister," he said. "She looks so sweet."

Meanwhile, the picture kept on running and you were having all kinds of trouble.

"She'll come out all right," somebody said. A lot of people shouted back, "You bet she will."

Your leading man in the picture (one of them, anyway) didn't seem to appreciate you, but everybody in the audience knew better. That lady in front of me said, "I'll bet his heart is breaking now."

And that's the way it went for about 90 minutes. There were "Ohs" when you got kissed on the lips. There were gasps when you were weeping.

And, whenever you sang, the audience tried to sing with you. Only a few knew the words of most of your songs, but when you sang "Old Folks at Home," that was different. Everybody helped out there. They didn't drown your voice out; they just made it sound louder.

When the picture ended, the lights went on. A lot of people, men and women, were crying. There was nothing sad about the picture, but they weren't crying because they were sad. They were crying because they were happy for you.

That was the nicest wedding present you could get, I think. So now you know, and lots of happiness.—L.K.

CHAPTER 14

Greetings from Mussolini (1941)

Not long after Deanna's wedding, reporter George Howard somewhat incredulously asked her about what had attracted her to Vaughn Paul. Deanna responded, "I think it was his unquestionable sincerity and his unwillingness to accept compromise. I liked, too, his insistence on being himself. In the company of an instrumentalist whose forté is classical music, he has courage enough to speak up and say he's mad about boogie-woogie. I wish I were more like him in that respect. I'm the tactful one, too tactful, maybe."

The reporter, sitting with Deanna in the Universal commissary, interpreted her statement as "a clear and definite view on marriage." Neither Howard nor Deanna seemed to realize that "unwillingness to accept compromise" could equally be interpreted as truculence. That "insistence on being himself" could be intransigence, and that publicly criticizing the genre of music that his new wife had studied for years was not an admirable trait. Instead, it showed a distinct lack of respect for Deanna and all that she had accomplished. But Deanna was still in love and wasn't yet able to recognize these truths.

When she returned from her honeymoon, Deanna was ready to become the chatelaine of "Chez Paul" and to successfully combine her career with the domestic duties of a young wife. Deanna's new house was designed by Allan Siple, an architect well known for his Los Angeles designs. A gift from Vaughn's father, it was situated in Brentwood on 1.5 acres of wooded hillside.

The house had a view of both the ocean and the city. By Hollywood standards it was a "simple" English bungalow with three bedrooms, three baths, servants' quarters, and a swimming pool. It featured an octagonal dining room, towering fireplaces, quilted chintz, and organdy flounces in the bedroom, with a Hammond organ in the recreation room. Deanna's bathroom was equipped with a "new-fangled" hair dryer. The house also had a twenty-foot steel-and-concrete "bombproof" shelter in the basement and Deanna invited all her neighbors, including Nelson Eddy, Gary Cooper, and Joan Crawford, to seek shelter in case of an attack.

Construction took longer than anticipated, mostly because Deanna's eager fans kept getting in the way. The address had been printed in a magazine story, and within a day, fans started flocking by the hundreds to the building site. "We have to sneak down there early if we don't want to be mobbed," Deanna told a reporter. "The other morning I found a girl pounding a big nail into one of my lovely pillars. I asked her what on earth she was doing. She said she wanted to go home and say that she had helped to build my house."

MUSSOLINI

Although Deanna represented the sweetness and innocence of American girlhood to the Allied soldiers fighting for freedom, she was also the darling of Axis leaders and was often used in their racist propaganda. Two years earlier, a photograph from *Life* showing Joe Pasternak, Henry Koster, and Deanna Durbin was featured on the cover of the anti-Semitic German magazine *Der Stürmer*. The photograph contained the caption, "Jewish Race Defilers at Work. This little artist is easy prey for Jewish gangsters. It is not necessary to explain what a little girl must do in order to attain fame and honor in Jew-infested Hollywood."

American films were banned in Nazi Germany and also in Paris and other occupied zones. But Deanna was extremely popular with Hitler, and later, with German prisoners in American POW camps. She was also the favorite American singer in fascist Italy.

During the war, Deanna's fan mail ran as high as ten thousand letters a month. Five full-time employees were assigned to handling her letters, and two of them did nothing but open envelopes. Possibly the most unusual fan letter ever received came to Deanna in June 1941. This was not only a fan letter, but was, as one newspaper columnist analyzed, "one of the cleverest pieces of propaganda that has been seen in America in many a day."

The letter came from Italy and was written on behalf of Il Duce by an official of *Popolo d'Italia*, Mussolini's newspaper and the official mouthpiece for the Italian dictator. The official also published the letter in the *Popolo d'Italia*, where it soon received international attention:

> *Dearest Deanna,*
>
> *In the past we always had a soft place in our heart for you. However, today we fear that you, like the remainder of American youth, are controlled by the president, and perhaps tomorrow will see fine American youth marching into battle in defense of Britain.*
>
> *If this is so, you don't know how hard life will be for the youth of tomorrow. Why doesn't American youth break the chains that are blindly dragging the entire nation into a war in which it will be defeated. To be able to gnaw the Axis, steel-tough jaws are necessary and not rosy ones used to chewing gum. If you only knew how good and beautiful are the children in Rome and Berlin and how much poetry there is in the youth of Europe, then you wouldn't listen to your and our enemies.*

The note—translated from Italian—was reprinted in American newspapers across the nation. And, as expected, the American press had much to say in response to this personal plea to their favorite movie star. On June 6, 1941, the *New York Times* responded with its own letter to Deanna:

> *Benito Mussolini's own newspaper has addressed an open letter to you, Deanna, chiding you gently for succumbing to the wiles of the president. He is leading American youth into a war in which they will be defeated, Benito warns you sadly. You don't realize how hard it will be, Deanna, for rosy lips like yours to try to gnaw at the Axis. You don't know how good and beautiful are the children of Rome and Berlin. Why doesn't American youth break the chains that are dragging the fine flower of America into battle in defense of Britain?*

This tender epistle shows how they like you in Italy, Deanna. Italian youth and their elders liked you so much that they could not be coerced to look at a home-made picture so long as you, or any American glamour girl for that matter, was permitted to be shown in an Italian theater. The Duce himself has such a soft spot in his heart for you that he longs to save you from the horrors of war.

If you should answer his billet-doux, Deanna, you might ask him why he is more tender of Americans than of his own youth. If war is so horrible for the young, why are those good and beautiful children of Rome snatched from the cradle and drilled to fight? They don't like being led to the slaughter, poor lambs; that's evident. What leader started the business of war for the young, anyway? And why don't the young of Italy break the chains that have dragged them into battle and death in defense of Germany?

But don't forget that the Duce is sincere about your boy friends, Deanna, he is afraid of American youth.

Meanwhile, H. J. Phillips from the *New York Sun* wrote a response to Mussolini on behalf of the star:

I have received your letter to me through one of your newspapers, chiding me for being among those young people of America who stand 100 per cent behind the president, and it makes me feel quite uncomfortable. The idea of me, a little girl in the movies, getting a warning from a great big Dictator like you! It's all so sudden. I had no idea you cared.

I always thought you were so busy answering orders from Hitler and trying to find out what you were expected to do next that you had no time for movie actresses. It would have made me awfully self-conscious just to have thought that, even on the screen, I was being glared at disapprovingly by you. I tremble even now.

You say I am making a big mistake in being against the Axis, because you and Adolf are unbeatable and that all Americans like me will be left behind the eightball, which hurts you because you like young people and hate to think of having to devour little American boys and girls. You think that I should keep out of any anti-Nazi movements and set that kind of example for the young people of America. You say the boys and girls of Berlin and Naples are much happier and face a brighter future than those of my country. Heigh ho and alackaday!

You wouldn't fool me, would you? I hope not, but I have read about your Italian boys and girls. It seems to me I have read that boys are trained for war from the cradle up. I've seen pictures of little school kids drilling in the hot sun when they ought to be out making mud pies or laughing at Mickey Mouse. And haven't I read about a little Italian duty being to do all the housework early, marry young and have more children than the Old Lady Who Lived in The Shoe?

Anyhow, Mister Mussolini, you are not half so sorry about me as I am about you. I know you are unhappy with Adolf. I know you would rather play in somebody else's yard. I am sure you are not nearly so hot for the Nazi way of life as you seem. I'll bet you would like to be a little boy or girl and come right out and give your honest opinion about German aggressiveness. I'll bet that if you could do it without anybody knowing it, you would love to go into a movie theater and boo newsreels of Hitler.

You're sorry for little girls like me, mister! Well, I am sorry for big boys like you! Don't worry about me anymore. I'll be all right.

P.S., Tell Adolf NOT to write me.

IT STARTED WITH EVE (1941)

The infectious gayety and charm of Deanna Durbin has never been demonstrated better than in her new picture. Where before there was a precocious youngster bouncing around the screen up there, now there is a finished, polished and enormously attractive light comedienne. Miss Durbin has indeed grown up, and in the process has ripened into one of the truly great stars of our day.

—*MORNING TELEGRAPH*

Deanna's next scheduled film was *Ready for Romance* with Charles Boyer. However, plans were changed to accommodate her honeymoon, and instead, the tenth Durbin picture was *It Started with Eve* (promoted in advance as *Almost an Angel* and *It Started with Adam*). This was the final movie Deanna made with Joe Pasternak and Henry Koster before they left Universal to work at MGM.

It Started with Eve was a light, sentimental comedy, reminiscent of Deanna's early pictures and very much an example of a "Durbin Formula" film. Koster came up with the idea for the movie. He recalled, "I read in the paper that General Pershing was dying, and somebody told me that they already had the front page of the *New York Times* printed and then he got better. That gave me the idea of an old man dying and somebody maybe wants him to be happy and tells him some lies, and then he doesn't die, and then the lies have to come true."

It Started with Eve opens at the deathbed of millionaire Jonathan Reynolds (Charles Laughton), where his doctor informs Reynolds's son Johnny (Robert Cummings) that his father is dying and that Reynolds's last wish is to meet Johnny's fiancée, Gloria. However, Johnny cannot locate her. In desperation, he asks a coat-check girl at the hotel, Anne Terry (Durbin), if she could play Gloria for an evening, offering her fifty dollars for help. The next morning, Reynolds suddenly improves. He asks to see Gloria again, and the romantic deception continues. After several misunderstandings and a growing familial closeness between Reynolds and Anne, Johnny and Anne acknowledge their true feelings for each other.

It Started with Eve was lauded by reviewers. The *New York Herald-Tribune* called the film "captivating comedy, brilliant direction and a delightful counterpoint of make-believe. A triumph for Durbin and Laughton." The *New York Times* wrote, "Fresh and pleasing . . . the perfect 8-to-80 movie." *It Started with Eve* played at the Radio City Music Hall in New York and was one of the year's top attractions, receiving an Academy Award nomination for Best Original Music Score.

Although the pairing of Deanna Durbin and Charles Laughton resulted in what was arguably Deanna's best film, *It Started with Eve* was plagued with difficulties from the start. The problems began with a disagreement between Henry Koster and Norman Krasna, the scriptwriter, who walked out on the project with forty pages left to write. Then, just three weeks into shooting, Richard Carle, the actor who played Reynolds's doctor, died of a heart attack. He was replaced with character actor

Walter Catlett. However, since Carle appeared in all the scenes that had already been filmed, a large part of the movie had to be reshot.

Then Deanna fell ill with a bad cold. After a week of shooting around her, production stopped for a month. Right after Deanna returned and shooting resumed, Laughton became sick, causing another delay. Meanwhile, an electrician broke a leg falling from the set and another got badly burned. Both Koster and Pasternak went through divorces. And, in the middle of all this, America entered into World War II, Pasternak accepted a contract with MGM, and Koster was declared an enemy alien.

Joe Pasternak loved Deanna. In many ways, she was like a daughter to him. And despite his inauspicious beginnings in Hollywood, Universal had been good to him. But although Pasternak had two years left on his Universal contract, he felt it was time to leave. There were several reasons for this decision. His movies had saved Universal from ruin and had made several people very rich. It was reasonable that he wanted a higher salary. Universal executives regularly undermined several of Pasternak's creative decisions, and he wished to have more artistic freedom. And then there was Deanna.

When Deanna ignored his advice about marrying Vaughn, Pasternak had been the one to abruptly change his movie plans and alter Deanna's on-screen persona. When she had been difficult with Koster on the set of *Spring Parade*, Pasternak had been the one to mediate so filming could continue. In his opinion, a producer's job was to make movies, not to placate a demanding star or calm a frustrated director. He also felt that Deanna didn't need him anymore, and that it would be better for them both if he moved on.

Meanwhile, MGM had offered Pasternak a generous contract. They wanted to make a star out of their young soprano, Jane Powell, and decided Pasternak was the man for the job. He had negotiated a deal with a high salary and creative freedom, and he eventually became one of the three most important people in the company, alongside Louis B. Mayer and MGM vice president Sam Katz.

For Deanna and Pasternak, each scene in *It Started with Eve* was tinged with an air of sadness, of finality. It was the end of something very special for both of them. When shooting began, Pasternak knew it was past time to tell Deanna he was leaving. He called her into his office and explained that MGM was offering him advantages that Universal would not provide. "It was the only time in our years together I saw her weep," Pasternak recalled. He tried to comfort Deanna as she sobbed, "You can't, you just *can't* do this to me!"

Pasternak stressed that his choice to leave wasn't about Deanna, but perhaps they both knew this wasn't entirely true. He recalled, "It was not easy to talk to her because a lot of water had flowed under the bridge. She had her life to live now and it could not be the same as before." When Pasternak finished speaking, Deanna tried to say "some nice thing" and ran out of his office. They did not have another personal conversation for over three years.

When describing the creation of *It Started with Eve*, Henry Koster recalled, "When we were doing that picture the war started. I had not become a citizen yet. You have to be in this country five years, and in 1941 I hadn't been here quite five years. I had to stay home after eight o'clock at night because of the curfew. Yes, although I was more of an American than most Americans I met, I was not only considered a foreigner, I was an enemy alien—a German."

Once again, the shooting schedule was changed, this time to accommodate Koster's curfew. But although he was officially seen as a potential foreign threat, the cast didn't treat him that way. "Every night at eight o'clock Mr. Laughton came to me and he would sit with me. The most wonderful part of the night was when he read to me . . . from the *Bible*, from Shakespeare, from *Alice in Wonderland*."

After *It Started with Eve*, Universal planned to cast Deanna in the role of Christine DuBois in a musical remake of the 1925 Lon Chaney film, *The Phantom of the Opera*. Koster would be assigned to the project as director and Charles Laughton would co-star as the Phantom. However, Deanna refused to co-star opposite a Phantom or anyone else. She turned down the project and a few months later officially went on strike.

ON STRIKE

Filmdom's No 1 star and biggest money-maker, 19-year-old Deanna Durbin, was suspended tonight by Universal, claiming a tiff which began when the grown-up child prodigy of the movies became miffed because her husband was ignored.

—*DAILY NEWS*

On October 16, 1941, Universal Pictures, which had earned over $20 million from Deanna's movies, suspended without pay its biggest star and greatest moneymaker on charges that she refused to report to work on *They Lived Alone*, a movie that was later shelved. Universal Pictures called it a suspension. Deanna called it a strike.

Matthew Fox, vice president of Universal, confirmed that Deanna had been removed from the payroll. He refused to comment on the reasons, claiming, "It would just exaggerate an unfortunate situation." However, Fox couldn't keep reporters, columnists, and fans from expressing a range of opinions about the situation. These included: Vaughn was causing the problem. Deanna's in-laws were making it a bitter family squabble. The studio was unfair. It was merely a token fight and would be over any time now. It was a fight to the finish and would go on for months. Deanna was "out of line" and needed a good spanking to bring her to her senses.

Three main stories were circulated about why Deanna was suspended by Universal, each spread widely by the press. The first involved Deanna's husband, Vaughn Paul. In 1939, Vaughn had declared to Louella Parsons, "I wouldn't marry a girl with all that money until I had a chance to earn a good living myself and carve a career of my own." Following Pasternak's example, when the executives at Universal Pictures had realized Deanna and assistant director Vaughn were serious about their relationship, he was once again promoted, this time to associate producer. Vaughn was assigned to the picture *Mermaid in Distress*, and even if he wasn't yet making as high a salary as Deanna, he was on his way.

But by October of 1941, *Mermaid in Distress* hadn't yet started production. Vaughn was weary of the interminable delay and feeling decidedly unappreciated at the studio where his wife was a shining star. And so, without proving that he was in fact capable of producing a film, Vaughn resigned and set about looking for a new studio connection, somewhere he could start at the top, equally as important as Deanna.

When Deanna went on strike soon after, newspapers reported that she had wanted her husband to produce her next film and the studio had refused. Pasternak was quoted, "When Deanna got married, I rather anticipated that something like wanting her young, inexperienced husband to come in on her career would happen. It's absurd."

The second—and most unlikely—speculation for the disagreement was Deanna's resentment of co-star Charles Laughton in *It Started with Eve*, and a not-unfounded impression that his supporting character had stolen the picture created to be a starring vehicle for Deanna. Laughton was considered by most to be the highlight of the film, and as Frank Morriss wrote, "When he is in front of the camera, nobody else has much of a chance."

Deanna agreed with Morriss. Decades later, she wrote to William Everson, a professor of cinema studies at New York University, "The sought-after new Durbin image was not meant just to show me grown up but to have a story which featured me in special and different circumstances, directed by someone exceptional. Instead . . . *Eve* was handed to Charles Laughton."

The third possibility was a professional disagreement between Deanna and Universal. Deanna had requested personal rights in the selection of stories, casts, songs, producers, and directors of her future films—the same rights less successful actors usually received. She felt the studio was treating her like a child when she was a seasoned professional. Deanna wanted to be allowed to know what was happening with her own career and to voice an opinion about things that affected her.

"I was suspended," she said, "for no other reason than that I wanted to grow up. The company was still treating me like a child instead of a married woman. And because I demanded the same prerogatives as any star, they suspended me. I believed that I had the right to see a script before I started work on a picture and that I had a right to some consideration in choosing a supporting cast. We couldn't get together, so I walked out."

Whatever the main cause of the disagreement, at the time of Deanna's strike she was considered a major asset in Hollywood. She was making a salary of over $3,500 a week, with a $50,000 bonus for every finished picture. Her contract with Universal did not expire until late 1942, so once

Universal suspended her, Deanna could not legally work for any other studio. And under the terms of what was at that time a standard Hollywood deal, she could be kept under suspension indefinitely.

Deanna spent her strike decorating her house and assisting with the war effort. Although she was not performing, Deanna expressed, "I feel swell. For the first time since I started working, I had time to do my own Christmas shopping." Although she was contractually forbidden from making movies, Universal allowed Deanna to appear in a short that was sent to Australia as a Christmas greeting to the American Forces. During the holidays, her records were dropped by parachute to almost every Allied camp in England and Africa.

The strike went on for four months. The cause of the breach was never made public and the terms of the agreement were also officially withheld. Reporters claimed that Deanna's demands—control of stories, songs, and directors—had been conceded to her in the settlement. The delays cost Universal $200,000, as the studio was forced to cancel two upcoming movie projects after being unable to find a suitable replacement for their star.

Deanna once again started making movies. She went back to being a media sweetheart and the beloved idol of millions. But the strike was not without consequences. Vaughn was annoyed that Deanna had conceded so easily. Universal became aware that Deanna was no longer a pliable ingénue. And Deanna was left with a mistrust of her studio, a pleasant taste of what life could be like if she didn't spend each day in the spotlight, and the dubious honor of *Photoplay's* 1941 award for "Worst boner of the year."

CHAPTER 15

Camp Tour (1942)

BY THE TIME AMERICA ENTERED WORLD WAR II, DEANNA WAS ALREADY considering leaving Hollywood. To her, freedom was more valuable than the stardom she had so easily achieved. And even after resolving the strike with Universal, she remained frustrated with her lack of personal and professional control.

However, once America plunged into war, Deanna felt she couldn't just walk away from the responsibilities and obligations of her stardom. As Deanna told *Modern Screen*, "I decided that this was no time for anybody to balk about work. Everybody has to co-operate now. My best contribution is to continue to make pictures. I'll wait until the war is over and maybe then I'll have a clearer view of things."

Because of the strike/suspension, Deanna didn't make any movies before the start of 1942, and none were released that year. But even though Deanna wasn't in front of the camera, there was still ample work off-screen for a movie star. Like all actors, Deanna "did her bit" to help the war effort. She worked for the Red Cross, she signed up for the Hollywood Victory Committee, and she entertained servicemen at Army camps and USO clubs.

Universal was besieged with G.I. requests for cheesecake pin-ups,[1] and the studio sent glamour photos and recordings of Deanna to military installations all over the world. Deanna learned to knit and started making socks, sweaters, and other comforts for the Red Cross. She knit on movie sets between takes, but since she appeared in so many scenes it took her almost three months to complete a sweater. Deanna later said that she recalled each picture by the garment she made while it was being shot.

She equipped a Red Cross center in her backyard for neighborhood use and started a Victory Garden in her yard where she grew beets so big they were featured in *Photoplay*. In the article, Deanna declaimed, "All it took was some new-fangled fertilizer and a bit of patriotism, and Bam! Five-inch beets were all over the place!" The vegetables needed to be dug out of the ground, and according to Deanna, "Pulling a five-inch beet out of adobe is like pulling a bowling ball out of cement!"

Deanna sacrificed her few weekly hours of leisure time to entertain soldiers visiting Hollywood. One enlisted man she met was Private Kenneth Wilkinson, the "Army's moviegoing champ," who had seen 312 pictures in the previous nine months and who was given a special leave of absence from the Army to meet Deanna. They were photographed together, Wilkinson's pale face stretching in a toothy grin and his eyes crinkling with pride behind his spectacles as he leaned in to his movie idol.

Deanna filmed a Red Cross "Roll Call" short supervised by Henry Koster, where she appealed for funds and performed the song "My Buddy." She donated profits from Deanna Durbin paper doll cut-out books to war charities and participated in several Command Performances. These special radio broadcasts, aired between 1942 and 1949, played on the Armed Forces Radio Network and were transmitted by shortwave to troops overseas. Performers were chosen by troop request, and there was a weekly listening audience of 95.5 million.

Deanna was featured in another *Betty Crocker* magazine column, "Deanna Durbin's Victory Dinner." The article suggested "a novel idea for combining a patriotic endeavor with social entertaining" by hosting a "victory evening," where the host would purchase defense stamps (a low-denomination type of war bond) and sell them to guests in exchange for the dinner: food a dollar, refreshments twenty-five cents.

Deanna donated six mobile canteen units, each equipped with hospital and kitchen facilities, for use in bombed areas of England. She cut up pieces of her dresses from *It's a Date* to send as mementos to soldiers overseas. Both she and Judy Garland were featured in the lyrics of a popular patriotic song, "Peggy the Pin-Up Girl," written by Glenn Miller:

> When he sees Lamoure or Grable on the screen
> Even a voice that's so disturbin'
> Like Judy Garland or Miss Durbin
> Can't compare to my pin-up queen!

Deanna was invited to England by the British Ambassador, Lord Halifax, for a Command Performance at Queen's Hall planned for early 1942 as part of a hospital benefit, as well as several performances for British troops. Deanna was excited about her first trip overseas and was looking forward to helping a nation that had already been at war for several years. She responded graciously, "It will be a great pleasure to do it, and a satisfaction, too. If I can help in the war effort, even in this small way, then I shall feel well repaid."

However, after the attack on Pearl Harbor on December 7, 1941, plans abruptly changed. Passengers could no longer travel safely by sea. The British embassy attempted to arrange aerial passage for Deanna, proposing an exemption to the rule that seats on official clipper planes be exclusively reserved for government officials. The request was denied. An attempt to secure a last-minute commercial reservation for Deanna on Pan American Airways also met with failure.

So Deanna changed her plans. Instead of performing for foreign troops in England, she decided to embark on a cross-country entertainment tour, visiting Army camps across the United States. The tour was arranged by the Motion Picture Division of the USO Camp Shows in cooperation with the Hollywood Victory Committee. Army camps on the tour included Fort Devens, Fort Dix, Indiantown Gap, Fort Belvoir, and Camp Edwards.

At the time, several disparaging insinuations appeared in the press about the questionable patriotism of film actors in Hollywood. Deanna countered the accusations by asserting, "We just have to do what we are best fitted to do. If it's fighting—and more Hollywood men are in the Army and Navy than people realize—or entertaining those in training, we do all we can."

Deanna was assigned to one of ten main touring units, while Judy Garland performed with another. Judy and her new husband, David Rose, had planned to make an extensive camp tour, with stops between shows to sell treasury bonds, war bonds, and war stamps. However, after performing at five camps and a hospital, Judy collapsed at Camp Walters, Texas, with a severe case of strep throat. She had to abandon the tour, but she returned later to perform with a different troupe after her recovery.

Deanna's troupe was a ten-act vaudeville program with USO Camp Show #4, titled *Razzle Dazzle*. Other performers touring with her included juggler Bob Ripa, tap dancer Johnny Barnes, "musical glasses" players Fayne and Foster, comedic singer Willie Sola, and mimic June Lorraine. There were also two MCs, Mary Lester and Milton Douglas, as well as a bevy of brightly costumed "Gae Foster Girls" dancing in choreographed routines.

Deanna was the headliner—in old vaudeville tradition, that meant the next-to-last performer. She was scheduled to sing two or three songs but often wasn't allowed to leave the stage before ten songs or more. "The boys are so grateful for these entertainments," she said. "It almost breaks your heart to see how happy you can make them with such small effort to yourself."

Just before Deanna left on tour, Vaughn was classified as 1-A, "eligible for military service," which meant he would soon be drafted and sent overseas. Despite this, Deanna did not hesitate "to go gladly" on the entertainment tour. To many, this was the first public indication that her marriage was not the fairytale it was thought to be.

Deanna entertained over fifty thousand troops on the tour, singing at service clubs, mess clubs, and dances. Theaters on the bases were large, with twelve hundred to fifteen hundred seats. They were well-lit, well-ventilated, comfortably heated, and equipped with state-of-the-art amplification systems. Deanna's troupe presented a ninety-minute show twice a night, six nights a week.

Sheilah Graham of the *New York Daily News* described the scene at one Army camp. "It rained here, and 800 soldiers proved they could take it by standing in line in front of the Camp Theatre the better part of an hour, hoping to buy 20-cent tickets to hear Deanna Durbin sing."

Instead of the arias, ballads, and art songs that Deanna performed in her movies, she picked songs that soldiers wanted to hear: "Amapola,"

"From Taps to Reveille," "Night We Love," and "Rose O'Day." Graham described Deanna's voice as "full and warm and youthfully fresh. It has a mature quality that could easily stir a variety of emotions. She could be one boy's sweetheart, and, if he closed his eyes, another boy's mother or a third lad's dream girl."

Deanna's account of her camp tour was published in *Hollywood*:

I have just lived through three of the most exciting weeks of my life. They were weeks packed with the hardest grind of work I've ever done, a few physical hardships, and a constant emotional strain. Translated into terms of salary, they added up to exactly zero. And yet, my reward was greater than money. It was something money could not buy. I was given a privilege which, in all sincerity, I wish every man, woman and child in this country could share. That privilege was seeing the fighting heart of America standing up to a job. It also made me proud to know I no longer was just a bystander in the struggle, but was doing my part of the job, small though it is.

She described how "at Indiantown Gap the boys rigged up a dressing room backstage . . . draping the walls with white target cloth tied with big red bows. Can't you picture hulking big buck Privates carefully tying on red bows because they thought it would please me?"

Deanna understood the efforts the soldiers made to show their appreciation. She recalled once, when signing autographs at a service club, "One of the boys shyly handed me a five-cent cupcake he had stopped to buy at the lunch counter. It was his way of thanking me. Two boys at Camp Edwards came backstage to present me with a gardenia corsage just before showtime. So what? Gardenias are gardenias and nothing ever extraordinary, you may say. Not to me! I knew it had meant obtaining leave, driving three-and-one-half hours to town and back to get the flowers, and three dollars out of a mighty slim paycheck."

At Fort Devens, Deanna paid a personal visit to one of the officers, whose quarters were located between two target practice fields. They could only be accessed at certain hours when the guns were stilled. "By accident we overstayed the time limit, but it was imperative we leave in time to make the show. That took a special telephone call to the firing range to hold their fire while our car made the dash, and I admit it wasn't the happiest ride of my life."

On a stop in Washington, Deanna was hosted by FBI Director J. Edgar Hoover, who showed her how to use a submachine gun. Deanna was also introduced to Massachusetts representative George Tinkman, a renowned game hunter. When they met, Tinkman exclaimed, "Why, I've seen you advertised all over Africa!"

Deanna was taken on her first "old-fashioned sleigh ride" behind two Army mules, and she attended a farewell dance for five hundred soldiers leaving that night for overseas duty. Just outside the dance, a train stood ready to carry the men away to their unknown destination. Deanna recalled, "They asked me to sing 'Embraceable You.' I tried, but the words choked in my throat. Then they asked me to say a few words. That was harder still. What can you say to boys at a time like that which won't make the going away harder? I talked about the fun I had had visiting them and my gratitude for the wonderful way they had received my efforts. I talked as if nothing was in the wind, and that I would see them again on the morrow. And all I could see was that train waiting for its cargo of youth, courage and determination."

HOLLYWOOD CANTEEN
The Hollywood Canteen was the best nightclub in the world.

Described by the *New York Times* as "a curious institution," this singular Los Angeles nightclub offered servicemen—usually on their last leave before being shipped overseas—food, entertainment, and a once-in-a-lifetime opportunity to meet, speak to, and even dance with their favorite movie stars.

Located in a converted barn at 1451 Cahuenga Boulevard in northern Los Angeles, the Canteen operated from October 3, 1942, until November 22, 1945, with almost three million visitors. The majority of the guests were Americans, but the Canteen was open to all enlisted men of Allied countries, as well as to women in the service. A soldier's ticket to admission was his uniform and everything was free of charge. The driving forces behind the Canteen's creation were actors Bette Davis and John

Garfield and composer Jule Styne. Renovations of the Canteen building and the labor to keep it running were all donated by members of various entertainment guilds and unions. The Canteen was staffed by volunteers from the entertainment industry, including Deanna, Judy, and several of their actress friends.

It was a hit. During its first month, soldiers packed away 25,000 pints of milk, 4,000 loaves of bread, 1,500 pounds of coffee, 70,000 oranges, 75,000 packs of cigarettes, and 100,000 pieces of cake. Over a million kisses were given. Music and dancing were provided by "big name" bands including Kay Kyser, Tommy Dorsey, and Duke Ellington. As reporter Kay Proctor wrote, "Millions of dollars' worth of hot rhythm was donated by the big names."

And then there were the girls. "After all," mused Proctor, "there must be girls for the boys to dance with. And there are. The sort of girls that the boys can't themselves believe they are holding to their palpitant hearts: Betty Grable, Ann Sothern, Deanna Durbin."

Deanna explained, "I wish I could say that I danced at the Canteen, but you could never call it dancing. I am yanked from one pair of arms to another and the orchestra is very loud, and I try so hard to have conversations—and then someone else cuts in and you begin all over again."

One night, Kay Proctor was volunteering at the Canteen. Her duties included moving food from the kitchen to the snack bar, answering questions, and spotting timid strays. Proctor noticed a tall, gangly soldier standing alone in a darkened corner of the room. There was a hungry look in his eyes as he watched the whirling dances and one foot tentatively kept time with music. He had a campaign ribbon with a battle star over his heart.

Proctor crossed the room to stand next to the soldier. She asked, "With so many pretty partners available, why aren't you out on that floor?"

A strange expression crossed the soldier's face. He introduced himself as George Brisco and explained that he had lost both legs in battle. He had learned to walk on his new artificial limbs and he did all right, now. But dancing, well, he hadn't the nerve to try it yet. Supposing he got out on the floor and made a mess of things? She could see how it was, couldn't she?

"Sure," Proctor said lightly. "But I tell you, I'm no great shakes of a dancer myself. So how about the two of us giving it a whirl? Right out in the middle where it's so crowded no one will notice us, anyway."

Brisco stammered for a moment and finally agreed. As it turned out, he managed exceptionally well, and no one could have guessed he didn't possess two good legs. When their dance ended, Kay introduced Brisco to Deanna, and they whirled off while Brisco's buddies stood by and cheered.

Later that night, Kay Proctor again approached Brisco. He was standing tall and appeared confident and smiling. "Gosh!" he exclaimed. "If I can dance with Deanna Durbin, I can dance with the world!" As Proctor later wrote in her column, "A man's courage regained at the cost of a few tired feet."

A soldier's impression of the Hollywood Canteen appears in a letter by Corporal Louis Lyne from Fall River, Massachusetts.

> *Someday, each and every one of us in the service will come face to face with tanks, planes and bullets—for some of us—death. For myself whether it will be a foxhole in the Solomons or a sand pit in Africa, my memory will stray to the grand people and stars of Hollywood.*
>
> *I recently spent a short furlough in Hollywood, and my greatest thrill was the Hollywood Canteen. Music by Kay Kyser, entertainment by Mickey Rooney, a dance with Deanna Durbin, a chat with Loretta Young, a cup of coffee with Irene Dunne, a heart-to-heart talk with that wonderful Martha Raye, and a motherly blessing from Faye Holden.*
>
> *Yes, some day from "No Man's Land," my memory will go drifting back to those people who took away the loneliness of a soldier 3,000 miles from home and sent me forward to what I have to face with a lighter heart. For those happy days, "God Bless You, Hollywood!"*

Then there was the story of Private Everett Scott and his dog.

Like millions of other young men, Everett Scott of Chanute, Kansas, joined the Army at the start of the war. And, like many other servicemen, he left his beloved pet behind. Scott's ten-year-old Airedale, Laddie, stayed at home when Scott departed for training at Fort Ord in California. Scott figured his dog would soon forget about him. But Laddie was so devoted that after a day spent sniffing hopefully around the house, he dropped in the dirt, closed his eyes, and refused to eat. For three months, heartbroken Laddie grew weaker and weaker, going from forty to twenty-five pounds.

The story of the faithful dog with a broken heart swept across America. In a time when millions of young lives were at stake, the tale of one wistful dog held a nation in thrall. Laddie became a symbol of the humanness of the men who command America's citizen Army. When the news reached him about the heartbroken pet, Major Stillwell, the Fort Ord Commandant, ruled that Laddie could come to stay with Scott.

Transcontinental Airlines flew the dog two thousand miles to the camp. As the airplane soared over the southwestern desert, a recording of Scott's voice played over the loudspeaker, repeating, "Hello, Laddie. How are you, boy?" In California, Laddie was taken to an animal hospital where a veterinarian kept an all-night vigil. When Laddie was reunited with Scott, he was overjoyed and seemed to be improving. Laddie was given a blood transfusion from Winky, a local Saint Bernard, and he managed to take a few steps unassisted. However, after just three days Laddie died.

Three weeks later the *United Press* reported, "Private Everett Scott of the 17th Infantry came to Hollywood today to accept a dog he didn't exactly need from Miss Deanna Durbin."

A woman in San Francisco already had given Scott a new dog, which he kept with him at Fort Ord. Scott politely declined offers from Hedy Lamarr, Paulette Goddard, and Gracie Allen. However, an offer from Deanna Durbin, the Army's sweetheart, was another thing entirely. Major Stillwell ordered Scott to put on his neatest uniform, travel to Universal, and accept Deanna's dog. Private Scott was a good soldier. He obeyed orders and went to Hollywood.

As one reporter described, "You could have cut your finger on the crease in his pants. Deanna was there, and there was also the dog, a six-month-old Airedale with a pedigree like a king's family tree. Miss Durbin said how-do-you-do. Scott blushed and said he was pleased to be here. They then posed for photos and went for lunch, where Scott toyed with a plate of pork chops and had to be persuaded to take dessert."

Deanna was doing her best to help and support the troops heading over-seas. But meanwhile, she was directly affected by the war. In February 1942, Vaughn was called up for naval service. After his departure, Deanna's sister Edith, her brother-in-law Clarence Heckman, and their baby, Dickie, moved in with her.

Deanna was considered a "war widow," and although she assured reporters and columnists that she missed Vaughn dreadfully, it didn't stop her from going to nightclubs with actors Anne Shirley and Craig Stevens. Perhaps, in truth, Deanna felt freed by Vaughn's absence. But whatever her true feelings about Vaughn or about her career in Hollywood, Deanna spent the next several years as a symbol of home to millions of soldiers, an inspiration in some of the darkest days of war.

CHAPTER 16

Deanna in WWII

THE JOY THAT DEANNA BROUGHT TO SOLDIERS AND CIVILIANS DURING the years of the Second World War deserves a chapter of its own. Soldiers stationed around the world were heartened, cheered, and even saved by Deanna. She was featured in dozens of war stories and she represented hope and freedom to millions.

Deanna was a favorite with leaders throughout the free world, particularly the British Prime Minister, Winston Churchill, who described Deanna as "a formidable talent" and arranged to see her films before they were released to the general public. Throughout the war, when Churchill achieved a military victory, he would retire into his private screening room with a brandy and a cigar to watch *One Hundred Men and a Girl*.

In Egypt, Admiral Sir Andrew Cunningham, Britain's Commander in Chief of the Mediterranean fleet, celebrated his smashing victory over the Italian fleet at the Battle of Taranto by going straight to the Alexandria opening of the new Deanna Durbin film.

The 330th Fighter Squadron in Glendale, California, made Deanna "Sweetheart" of the squadron. She was named an honorary captain of the 160th Infantry California National Guard and an honorary member of the American Legion. She christened the James Cook tanker at Terminal Island and was presented a pair of wings by the Dallas Aviation School. Deanna was given the rank of honorary colonel in the US Army Air Forces and elected honorary president of the "Blue Stars" group, an organization of airplane-building wives of servicemen. She was made an honorary colonel of the "Univets," the Universal war veterans. The House Guards of Great Britain's 'civilian Army' named Deanna their "Most Popular Star," while a quartermaster truck regiment at Fort Devens elected her, "The girl they'd like most to come home to."

One Hundred Men and a Girl was the last American film sold to Russia before World War II, and Deanna had fiercely loyal Russian fans, numbering in the millions. During the terrible siege of Leningrad, starving civilians lined up for hours at bomb-blasted cinemas to see Deanna find romance in *Spring Parade*.

One Hundred Men was also a favorite in pre-war Japan, and during World War II, Deanna was used as a propaganda figure in Japanese-controlled territories. When the Japanese besieged Hong Kong, they set up loudspeakers across a narrow stretch of water in Kowloon where a garrison of Canadian troops was stationed. The soldiers then played Deanna singing "Home, Sweet Home" and "The Old Folks at Home," the music punctuated with amplified taunts of, "Think of what you're missing back home!"

DEVOTEES IN WWII

The Deanna Durbin Devotees were also affected by the war. Because of an American government order forbidding the use of sterling silver and gold, club pins could no longer be manufactured. Instead of sharing letters about scrapbook collections and trips to the cinema, the Devotees' newsletter printed notes expressing how deeply the fans' devotion ran. One letter, written by seventeen-year-old Ruth Mitchell from Manchester, England, read: "After an air raid early this year, I returned to my home to find my bedroom thrown into a shambles by the blast from a land mine which just missed the house. I managed to extract some of my Durbin pictures from under the debris, but few weren't spoiled."

One wartime edition of *Deanna's Diary* printed a photograph of nineteen-year-old English Devotee Raymond Hill. Hill, who had recently become a bomber pilot for the RAF, wrote in an accompanying letter: "I have an invitation to a German party tonight, complete with musical pom-poms, ack-ack, and lightning effects by search-lights. Flying over Berlin beats a Hollywood premiere for searchlight displays."

In 1943, the British magazine *Universal Outlook: The Magazine for All Interested in Deanna Durbin* was discontinued when the editor, James

Stannage, joined the RAF. Although the Devotees continued throughout the war, the final issue of *Deanna's Diary* was published in 1943 when an American postal edict forbade American magazines to be mailed overseas. It contained a personal note from Deanna: "In these grim days all of us are busy concentrating the best we can on aiding the war effort, so knowing how much all of you are doing, your continued cooperation and loyalty mean twice as much to me."

Deanna and her family still remained astonishingly accessible to the loyal fandom. Philip Hozak, a member of the Devotees who served in the US Navy, wrote the following story:

Having just been transferred to San Pedro, California, from the Hawaiian Islands, I felt as though I had been suddenly transported from the underground realm of the devil into heaven itself, as the horrors of war hadn't as yet touched California. Two years ago I had the pleasure of meeting Mr. Durbin and seeing Deanna at the studio. They still remembered me and invited me to visit them.

The Durbin residence is a beautiful home, modern and spacious, right in every detail. After lunch, Mr. Durbin drove me to Universal Studios to watch Deanna at work. We watched Deanna with great interest while she and fellow workers did a scene about seven times in succession.

During a change of the set and lighting, Deanna was free to visit with us. She looked much too gorgeous for her own good in a form-fitting, white sequined evening gown, with an ornate white and silver bird on the shoulder for trim. Her smile and sincere cordiality makes you feel as though you've been friends with her always, and that you are just now renewing that friendship. She asked me if there were anything I would especially like and I chose to have my picture taken with Deanna. She called the still man over and some shots were taken.

We left the sound stage to go back to the Durbin's for dinner and I was asked to spend the night. It was necessary to rise at 6:00 a.m. the next morning, in order to reach San Pedro before my liberty was up. Mrs. Durbin came down and fixed us a grand breakfast and Mr. Durbin drove me back to the station. I can safely say that the Durbins are the most hospitable and charming people I have ever met.

During the war, more than two-thirds of Deanna's correspondence came from abroad, and more than 30 percent of the letters were from men in service. Hundreds of items were sent to Deanna with requests for autographs, including helmets, parachutes, and scraps of khaki shirttail. Soldiers also mailed souvenirs from overseas. A Canadian sergeant sent an aluminum ring made from a scrap of propeller from a German Dornier plane shot down in the Battle of Britain. In 1940, Deanna received a letter written by a serviceman with the Royal Air Force. Inside was a second, sealed envelope, which the pilot asked Deanna to forward to his parents in Kaatsheuvel, Holland, as mail could not be sent from Britain to occupied Europe.

Deanna also received a letter from a young soldier in West Virginia. He wrote that when he registered for the draft, he had given her name as the person who would always know his whereabouts. The soldier explained that he would be writing to Deanna regularly and based on the return addresses on his correspondence, the government would always know where to find him.

Another letter came from Private Howard Jones, a truck driver with a machine gun battalion of the Australian Imperial Force stationed in the Libyan Desert: "Dear Deanna, I want to tell you about my truck. The engine sings so sweetly that I decided to name the truck 'Deanna' after you."

A British soldier wrote about his flight from Dunkirk during the historic retreat. He explained that the only thing he managed to save, besides his own life, was his autographed photo of Deanna.

Pilot Officer C. P. Hulton-Harrop sent a postcard that read: "I am a British prisoner-of-war feeling a little bored with life, and wonder if you would be very kind and send me some stills from *It's a Date*, to add a bit of hominess to our room."

Back in 1939, high school student Donal Engen was so eager to meet Deanna that he wrote and sold a book about his high school's history to raise the fare to travel from Sioux Falls, South Dakota, to California to meet his screen idol. By the time America entered into World War II, Engen had graduated high school and left the University of Wisconsin to join the Air Corps as a bomber pilot. On his final leave before being shipped out, he traveled to Hollywood with his entire crew. Deanna gave them star treatment, including luncheon in a studio restaurant, a tour of the studio sets, and a preview of her latest picture.

During the luncheon, Donal shyly asked Deanna if, once he was overseas, he could name his airplane after her. Permission was granted, and the plane, a B-24 Liberator bomber, became christened *Deanna's Dreamboat* with a color portrait of Deanna painted on one side. The plane was based in the Philippines and was regularly sent on missions to attack Japanese bases in Formosa and China.

Another serviceman, Lieutenant Patrick Tolson, named his Liberator bomber *The Demi-Durbin* after seeing photographs of Deanna in *Life* magazine. According to Tolson, "Fully armed, the B-24 in which we are training for combat packs only half the wallop of Deanna."

Knud Petersen was a Danish artist and a teen-aged resistance leader. He recalled: "Jens was my brother. . . . We competed over everything, and it could get ridiculous. Living in Odense during the war, we both fell in love with American movie star Deanna Durbin. We had one photo of her, and we tore it in half so that neither of us could have her to ourselves. Same thing with our record player, a gramophone. It had a detachable crank arm that you had to use to get it started. I would take the record of Deanna Durbin singing and Jens grabbed the arm. We could only hear her when we were together, the last place we wanted to be."

Leslie Wood, a British Home Guard soldier, wrote this letter to an American movie magazine to describe his experience during the London Blitz:

> *It's a long way from this neck of the woods to Hollywood, but now we're all in this war together, I thought it wouldn't be out of place for a London Cockney to send you a thank-you note—not just you but to the whole motion picture industry—for what you did for us in the blitz.*
>
> *We've all been through a lot—the Jerries bashed us half but not quite all the way to hell, yet we still went to the movies. This wasn't just plain moviegoing. Every morning when we'd get to the shop or office, we'd learn another stalwart neighborhood movie house had been crushed to rubble. . . . Maybe half its audience was in the hospital or*

the morgue, yet just so long as you sent us pictures, we were there to see them.

Under every cinema screen there are two flashers. One says "Alert" in red and the other "All Clear" in green. Nobody takes any notice of them. I'd taken a duck under the seat when the glass started falling off the lights the afternoon Jerry bombed Buckingham Palace. But what the heck, the show went on and soon Deanna Durbin's voice, unforgettably lovely, made the rumble of bombs and guns less frightening and soon forgotten.

Cyril Grant, a Canadian anti-aircraft gunner on the cruiser HMS *Frobisher*, described his ship's arrival in France during the invasion of Normandy: "It was about 7:20 a.m. on June 6, 1944. Loud music was being played over all the public address systems, as a morale lifter I suppose. And just before the first landing craft hit the Normandy beaches in the Sword Sector, I was suddenly aware of Deanna Durbin's lovely voice singing, 'Say a Prayer for the Boys Over There.' Perfect timing!"

British pilot John Vickers described how the hunt for a Durbin album saved his life: "I flew Mark 8 Spitfires in Burma with several chums near Sinthe, an airstrip 50 miles north of Burma's largest river, the Irrawaddy. On February 12, I did a 'Grog Run' to Calcutta, spending two days buying grog and tracking down a record of Deanna Durbin singing, 'The Lights of Home.' As I landed at Sinthe on February 15, there was no sign of anyone. I climbed out of the aircraft and was told that, during the night of February 13 as I hunted for Deanna's newest album, a lone Japanese aircraft had bombed the campsite, killing eleven of our lads and wounding another thirty."

Arthur Iles, a British Naval gunner on the dangerous Arctic convoy route from Britain to Russia, fought a dangerous battle, accompanied by the sound of Deanna's voice:

In mid-February 1945 I was on watch behind 'B' Gun on HM destroyer Zealous *as it escorted a convoy bound for Murmansk, North Russia. Suddenly the bells rang out for "action stations" as a squadron of German torpedo bombers appeared through the leaden skies and came diving down to attack with machine guns blazing. The sound reproduction equipment had been churning out recorded music during the few hours of Arctic daylight and the delectable Deanna Durbin was putting her heart into "There's No Place Like Home." As the guns opened up, loud bangs, orders and imprecations could be heard as the guns' crews struggled to remain upright on the icy decks. And meantime Deanna was still pressing on with her song. The irony of it! I could not help seeing the funny side of the situation, when at any moment we could be blown to atoms!*

A private from 49th Air Base Squadron at Harding Field, Louisiana, described a "terrible incident" in which a windstorm blew down the cherished photo of Deanna, resulting in "a shattered glass frame and six shattered hearts." Another private wrote, "I am a medical soldier in the South Seas war. The other night, with a makeshift screen and seats of mounds of white coral, we saw *It's a Date* against a tropical sky. We are fighting a war for the preservation of all that is represented in the picture. It is worth it all."

From Syria, four British soldiers wrote to tell Deanna, "We have an old battered gramophone here in the camp and a few of your popular records. When we play them of a night in our tent and the liquid notes of your golden voice float through the olive trees of this strange land, the noise of the camp is hushed as the boys all stop to listen. Many a heart is stirred and many eyes are dimmed with tears as they think of their former homes when they listened to your voice in happier surroundings."

Another English soldier explained, "You epitomise everything that is missing from my present existence: sincerity, tenderness, music, and laughter. I am a tank driving instructor in the British Army, and perhaps you can imagine how, after a day of struggling with one of those filthy lumbersome beasts through seas of mud, it is just a little piece of heaven to be able to visit the garrison cinema, see you and feel the sweetness and peace which surrounds you."

Deanna not only heartened soldiers, but the cheerful, plucky characters she played in her movies also gave hope to girls and women overseas, victims of the Nazis and their Axis allies. For some, Deanna's movies were the only concrete images they had of a normal life through the long years of war.

In 1941, ten-year-old Ester Rudomin and her "capitalist" Jewish family were taken from their home in Vilna, Poland, by invading Russian troops and were sent to Rubtsovsk, Siberia. Although this exile saved Ester from the Nazis who later invaded Vilna, their years in Siberia were a constant struggle. Ester's father was drafted into the Russian Army, her mother worked in a slave labor camp, and Ester lived for several years in terrible conditions, fighting to survive:

> *The second summer in Siberia was hot and dry, a summer of severe drought. It was also a summer of typhus. People were dying by droves. It was also the summer I saw Deanna Durbin in* One Hundred Men and a Girl *four times at the village movie house. In the annals of movie fanatics this would not rate me a mention, but in order to get the sixteen rubles needed, our menu became more austere than ever. Whatever my parents thought of my self-indulgence, they never said a word; they must have realized how great this other hunger was.*
>
> *That summer, Deanna Durbin was our super-heroine. We sang her songs and we talked about her smile, her walk, her hairdo. But mainly we talked about her clothes; when the war was over, we would all dress like Deanna Durbin. How this was to be accomplished in Rubtsovsk was no concern of ours; there had been a scarcity of clothing even before the war . . . but we dreamed on and on and sang Miss Durbin's songs.*

Deanna even gave hope to the famous young Jewish diarist, Anne Frank. In a lot of ways, Deanna and Anne were very much alike: they were both clever, vivacious, talented girls. However, the circumstances of their lives couldn't have been more different. Deanna was known around the world. She was arguably the most universally loved juvenile star to ever grace the movie screen, and the smallest details about her were avidly consumed by fans of all ages.

Anne's life was a harsh contrast. She was forced to hide for survival, crowded with her family in secret attic rooms. Once discovered by the Nazis, she was shipped to Auschwitz where she and her mother and sister died of typhus.

Growing up, Anne dreamed of seeing Hollywood and becoming a screen star. Her playmate, Eva Schloss, said that before the war, Anne saw all Deanna's films. Nineteen-thirties Hollywood was an artistic realm that took the dreams of teen-aged girls very seriously, and it was a culture created largely by American Jews, Anne's own people, separated only by distance and circumstance. During the war, the fairytale of Deanna Durbin helped to inspire and hearten Anne, even as she lost everything else that she treasured.

Anne Frank's annex was emptied after her family's arrest, and when her father returned over a decade later, almost nothing was left. However, Anne's small bedroom was still decorated with photographs and carefully cut newspaper clippings she had posted on the wall: a posed shot of Deanna and two images from *First Love*. The clippings remain there today.

Margaret Sams grew up in California. In 1936, she and her husband Bob Sherk journeyed to the Philippines. When World War II broke out, Bob was arrested and Margaret and her four-year-old son David were sent to the Santo Tomas internment camp. In 1997, almost five decades after the war, Margaret wrote a letter to Deanna:

I am an old lady (a great grandmother) and for a long time I have wanted to tell you a story that involves you. In 1936 I was twenty years old and I longed to see the world. I had an opportunity to move to the Philippine Islands and I took it. As you know, Cavite, a Naval Base in the Philippines, was bombed on December 10, 1941. In less than a month, my young son and I were inside a fenced area in Manila. There were no facilities to take care of the hundreds of men, women and children. My husband had gone to join the armed forces and I never saw him again.

The Japanese tried in every way they could think of to intimidate, to demoralize and demean us. One subtle way of intimidating a conquered people is making them think that their homeland is no longer what it once was. An outstanding example of this everyone who was there will still remember. One morning, during the first hectic weeks of internment, we all read with great sorrow that Deanna Durbin had died a horrible death when she was giving birth to a child. We felt as if someone very near and dear to us had died and the whole camp mourned. We felt so keenly about it, as a matter of fact, that we had a memorial service. We all felt as if we'd had a real blow.

[In the camp, I met] Jerry Sams. I am sure that Jerry was the most daring man in that camp. He made from scratch a radio that could receive news from KGEI in San Francisco—with one tube. On Christmas Eve, 1944, Jerry (now my dear husband for 52 years) was just starting to listen to the news, when all at once he jerked his headphones off and hissed at me, "Come here!" He put his ear phones on me. I was actually electrified to hear a woman's voice saying, "Good evening ladies and gentlemen, this is Deanna Durbin speaking to you. I am dedicating this evening's music to the women of the Philippine Islands." And then she started to sing.

I still cry when I think of that night. It isn't that I'd ever seen you in my life, but we had thought you dead for almost three years. Suddenly, to hear you talking to the "The Women of the Philippines"—to ME—I could hardly keep from shouting it from the rooftops. We have loved your singing forever, it seems, and we still listen to your tapes and remember and remember. . . .

Nineteen days later, this letter arrived from Deanna Durbin in response:

Your letter told me so beautifully of your feelings . . . now, I shall try and tell you mine. To start with, there were tears. Then a sort of overwhelmed happiness that you managed to contact me and that after

all these many years I am able to keep and cherish your letter with its fabulous happy ending! It was written by someone whom I consider a very dear friend.
Always, Deanna.

CHAPTER 17

War-Themed Movies (1943)

At twenty-one, there are few girls who have lived as completely as Deanna. At fifteen, she was a star with a million-dollar invest-ment behind her. At nineteen, married and the mistress of a home; at twenty-one, a woman experienced in the emotion of parting from her husband when he went off to war. Yes, Deanna has packed a lot of living into her twenty-one years.

—*Photoplay*

For eleven months and eighteen days, Deanna didn't make any movies. She had spent the time on strike, establishing a home, volunteer-ing at the Hollywood Canteen, seeing her husband off for duty, and sing-ing at dozens of Army camps.

And then—as suddenly as she'd left—Deanna was back. Six years before, a beribboned fourteen-year-old girl dressed in a crisply ironed sailor suit had reported for the first time to Sound Stage Twelve at Uni-versal City. On June 15, 1942, Deanna reported there again: older, more independent, but still very much the property of the studio that had cre-ated her.

Moviegoers around the world had lamented the year without Deanna and were eagerly anticipating her return to the screen. They were also a bit apprehensive. Deanna was married now and could no longer play a child. She was no longer being guided by Pasternak and Koster and had negoti-ated at least some measure of story and director approval on her pictures. What sort of film would come out next?

THE AMAZING MRS. HOLLIDAY (1943)

From the outset, nobody seemed to know what *The Amazing Mrs. Holliday* was supposed to be. The movie was originally intended to signify Deanna's debut as a dramatic actress; however Universal insisted on adding songs to the film, making it a musical instead. Working titles included *The Divine Young Lady*, *Call Me Yours*, and *Forever Yours*. The plot was based on an original story by Sonya Levien, with a screenplay written by Frank Ryan and Hans Jacoby and a finale later rewritten by Robert White.

The Amazing Mrs. Holliday was produced by Bruce Manning, who had cowritten the screenplays to several of Deanna's earlier films. However, Manning also ended up directing this movie, the only time in his career that he stepped into a directorial role. Cinematography was by Elwood Bredall, Vaughn Paul's half-brother—the same cameraman Pasternak had turned down because he insisted on "only the best" for Deanna. The movie could—and should—have been a mess, and although the result was not close to Deanna's usual standard, her charm and talent still shone through.

Initially, *The Amazing Mrs. Holliday* was directed by Jean Renoir, son of Impressionist painter Pierre-Auguste Renoir. Already an acclaimed director, two of Renoir's French movies, *La grande illusion* (1937) and *La règle du jeu* (1939), were cited by critics as being among the greatest films ever made. Renoir himself was ranked as the fourth-greatest director of all time and was one of the first auteurs, a filmmaker whose personal influence and artistic control was so great that he became regarded as the author of the movie.

Renoir had signed a one-picture contract with Universal, and for that picture he was, inexplicably, assigned to *The Amazing Mrs. Holliday*. Production began in May 1942, with a shooting schedule of forty-nine days. On the first day the writers still hadn't provided a script, just the beginning of a storyline and some vaguely sketched generalities. After forty-seven days of shooting, the movie had fallen over ten weeks behind schedule, and Renoir and Manning realized they were heading for a disaster. They stopped shooting for the day and called an emergency meeting.

Manning offered to ask Universal to shelve *The Amazing Mrs. Holliday* and start fresh. He suggested another idea, outlining an adaptation of

Shakespeare's *The Taming of The Shrew* transposed to a present-day Texas gas station. Its owner would have two daughters, with Deanna playing "the shrew."

Renoir initially agreed, and the two men spent the evening sketching out the new idea. However, the next day Renoir quit. He claimed he was leaving due to recurring pain from a World War I leg injury, but there were rumors he was being fired for his slow filming pace. Renoir walked out of his contract with Universal and immediately directed another film, *This Land Is Mine* (1943), at RKO. Again, Deanna felt abandoned. In her words, "Not even in Hollywood does a captain abandon a sinking ship."

With no director, filming halted. Deanna suggested to Manning that he step in to direct the film. After all, Manning had observed Deanna and Koster working together for years and was the closest thing to Koster Deanna had. So Manning became a director for the only time in his career and pulled off what one reviewer called, "a near-miraculous salvage job."

When Manning took over, the shooting schedule was extended by seven additional weeks. After seventeen total weeks of filming, the finale was rewritten and filming was finally completed. On February 19, 1943, after what one newspaper called "a seemingly endless production schedule," *The Amazing Mrs. Holliday* was released.

The film begins with a missionary schoolteacher named Ruth Kirke (Durbin) and sailor Timothy Blake (Barry Fitzgerald) aboard a steamship, transporting eight war orphans from China to San Francisco. The journey had begun on a cargo ship commanded by Commodore Thomas Holliday (Harry Davenport), a ship that was sunk in a torpedo attack.

When the steamship docks in America, an immigration official informs Ruth that a $500 bond is required for each orphan, and Ruth and Blake rush to the home of Commodore Holliday, who they believe had perished during the torpedo attack. Desperate to help the children, Blake misleads the Commodore's wealthy family into thinking that Ruth was Holliday's widow. The family pays the bonds, and Ruth and the children move into Holliday's mansion. Ruth soon falls in love with the Commodore's grandson, Tom Holliday III (Edmond O'Brien). During a China Relief ball at the mansion, Commodore Holliday suddenly appears. He offers to marry Ruth; however upon learning that Ruth and his grandson are in love, Commodore Holliday agrees to let Ruth wed Tom if they leave the children with him.

The movie received óne Academy Award nomination for Best Music Scoring. Despite months of anticipation and a significant publicity campaign, *The Amazing Mrs. Holliday* was not a critical success. Reviews lamented Pasternak and Koster's absence. *Screenland* wrote, "For the first time in her brilliant career, Deanna has to cope with a poor story. Universal, do better by our Deanna!" The *New York Times* didn't even attempt to be kind: "Credit Universal for the clumsiest trick of the week. Not only have the authors exploited the cruel story of children in war, but they have made a film that is totally slapdash in construction. It has tried to be popular; it has succeeded in being cheap."

Deanna, too, was disappointed. In a 1990 note to NYU cinema studies professor William Everson, she commented on the movie:

> *I went on a six-month suspension at that time and came back to what I thought would be a picture written by Bruce Manning and directed by Jean Renoir. We were on the shooting stage for about six months with numerous script changes every day. [I was] enthusiastic and raring to go, and the disappointment of a bad film hurt all the more. Even if a film I made was not good, it represents a great deal of hard work and I can't help having certain fond memories and thoughts about it.*

HERS TO HOLD (1943)

After *The Amazing Mrs. Holliday,* Felix Jackson, who had worked as screenwriter on several of Deanna's movies, was assigned by Universal as her new producer. Jackson read the criticism of *Mrs. Holliday* and decided the public wanted familiarity. They missed the Deanna who had captured their hearts back in 1936. Yes, the child actress had grown up, and yes, there was now a war on. But that could all be incorporated into the next film, while still giving them the Deanna they wished to see.

For years, Jackson had wanted to create a third *Smart Girls* movie about Penny Craig and her sisters. Now that *The Amazing Mrs. Holliday* was finally complete, he returned to the idea. But first, he needed to locate RAF pilot Derek Bolton.

Born in 1916, Bolton had joined the Royal Air Force at the start of the war. He flew over eighty operations, mostly night missions, and was known and respected as a fearless bomber pilot. He was also a huge fan of Deanna. When Deanna was on strike, Bolton wrote to the Universal London office suggesting an idea for a patriotic "Deanna Durbin" movie, *Three Smart Girls Join Up*. Why not make Deanna a mechanic in an aircraft plant and do a picture about women in the defense industries? In his scenario, the leading man was an English RAF flyer and his heroine was an American girl.

The London office was intrigued with Bolton's idea, and forwarded the two-page suggestion to New York. Recognizing its potential, the proposal was sent by teletype to Hollywood. At the time, Jackson felt the idea didn't match his vision, as he wanted to focus on the girls at home. But when the movie idea was later revived, patriotic films were all the rage. The world had changed, and so had Deanna. The plot of the new *Smart Girls* movie could reflect these changes while recapturing the magic of the earlier films.

Jackson decided to move ahead with the movie, but he had a problem: he couldn't locate the young author. Even though *Three Smart Girls Join Up* was not an actual script, the story idea needed to be legally purchased before the movie could be made. But Bolton had been transferred and couldn't be found. Letters to Bolton from Jackson were merely returned to the movie studio. Universal persisted, pressuring the RAF to locate this one flyer.

At first, the RAF refused to help.

"But all we want to do is to pay the guy some money," said a staff member at Universal.

"Can't help it," replied his contact in the RAF. "We can't tell where anybody is."

"Just tell us when Bolton will be on leave," the staffer responded, "because we have his home address."

"Can't do that either."

Finally, a British official volunteered to be an intermediary, and after a two-month search, Bolton was found and the papers were signed.

In *Hers to Hold*, the film's final title, pilot Bill Morley (Joseph Cotten) is awaiting his commission with the United States Air Force. He encounters socialite Penny Craig and kisses her, causing Penny to immediately fall in love. Morley and Penny spend a romantic evening together, and afterward, when Penny sees an advertisement for riveter jobs at the aircraft factory where Morley is employed, she decides to apply. Penny learns to manufacture planes and during her breaks she performs for the workers at the factory. Soon Morley is called up to go overseas. After a brief misunderstanding, Penny races to the airport, arriving just in time to say goodbye. She sends Morley on his way with a smile, declaring, "If you fly 'em, then I'll build 'em."

Hers to Hold was filmed at the Vega Aircraft Factory in Burbank, California. It was shot on Sundays to avoid disrupting the actual manufacturing of aircraft. The airplane shown in the film was a Boeing B-17 Flying Fortress named *Tinkertoy*, which flew several combat missions with the Eighth Air Force over Europe. *Tinkertoy* was considered a "jinx ship" that no one wanted to fly, as its crews met with frequent and gruesome deaths. On December 20, 1943, the battered plane was finally lost on a mission over Germany.

Although *Hers to Hold* was officially the third movie in the *Smart Girls* trilogy, the other sisters didn't appear in the film. It was rumored that the reason for their absence was Deanna's refusal to appear in an ensemble movie where she was not clearly the star.

The movie received one Academy Award nomination for Best Song. Reviews of *Hers to Hold* were largely positive. *Motion Picture Herald* wrote, "Deanna Durbin is back with a combination of romantic gaiety and lilting voice that may well top her first hits." *Photoplay* called the movie, "A charming, timely love story." Frank Morriss wrote, "Deanna's acting has poise, and her singing is, as ever, delightful. A swell film."

Hers to Hold provided an interesting look at the war industry on the home front and encouraged women to sign on for factory aircraft work. However, instead of focusing on the acting, the music, or the movie's social influence, Deanna's public watched as she became the target of Hedda Hopper—syndicated newspaper columnist, rival of Deanna's champion Louella Parsons, and queen-bee gossipmonger.

HEDDA HOPPER

Nobody's interested in sweetness and light.

—HEDDA HOPPER

Most people in show business agreed that Hedda Hopper was an awful person. An actress-turned-gossip columnist with a daily readership of thirty-five million, Hopper could—and often did—gleefully ruin the careers and marriages of Hollywood's elite.

Born Elda Flurry in 1885 to a butcher's family in Hollidaysburg, Pennsylvania, as a young woman, Elda ran away to dance in a New York City chorus line. In 1913 she met and married matinée idol William DeWolf Hopper, twenty-seven years her senior. William Hopper had already been married so many times that he was nicknamed "the husband of his country." To avoid confusion with previous wives Ella, Nella, Ida, and Edna, Elda changed her name to "Hedda." In 1915, Hopper followed her husband to Hollywood, where she appeared in more than 120 films. In 1933 she was hired by Cissy Patterson, one of the first women to head a national newspaper, to write the column, "Letter from Hollywood."

Hedda Hopper set herself up as judge and censure of everything that happened in Hollywood. With frequent disdain for grammar, logic, and truth, she skewered the reputations of the beloved and powerful for over twenty-eight years. Hopper was loathed by most Hollywood stars. Joan Bennett sent her a skunk on Valentine's Day, and Spencer Tracy actually kicked her in retaliation for reporting on his affair with Katharine Hepburn. In the early 1940s, Hopper was at the height of her career. Possibly to scoop her nemesis Louella Parsons, who had always made a pet of Deanna, or possibly because of her innate inability to pass up juicy gossip, Hedda "tattled" on actor Joseph Cotten for trysting with Deanna while filming *Hers to Hold*.

The short column contained heavy hints that Cotten had been caught by the Malibu Beach Patrol in the back seat of his car astride young Deanna Durbin, and that they had stayed together overnight on the Universal backlot.

After almost two years of marriage, Deanna was already feeling she'd made a mistake with Vaughn. But whatever she chose to do about it, and whether or not Hopper's allegation was actually true, Deanna still needed to protect her reputation. She refused to comment or to speak about the matter and hoped the rumors would just go away. Joseph Cotten, on the other hand, had been married for more than a decade. And he was a man of action:

> *I told Hedda that as a journalist she had every right to air her opinion of my professional behavior on the screen but that my personal life was none of her business. She replied that I was wrong, and went on with an earful of trite reasons: "free speech," "duty to the reading public," etc.*
>
> *"Would you like me to deny it, dear?" she asked.*
>
> *"Yes," I said.*
>
> *"Fine. I'll simply say you said you did not have a midnight tryst on the lot."*
>
> *"Forget it, Hedda," I said. "And forget it forever. If you mention my name in your column personally again, I'll kick you in the ass."*
>
> *She did. And I did. The kick was not a boot that would have carried a football over the crossbar, but neither was it a token tap. Hedda was sitting in a cane-bottomed chair and contact was positive enough to disturb the flower garden on top of one of the outrageous hats for which she was renowned.*[1]

The kick took place at a party at the Beverly Wilshire, the same hotel where Deanna had received her Academy Award and had held her wedding reception. Hopper had just published another article, making further insinuations about the two actors. Cotten strode toward Hopper, saying, "I've got something for you." He then kicked right through the seat of Hopper's gold party chair and the chair's legs buckled, knocking Hopper to the floor.

After the kick, a "group of gentlemen" carried Cotten shoulder-high into the bar to toast his health. The next day, telegrams and bouquets filled his house, congratulating him on the kick. Cotten pasted the telegrams on his bathroom wall.

Somehow, in the gossip-hungry world of Hollywood, the Durbin/Cotten story didn't go any further. Perhaps there was no solid proof.

Perhaps the Universal press office called in some heavy favors. Perhaps reporters, remembering the sweet thirteen-year-old in *Three Smart Girls*, were reticent to ruin her reputation. Deanna did not ever say anything, write anything, confirm or deny anything about these accusations. Not then. Not ever. But she also never again appeared in a movie with Joseph Cotten.

HIS BUTLER'S SISTER (1943)

Universal has had rather a tough time bringing Deanna Durbin to adult flower. Maybe Miss Durbin's elusive charm is strangely inconsistent with maturity and with the sternly pressing problems of today. Anyhow, the boys at Universal have turned the clock backward as far as possible for Miss Durbin's latest film.

—*NEW YORK TIMES*

Hers to Hold and *The Amazing Mrs. Holliday* were both rooted in wartime themes. They contained only a few songs and featured a far more mature Deanna than before. However, by 1943, audiences were tired of war movies. They were looking for an escape, an on-screen fantasy to follow the newsreels presenting the stark reality of war.

In the 1930s, Carole Lombard, wife of Clark Gable, was the highest-paid star in Hollywood. She was known for both dramatic roles and for her "screwball" comedies. *His Butler's Sister* was originally slated for Lombard under the title *My Girl Godfrey*, as a sequel to Lombard's 1936 hit, *My Man Godfrey*. However, Lombard never made the film.

In early 1942, Lombard and her mother were returning to Hollywood after a successful war bond drive. Lombard had initially planned to travel by train, but at the last minute she chose to fly. Lombard's mother objected that airplanes were unsafe, but a coin toss in Lombard's favor decided it. The plane crashed into the mountains near Las Vegas just after take-off, killing everyone on board, and *My Girl Godfrey* was rewritten, renamed, and assigned to Deanna.

His Butler's Sister was produced by Felix Jackson and directed by Frank Borzage. As the *New York Times* put it, the studio was "cooking up a fluffy little pastiche which is openly a Cinderella tale." With this film,

Universal went back, as closely as it could, to the old "Durbin Formula," featuring Deanna in a role much closer to the Penny of *Three Smart Girls* than the Penny of *Hers to Hold*.

Ann Carter (Durbin) has a pretty voice, ambition, and an older half-brother Martin (Pat O'Brien) who lives in New York. Arriving at Martin's fancy Park Avenue address to stay with him while she pursues her career, Ann learns that her brother is not wealthy, but is employed as butler to composer Gerard (Franchot Tone). Ann is ecstatic to be in the famous composer's apartment, but Martin warns Ann that she is forbidden to put his job at risk by singing for Gerard.

The next day, while Ann is helping vacuum the apartment, Gerard returns and assumes Ann is the new maid. After speaking with Ann, Gerard feels intrigued by her and newly inspired in his work. Ann and Gerard spend an evening nightclub hopping, but a misunderstanding ensues and Ann, heartbroken, plans to leave town after singing at the annual Butler's Ball. When Gerard arrived at the ball in search of her, their eyes meet, and Ann rushes into the arms of her love.

His Butler's Sister was released on November 26, 1943, with a sixty-minute "Lux Radio Theater" adaptation airing on February 7, 1944. The movie was nominated for an Academy Award for Best Sound Mixing.

Although *His Butler's Sister* was not as big a hit as Deanna's earlier pictures, reviewers rated the film highly. *Variety* praised the "neatly-contrived situations, consistently good pace, excellent cast . . . a top attraction of the Durbin series." The *New York Times* asserted, "She makes very crystalline music and acts more simply and shyly than she has done in several films. It would be nice for Miss Durbin—and for us—if she could just go on being the center of such genial idolatries as this."

As part of a cultural exchange representing the alliance between America and Russia during World War II, President Roosevelt presented Stalin with a copy of *His Butler's Sister*, and the movie soon became the most popular Durbin film in Russia.

Judy Garland was also busy during the war, making the patriotic films *For Me and My Gal* (1942) and *Thousands Cheer* (1943). She also finally got her chance to work with Joe Pasternak. When he and Judy first met,

Pasternak recalled, "to my surprise I learned that she had been following Deanna Durbin's career under my guidance with a lot of interest."

"A lot of interest" was an understatement. Judy had won her stardom through years of heartbreaking struggle at a hostile studio while Pasternak had handed Deanna overnight success. Not long after establishing himself at MGM, Pasternak produced Judy in *Presenting Lily Mars* (1943), the film that represented her on-screen coming-of-age. But even with Pasternak at the helm, *Lily Mars* was not nearly as successful as any of the films he had made with Deanna. The *New York Times* said the movie had "the unfortunate air of a children's recital in which mama, or in this case MGM, is pushing her precocious child out front and telling her to knock them dead. . . . It is glorified monotony."

By 1943, Deanna had earned over $1.6 million, and Felix Jackson had taken over the management of her career. Her new contract with Universal made her the highest-paid actress of the time. In 1943, Deanna received $115,000 from her weekly salary, plus $150,000 for the three films she completed. In total, Deanna earned almost three times more than President Roosevelt's $75,000 annual income.

Although Deanna was Universal's top star, she still didn't feel the studio was giving her the respect she deserved. In mid-1943, Deanna was approached about starring in *Oklahoma!* on Broadway. This wasn't opera, but it *was* live theater, something Deanna wanted very much to do. Universal executives refused to even discuss the offer.

This blunt refusal made Deanna feel more constrained than ever. She considered another strike; she considered publicly battling the studio for control of her own life and her own career. But Deanna was already fighting for a different freedom, one vitally important to her.

Divorce
Deanna and Vaughn Paul were divorced on December 15, 1943.

After his marriage, Vaughn had expected to quickly rise to the top of the movie world. He pictured hosting stars for drinks and cigars after a day spent making deals on the golf course. He figured that soon "Vaughn Paul" would be one of the top names in Hollywood. Instead, when

Deanna's co-star Robert Cummings introduced the couple at a party, he referred to them as "Mr. and Mrs. Durbin." Vaughn was incensed. How dare people only know him as Deanna's husband? He was so much more important than that.

Vaughn was bitterly disappointed that after he quit Universal, no other studio would hire him. He was angry that newspapers and magazines saw him as "Mister Deanna Durbin." He was annoyed that his pretty young wife wasn't the same staunch but dependent young girl that she portrayed in her movies. The real Deanna had opinions; the real Deanna could fight back.

Louella Parsons was the first to report Deanna's marriage, and she also got the scoop on her divorce. In Parsons's column, Deanna explained, "Vaughn and I have been drifting away from each other for the past year. Perhaps it is his long absences. Perhaps it is the misunderstandings we never have been able to adjust. I am sorry and I know Vaughn is, but there seems to be nothing either of us can do to avoid a break."

To the rest of the press, Deanna issued a formal statement: "It is with deep regret that Mr. Paul and I have found it impossible to continue our marriage. As a result, I am taking legal steps to have the marriage terminated. Our marriage was embarked upon with all the sincerity and hopes that should go with marriage. But circumstances that neither of us have been able to solve now make it imperative to part to assure our individual welfare and happiness."

In court, where Vaughn was absent from the proceedings, Deanna was far less diplomatic. She stated mental cruelty as the reason for the divorce. "Although I am normally a very happy person, I was in a constant state of depression caused by his criticism of me and everything I did." Deanna testified that throughout their marriage, Vaughn had criticized her work and kept her in a state of constant nervous distraction. "I work very hard; very hard trying to make good pictures. But no matter how good the critics thought they were, Vaughn would always find fault with them. It was very discouraging."

Both Louella Parsons and Hedda Hopper painted Deanna as an innocent girl who had been blinded by love. Hopper used Deanna's "failed marriage" as a cautionary tale of what happens when girls ignore the advice of their mothers. But she also called Deanna "the ideal of American girl-hood." According to Parsons, "When Deanna said her wedding vows, she was . . . as unsophisticated, as pure in heart and as sweet as is the little girl who lives next door to you in your hometown. She had saved herself for the man she married. No breath of scandal had ever touched her."

Despite all that she endured in this short marriage, Deanna remained publicly diplomatic, explaining to Parsons, "I hibernated all my life, and when I married Vaughn Paul it wasn't any different. I was sheltered, every-one thought for me, and at the age of nineteen I stepped from the clois-tered girlhood into a marriage that gave me the same sort of protection. Every girl should be allowed to think for themselves. It wasn't Vaughn's fault or my fault that we failed to make a go of our marriage. He, too, was spoiled and an only child. If I'd had other previous romances, I might not have married the first man I was permitted to see. That would have saved him unhappiness and saved me from a marriage that should never have taken place."

Somehow, Deanna avoided scandal once again. She even kept the house. After the divorce, Hollywood forgot Vaughn, and fans soon man-aged to overlook the fact that their beloved star had ever been married at all. Deanna emerged from the marriage publicly unscathed and with her reputation intact, still one of Universal's biggest stars. Vaughn was not credited as working in Hollywood again.

CHAPTER 18

The "Nightclub Singer" (1943/1944)

CHRISTMAS HOLIDAY (1943/1944)

She has never had a failure. Every one of her pictures has been a hit. That scares you, you know. You say to yourself: "Now someday she's going to make a failure—everyone has a failure."

—WILLIAM SEITER

CHRISTMAS HOLIDAY WAS DEANNA'S FIRST OF TWO ATTEMPTS TO MAKE A firm transition from adolescent comedy-musicals to serious drama. It was the first picture in which she played a married woman, and the first time her singing was subordinated to her acting. In Deanna's opinion, her role in *Christmas Holiday* was the only worthwhile performance she ever gave. At the same time, it was—at least according to some—Deanna's first failure.

When Felix Jackson took charge of the "Durbin pictures," he realized that Deanna couldn't just continue to play ingénue roles. It was almost a foregone conclusion that child stars didn't continue their success as adults. But Jackson felt the transition was possible for Deanna, and he set about to make it happen.

In 1938, Jackson had read *Christmas Holiday*, a book by English novelist William Somerset Maugham that had sold over a hundred thousand copies in America. At the time he'd thought, "What a good gutsy picture it would make for some dramatic star." Walter Wanger at Paramount Pictures planned to turn *Christmas Holiday* into a film, but the Hays Office rejected his proposal, as they felt the plot of an Englishman meeting a beautiful Russian prostitute in a Paris brothel was "too sordid, presenting a story of gross sexual irregularities."

When Jackson first read the book, he hadn't even considered it as a vehicle for Deanna. However, in 1943 Universal bought the movie rights, and *Christmas Holiday* became an integral part of his plan to broaden the scope of Deanna's roles. To get around the Hays Office, the setting was changed to a nightclub in New Orleans and the lead was changed to a naïve girl working as a nightclub singer. However, despite the revised script, it was clear that the story was set in a brothel and that Deanna's character was employed as a prostitute.

Deanna wasn't the only actress making a first attempt at a dramatic role. At almost the same time *Christmas Holiday* went into production, Judy Garland's second husband, Vincente Minnelli, directed her in *The Clock*, a movie about a soldier on a forty-eight-hour leave who meets a girl at Pennsylvania Station and falls in love with the lovely New Yorker. The *New York Times* called *The Clock* "a tender and refreshingly simple romantic drama," but the film was far less successful than *Meet Me in St. Louis* and other musicals Judy shot around that time.

Not only was *Christmas Holiday* Deanna's first dramatic role, but it was also the first Durbin movie adapted from a novel. The screenwriter, Herman Mankiewicz, had recently written the screenplay to *Citizen Kane* with Orson Welles and was fired from *Christmas Holiday* after executives caught him drunk several times on the studio lot. Another writer, Dwight Taylor, was hired to replace him. A week later, Mankiewicz walked into Felix Jackson's office and said, "Felix, don't you think Herman Mankiewicz drunk still writes better than Dwight Taylor sober?" Jackson agreed and promptly hired him back.

For the male lead, Jackson chose a relatively new actor. Gene Kelly had only been in pictures for two years, but he had already gained a reputation as a cheerful hoofer and talented choreographer. The part of Robert Manette was completely out of character for him, but for some reason Kelly was the exact actor Jackson wanted for the role.

"I was scared to death to do the film," Deanna admitted. "But I wanted to do it more than any picture I have ever made. I've done thirteen pictures the nine years I have been on the Universal lot, and I've always played a sweet young thing with no problems. The roles were so easy I just found myself walking through them. But I knew *Christmas Holiday* would be a real test of my ability. When I heard that Gene Kelly had been signed, I was even more excited because I felt that Gene was absolutely perfect for the script."

In *Christmas Holiday*, Army officer Charlie Mason (Dean Harens) has an unexpected stopover in New Orleans on Christmas Eve. He visits "nightclub" Maison Lafitte, where he meets Abigail Manette (Durbin). In a series of flashbacks, Abigail tells Mason the story of her marriage with the charming but unbalanced murderer, Robert Manette (Gene Kelly). Meanwhile, Manette escapes from jail. He finds Abigail, accuses her of being unfaithful, and is about to kill her when he's shot by a policeman. Manette dies in Abigail's arms, leaving her to forge a new start with Mason.

Although director Robert Siodmak said that "Deanna ... flinched from looking like a tramp" and instead, "wanted to look like nice wholesome Deanna Durbin pretending to be a tramp," Deanna committed herself fully to the character of Abigail Manette. In her earlier movies, she had read the day's scenes for fifteen minutes under the hairdryer and was ready for the camera. She had been taught by Koster to strive for naturalness and to let the director do the coaching. But Deanna explained that with *Christmas Holiday*, she "would take the script home every night and rehearse every scene five million different ways." In a scene portraying the Midnight Mass in St. Louis Cathedral, Deanna forced herself to stay awake the entire night before so it would be easier to look harried and to weep convincingly on camera.

And then there was the slap. During one of the scenes, actress Gale Sondergaard was supposed to slap Deanna's face. Hard. Sondergaard tried faking the slaps but it just didn't look real. "I guess you'll have to take some really hard hitting," Siodmak told Deanna. "That's the only way it will be effective."

They launched into the scene and Sondergaard landed a "solid right" on Deanna's cheek. And again. And *again*. By the time the scene—with accompanying close-ups—had been filmed, Deanna had been struck eight times. Then the still photographer stepped in to take pictures of the slap. So they did it twice more. By this time, Deanna's face was swelling noticeably and only long shots could be filmed for the rest of the day.

Christmas Holiday was nominated for one Academy Award for Best Musical Score, although it contained minimal music. The movie had a misleading title and a confusing June release date, and critics were not impressed. The *New York Times* called the movie "a moody and hackneyed yarn, a dramatic farrago that was being played by faded stars ten years ago," with Deanna "painfully weak, empty of quality and attitudinized." Very few reviewers disagreed.

In *Chestnuts in Her Lap*, a book about "failed" films of the 1930s and 1940s, Caroline Alice Lejeune wrote:

> Christmas Holiday *is a jolly title for a Deanna Durbin film, but the title is the only jolly thing about it. Miss Durbin is an accomplished singer, so they cut her songs down to two and made them blues numbers. She has a naturally modest and ingenuous manner, so they cast her as a hostess in a seedy night club. She is at her best in simple comedies, so they give her a heavy drama about a wife whose homicidal husband believes her to be unfaithful. She has a youthful figure, so they dress her in sophisticated gowns. Her face is fresh, so they plaster it with makeup. She has a limited range as an actress, so they ask her to express, in ninety minutes, anguish, rapture, fear, world-weariness, and spiritual catharsis, apart from one or two other emotions you may find difficult to identify. Does this seem to you the best way of making a Deanna Durbin picture? No? No.*

Deanna expressed to Louella Parsons, "I loved all the controversy and I think Felix Jackson was awfully smart. Instead of gradually changing me from a goody-goody girl into a woman of the world, he let me take a complete break. I've never been so happy in any moment of my career as I am now. I want to play every sort of character—I want to be a great comedienne, a motion picture actress as well as a singer."

Although the movie was panned by critics, *Christmas Holiday* was Universal's highest-grossing film of 1944, overtaking *Arabian Nights* by almost $300,000. On the opening day at New York's Criterion Theatre,

12,644 tickets were sold. By the end of July 1944, the film had grossed $2 million, surpassing every other Universal release at that time.

Just after filming was completed for *Christmas Holiday*, Universal signed Deanna to an exclusive six-year contract. It was the last movie contract she ever signed.

DEANNA DURBIN HOME
"The Deanna Durbin Model Home May be Yours for $1.00!" the headlines cried.

In Deanna's birthplace, the war effort was in full swing. Canada had been at war since 1939, and in the past several years Winnipeg had promoted fundraisers to support their own troops as well as at least a dozen other charitable causes. The Deanna Durbin Model Home was a project of the local Kinsmen Club in support of the Milk for Britain fund. This initiative, spearheaded by Kinsmen founder Hal Rogers, raised funds to purchase powdered milk for British children. The campaign involved a raffle with an actual house—or $10,000 in war bonds—awarded as the grand prize. The house was located at 8 Kingston Row in St. Vital, Winnipeg, not far from where Deanna was born. The lot was donated by the municipality and the building supplies funded by Deanna herself.

Deanna was photographed presenting the property deed to a former Kinsmen member who had moved to Los Angeles, and Ada Durbin traveled to Winnipeg for the official "sod turning" at the construction site. In the photograph of the event, Ada was dressed in a white coat with a wide fur collar and was surrounded by Winnipeg dignitaries. Although the construction site on Kingston Row was just a few streets from the small house by the railway where she used to live, it must have felt a world away.

The Deanna Durbin house was won by William Campbell, a twenty-eight-year-old "bachelor farmer" living five hundred miles away from Winnipeg in Neville, Saskatchewan. Campbell announced that he didn't need a house in Winnipeg and would instead take the $10,000 bond. Overall, the "Deanna Durbin Model Home" draw raised over $25,000, enough to buy over three-and-a-half million individual cups of milk.

Months later, a real estate ad in the *Winnipeg Tribune* featured the Deanna Durbin Model Home: "Situated in beautiful St. Vital, this sensational new-type home, built by an outstanding construction company, with every one of the most modern and up-to-date features. Selling tastefully and well-furnished for $15,000 or unfurnished for $12,500."

CAN'T HELP SINGING (1944)

After the release of *Christmas Holiday*, Felix Jackson planned to film *Strangers*, a romantic drama for Deanna with French-American actor Charles Boyer. However, after receiving an avalanche of mail from fans demanding a less dramatic vehicle for their idol, Jackson instead decided to shoot a lavish, full-color musical.

Can't Help Singing was Deanna's fifteenth movie, her only film shot in Technicolor, and the most expensive film in Universal's history. A publicity brochure announced, "For the last eight years, Deanna has been in a black-and-white shadow on the screen before them. Now she is being brought to them in all the beauty of her natural coloring." Costumes were designed by Walter Plunkett, the designer for *Gone with the Wind*. Jerome Kern, who was celebrating his fortieth anniversary as a composer, wrote the score. The movie was based on the novel *Girl of the Overland Trail* by Samuel and Curtis Warshawsky. It was made to cash in on the success of the Broadway hit *Oklahoma!*, which, after Deanna had been forced to turn down the lead role, ran for a record 2,212 performances.

Can't Help Singing was set during the California Gold Rush and recounts the adventures of Caroline Frost (Durbin), the willful daughter of a senator (Ray Collins). To discourage their romance, the senator arranges for Caroline's beau, Lieutenant Robert Latham (David Bruce), to be posted in the far West. Fueled by her desire to be with Latham, Caroline joins a wagon train heading overland. She shares a wagon with Johnny (Robert Paige), a debonair gambler. Caroline and Johnny eventually reach Sonora, California, they fall in love, and all ends happily.

The movie garnered two Academy Award nominations, Best Music Scoring of a Musical Picture and Best Music Original Song. The film had an advertising budget of $300,000, which was the most Universal had ever spent promoting a film. The main poster tagline read, "The Thrill Your Eyes Will Prize Forever." Over its December 1944–January 1945 run at the Criterion Theatre in Manhattan, *Can't Help Singing* broke the record for tickets sold.

The movie was a relief to both Deanna's fans and to the reviewers. *Screenland* lauded Deanna for "doing all the things her fans enjoy so much." The *New York Times* wrote, "Those Yuletide herald angels hit some vocal competition yesterday. . . . Miss Durbin's generosity with songs was more seasonal and triumphant than that of the seraphic choir."

After the movie's release, Deanna received a fan letter from up-and-coming crooner Frank Sinatra: *I had scheduled that song of yours and Jerome Kern's "More and More" for my next radio broadcast. But after hearing you sing it, lady, I dropped it like a hot potato. It made me feel that I want to hear "more and more" of Durbin singing—and "less and less" of Sinatra!*

The end of 1944 found a much different Deanna than the year before. She was legally free from Vaughn Paul, and she now exercised a measure of control over her movie career. She had made a sincere effort as a dramatic actress, and although the reception had been mixed, she was still proud of *Christmas Holiday*. Also, her first large-scale Technicolor musical had been widely praised.

Two events near the end of the year affected Deanna greatly. On Christmas Eve, her grandmother, Sophia Read, died at the age of eighty-four. Sophia had been so proud of Deanna and had even made the difficult journey to California for her granddaughter's wedding. Deanna had meant to travel to Winnipeg to see her, but there just hadn't been time. And now, it was too late.

Then Deanna received a wire from the Chicago Civic Opera Company asking if she would consider a guest concert appearance at the Chicago Opera House in January 1945.

Deanna had always dreamed of being an opera singer. When she was offered an audition at the Metropolitan Opera eight years earlier she had turned it down, feeling she wasn't yet ready to compete vocally on a world stage and certain she would have another chance to audition. But although Deanna took regular singing lessons and performed classical pieces in her films, she hadn't been able to devote the undivided attention to her vocal training that was necessary to prepare for an operatic career.

When Deanna signed her new Universal contract, she knew that committing to several more years of making movies would further delay her musical ambitions. And although Deanna had taken the studio's *Oklahoma!* refusal very much to heart, Broadway wasn't her dream. But here was a chance for a classical concert appearance. She could prepare the songs in California, and Chicago wasn't that far away. Surely the studio would allow this opportunity that meant so much to her.

Felix Jackson was sent to break the news. He explained to Deanna that he had tried to rearrange her filming schedule. He was truly sorry the concert appearance wouldn't work out, but he was certain there would be other similar chances.

Deanna wasn't so sure.

CHAPTER 19

Two New Mothers (1945)

Deanna is now 23; she's prettier than ever. Her figure is slim and shapely with no suggestion of the childhood plumpness from which both she and Judy Garland suffered when they were youngsters singing their way to fame. She has a dazzling pink-and-white complexion, clear blue eyes, well-cut features, with evenly-spaced brows and lips and white, even teeth. Her disposition, one of the evenest, gives her a calm expression, but her eyes still hold the twinkle that made her first pictures so memorable.

—ROSALINE SHAFFER, *CEDAR RAPIDS GAZETTE*

AT TWENTY-THREE YEARS OLD, DEANNA WAS JUST AS MUCH IN THE public eye as when she was a child. She was now seen as an elegant woman, so popular with troops that her photograph was featured on the cover of the January 1945 edition of the Army magazine *Yank*. Although her life was still scrutinized, she had achieved some measure of independence. Deanna still lived in the house she had built with Vaughn, but now she lived alone, her solitude "a beautiful relief."

Deanna explained, "I'm enjoying my girlhood, because I never had any. Now I have my own household, my housekeeper and maid, the cocker spaniel and my first freedom to live exactly as I like."

And yet, nobody believed she would stay alone for long. According to columnist Dorothy Kilgallen, "Deanna Durbin is running the gamut of Hollywood eligibles." Newspapers romantically linked her to co-stars Robert Paige and Dean Harens, as well as actors Alan Curtis, Fred de Cordova, and Steve Crane.

Then there was Robert Landry: six feet tall, with dark brown hair and "laughing" blue eyes. Stationed on a Pacific cruiser during the attack on Pearl Harbor, Landry had captured iconic images of the event and had distinguished himself as a war photographer. Before the war, Landry had photographed Deanna several times for *Life*. He became reacquainted with her when he attended a party at Deanna's home while on leave. After that, they were inseparable. When it was time for Landry to return overseas, Deanna saw him off at the airport, and he cabled her from England when he arrived.

The relationship appeared to be serious, but Deanna insisted she had no plans for another marriage. "Almost every time I pick up a paper I read that I'm on my way to the altar with this man or that man. Seems all the reporters have to do to keep busy is to find me a husband."

Although officially she remained unattached, Deanna plunged into Hollywood nightlife. She went to Ciro's Nightclub, Mocambo, Chanteclair. She was photographed drinking and dancing: sometimes accompanied by dates, but more often just with Felix Jackson. Jackson was a man twice Deanna's age, and as her longtime producer he was seen as the perfect chaperone.

END OF WWII

At the end of World War II, Deanna was still seen as a symbol of freedom. She was a reminder of a simpler time, smiling proof that life would soon return to normal. In postwar Germany, *One Hundred Men and a Girl* was one of the first American movies shown to the defeated citizens. When American soldiers liberated Italy from the Nazis, one Italian was overheard crying, "Ahah! Now we get Deanna Durbin pictures again!"

The first postwar movie played in Manila, Philippines, was *His Butler's Sister*. According to the Office of War Information, the movie "created quite a stir" because the Japanese Army "had very effectively circulated propaganda, in the Philippines to the effect that Miss Durbin was dead of tuberculosis."[1] It was also the first American movie the American Occupation Committee permitted in Japan. It was hugely popular, not only because of Deanna's singing, but also because *His Butler's Sister* featured several kissing scenes, something not usually shown in Japanese films.[2]

In Russia, the Soviet Film Commission purchased several American films starring Deanna Durbin. Two American GIs stationed in Moscow attended a memorable showing of *One Hundred Men and a Girl*: "We knew enough Russian to read the subtitles they'd put on it. Poor old Deanna was the victim of capitalist exploitation; then in that place where she gets something to eat, they're only giving it to her to watch her make a fool of herself so they can laugh at her bad manners. It was all we could do to stay in our seats."

Deanna's early films had heartened soldiers, and were still providing inspiration and hope around the world. But the war was over, the world had changed, and Deanna once again tried to move into a serious role, to get away from the plucky "Miss Fix-it" character that defined both her personal and professional life. And that second effort was the musical film noir mystery, *Lady on a Train*.

LADY ON A TRAIN (1945)

Deanna Durbin, Hollywood's 20-carat voice, used to play Miss Fix-it, but now she's in worldly roles. . . . It may not be art, but, man, how it pays.

—KATE HOLLIDAY, *MACLEANS*

Lady on a Train was released on August 3, 1945. It was based on an original story by Leslie Charteris, produced by Felix Jackson, and directed by Charles David, a French director working with Deanna for the first time.

The movie was billed as a comic mystery featuring Nicki Collins (Durbin), an avid reader of "whodunit" books. Nicki accidentally witnesses the murder of shipping magnate Josiah Waring (Thurston Hall) from the window of a train. She seeks out mystery writer Wayne Morgan (David Bruce) for assistance, but when he initially refuses to help her, Nicki sets out to solve the crime herself.

Nicki is caught spying on Waring's family and is mistaken for a nightclub singer who is also Waring's fiancée. Nicki and Morgan case the nightclub where his actual fiancée works and are arrested for murder. After Waring's son, Arnold (Don Duryea), bails Nicki out of jail, she mistakenly seeks the protection of the murderer, Arnold's brother Jonathan

(Ralph Bellamy). Luckily, Morgan arrives just in time, followed by the police. Jonathan is arrested, and Nicki and Morgan fall in love.

One of the poster taglines, reinforcing Deanna's new image, was: "SeX Marks the Spot." The black satin dress Deanna wore in the movie was considered so iconic that it was donated to the National Museum of American History. And to publicize the film, Deanna became the first screen star to have her name adorn the side of a Pullman car.

Lady on a Train received an Academy Award nomination for Best Sound, but the film was not a critical success. The *New York Times* called the movie "an embarrassment," describing this "empty and careless little fable [as an] exhibition of the little lady falling flat on her histrionic face." *Photoplay* noted, "Even if you're a Durbin fan you'll probably wonder how Deanna ever got so precocious and artificial that it will almost embarrass you."

Deanna was disappointed with the negative reception to *Lady on a Train*, but compared to the excitement she was experiencing off-screen, the critical reception of her latest film didn't seem all that important. For again, Deanna was in love.

FELIX JACKSON

In April 1945, Deanna declared to United Press that she had no plans for marriage. She firmly asserted, "I've decided to live my own life for a while." Less than two months later, Deanna unexpectedly married again. The groom was Felix Jackson, her producer, a forty-three-year-old divorcé.

When Jackson became Deanna's husband, he was already widely respected in his own right. Born Felix Joachimson in Hamburg, Germany, he worked on a local paper and managed several Berlin theaters. In 1933, he fled Germany and worked with Pasternak and Koster in both Austria and Hungary. At that time, he wrote and directed the Austrian-Hungarian comedy film *Kleine Mutti* (1935), which was remade in Hollywood as the Academy Award–nominated film *Bachelor Mother* (1939), starring Ginger Rogers.

Felix Jackson seemed an unlikely choice for a love interest. He had worked with Deanna for so long that many colleagues called him Deanna's "second father." As one article reminded her fans, Jackson had been instrumental in guiding Deanna's career "from pigtails to black satin sophistication." He had been married three times before, and his third divorce was finalized just a few months before he wed Deanna.

Deanna and Jackson eloped to Las Vegas on June 13, 1945. They were married in the Little Church of the West, the oldest building on the Strip.[3] Deanna's brother-in-law was her witness, and her sister, Edith, was her attendant. She wore a gray chiffon frock and pale pink shoes and carried a bouquet of pink roses. Her wedding ring was platinum, set with baguette diamonds.

The newlyweds drove back to Los Angeles that night for a ten-day honeymoon, which they planned to fill with "romance and discussing the bride's next picture." They bought a house on a six-acre property in the Pacific Palisades with a view of the sea, seven fireplaces, and a stable.

Although Jackson and Deanna were seen as professional equals, in the first year of their marriage, Deanna earned $310,728 and Jackson $114,875, a clear economic disparity. The couple continued to work together with Jackson producing and casting Deanna's next film. Tabloid writers were delighted, and one headline blazed, "Deanna's Husband Picks Her Lovers!"

Magazine columnists, newspaper reporters, and Deanna's fans were confused about why Deanna, who had been so vehement about remaining independent and unattached, had suddenly chosen to get married to a man almost twice her age. And that confusion only deepened when, on August 13, 1945, the world learned that Deanna was expecting a baby— exactly nine months after her wedding day.

Because of Him (1945/1946)

Universal's production of a gay comedy to be entitled Because of Him *is also fondly called, by members of the publicity department, "the Stork Club."*

—LOUELLA PARSONS

Newspapers around the world buzzed excitedly over the announcement of Deanna's upcoming motherhood. Letters poured into Universal, offering congratulations and advice to the mother-to-be. Magazines wrote that Deanna had started knitting "soakers," and to ensure her child would be musical, she was "keeping up with her music and holding 'rhythmic thoughts.'" Deanna couldn't wait for her baby to arrive, but first, she had a movie to complete.

Because of Him, originally called *Catherine the Last*, was Deanna's seventeenth movie. It was filmed in the second half of 1945 and released on January 18, 1946. The film was known as somewhat of a "stork club," as Deanna was pregnant and the wife of co-star Franchot Tone gave birth to a son while the movie was being shot.

The movie follows Kim Walker (Durbin), a waitress and aspiring actress. When legendary actor John Sheridan (Charles Laughton) visits her restaurant, she asks for his autograph. Sheridan signs what is actually a forged letter of recommendation, and using the letter as an introduction, Kim is offered a role in a new play by writer Paul Taylor (Franchot Tone).

Sheridan is initially furious; however, after hearing Kim sing, he agrees to keep her in the play. That night, Taylor visits Kim's apartment and they kiss. However, when Taylor realizes Kim lied to get the role, he storms out, demanding his name be taken off the play. At opening night, Taylor overhears that the play is a hit and he sneaks backstage. When Kim sees Taylor, she rushes into the wings and into Taylor's arms, and the movie ends with Sheridan pulling back the curtain, revealing Taylor and Kim kissing.

Critics were not kind to this movie. The *New York Times* called it "an utterly pointless fable." *Varsity* stated, "Deanna Durbin sings, but why she sings is something you may be able to figure out, but apparently the writers couldn't. What Laughton does with this picture is nearly a miracle and drags it out of near-zero class."

After *Because of Him* was released, Thomas Pryor of the *New York Times* asked Deanna about her recent movie choices. Deanna replied that she would much rather "meet with complete failure trying to do something different than to be successful just doing the same old thing over and over." She went on to remind him, "I'm not fourteen anymore."

"But how about your fans?" the reporter persisted.

"They appear to like the change. Of course, I got a lot of letters in the beginning from people who thought I should continue to be the wide-eyed innocent of my earlier pictures. But I think I have another audience now ... one that I might not have if we hadn't tried something different."

Deanna wasn't worried about the critical reception to her latest film. There would be other movies. Besides, she was done acting for now, at least until after her baby was born. And, wildly excited, Deanna threw herself into preparing for her upcoming motherhood.

Two New Mothers

Deanna Durbin and Judy Garland are not copycats. Anyone will agree to that, but for some uncanny reason, both their careers and their private lives have run virtually identical. Never in Hollywood have there been two stars whose lives have run so parallel.

—John Todd, *In Hollywood*

From the day Deanna and Judy first met on the MGM backlot, their careers had, in many ways, "run parallel," and the two young singers were still being constantly compared, both on-screen and in their personal lives.

Judy had married David Rose just three months after Deanna wed Vaughn. Deanna divorced in December 1943, and Judy followed six months later. Both were June brides for their second marriages, and Felix Jackson and Vincente Minnelli both had professional working relationships with their new wives. And then, both Deanna and Judy announced they were expecting babies. With due dates only a week apart.

Deanna said, "I see that Judy Garland has announced that she is expecting, too. It is amazing how our careers have paralleled. We both started in pictures as singers while we were early teenagers; both were married, divorced, married again, and now we're to become mothers. I hope she is as happy and contented as I am."

Liza May Minnelli was born just a week early on March 12, 1946. But, as one magazine put it, "The stork flew in at Deanna's over four weeks earlier than expected." Jessica Louise Jackson was born on February 7, 1946, just under eight months after Deanna's wedding. She was delivered at the Cedars of Lebanon Hospital and weighed six pounds and five ounces.

Deanna explained, "Ever since I outgrew the kid stage myself, I've wanted a baby. I have a competent nurse, but I love doing things for her myself and have become rather expert. Of course, I sing to her because I couldn't live without singing. . . . Jessica should have musical talent, for she gets it on both sides. If she reveals this talent, we will do everything in our power to develop it. But right now, she seems to excel in eating and sleeping."

In a business where salacious gossip was hard currency, it was shocking that nobody publicly questioned how unusual it was for a healthy, normal-weight baby to be born less than eight months after Deanna's wedding day. There were a few whispers in Hollywood about whether Deanna "had" to marry Jackson, or if perhaps she should have "had" to marry one of the other young men she frequently saw before her second marriage.

According to Felix Jackson, after Jessica arrived, "Louella Parsons phoned to see if it was true that now the baby was born we were getting a divorce."

However, the whispers were few and they soon died away. Once again, Deanna had escaped scandal. By 1946, she was the second-highest-paid woman in the United States, behind Bette Davis, and her salary continued to increase. She had a beautiful baby in her arms, a talented man at her side, and she was ready to prove to moviegoers that their beloved ingénue could still make magic on the silver screen.

CHAPTER 20

Highest-Paid Woman in America (1947)

Deanna Durbin is the highest-paid movie actress. A "song" can no longer be the synonym for "cheap."

—PORT ARTHUR CHRONICLE

IN 1947, AT THE AGE OF TWENTY-SIX, DEANNA DURBIN WAS LISTED BY the United States Treasury Department as the nation's highest-paid woman, with an annual salary of $310,728.33.[1] She had a sprawling estate and a cherished baby girl. To her fans, Deanna's life seemed perfect.

However, after recovering from Jessica's birth, Deanna returned to a significantly different studio than the one she had left. Universal had merged with another motion picture company, International Pictures, and much of the management had changed. The new company, Universal-International, had become financially secure in the postwar boom and there were several newer, younger, and cheaper stars on the lot. Just before coming back, Deanna expressed, "I don't know if I'll be able to recognize the studio. . . . It used to be like one happy little family. I knew practically everyone by his first name and telephone number."

Deanna was right to be concerned. Instead of showering her with respect for her significant talent or gratitude for saving their studio, executives now felt less of a need to cater to Deanna. She could feel this change the moment she arrived back, but Jackson assured her that everything was fine and advised her to concentrate on her upcoming film.

I'LL BE YOURS (1947)

If I were Queen, I would toss half a dozen of Hollywood's best scribes into a custom-built dungeon and I'd keep them there for a year and a day, or as long as it took them to turn out a really good script for that long-suffering lass, Deanna Durbin.

—DOROTHY KILGALLEN, *MODERN SCREEN*

I'll Be Yours, originally titled *Josephine*, was released on February 2, 1947. It was Deanna's first film following the birth of her daughter, as well as the first movie made by Universal-International. It was a remake of the 1935 Margaret Sullivan comedy *The Good Fairy*, which was based on *A jó tündér*, a Hungarian play that ran on Broadway in 1931. The film was produced by Felix Jackson and directed by William Seiter, who had worked on two of Deanna's earlier hits. The movie was originally planned as a Pasternak/Koster production in 1940; however it was postponed after they left Universal.

In the film, Louise Ginglebusher (Durbin) comes to New York to make it in show business. On her first day in town, she meets poor but honest attorney George Prescott (Tom Drake). After Louise crashes a party at the Savoy Ritz, the host, Conrad Nelson (Adolphe Menjou), invites Louise to his private suite. He offers to star her in a Broadway musical in exchange for letting him indulge his "fondness for young girls." To discourage Nelson, Louise claims she's married, and when Nelson offers to buy her out of her marriage, she names Prescott as her husband. Many complications ensue, but Prescott eventually saves Nelson hundreds of thousands of dollars through his honesty, and Prescott and Louise fall in love.

I'll Be Yours was not a critical success. *Photoplay* called the plot "virtually non-existent, the unending story-lags filled with vacuities, and the few comic lines remaining thrown in without regard to time, place or story." The *New York Times* wrote, "*I'll Be Yours* is at best just a pleasant diversion, thanks mostly to Miss Durbin."

Usually, when one of Deanna's movies was released, she would discuss the film's reception with her producer. But Felix Jackson, Deanna's producer—and husband—was gone.

In November 1946, Jackson received a release from his contract with Universal-International, and in January 1947, nineteen months after he wed Deanna, Jackson moved to New York. Permanently. He planned to work in theater and announced he was writing a musical parody of the Emily Post etiquette book.

From the day Jackson left Hollywood, he showed no further interest in Jessica. And as for Deanna, either Jackson had thoughtfully remained with her just long enough to ensure her career was secure and to avoid any scandal around an accidental pregnancy (possibly with another man), or he had callously abandoned his wife and young child.

Nobody knew the true story, and Deanna wasn't telling. But losing Jackson was a huge professional blow. He had championed Deanna for almost a decade and had personally overseen her career since Pasternak departed for MGM. With Jackson gone, Deanna was left with ambivalent Universal-International studio executives and no defender to look out for her personal or professional interests.

And then, Deanna had to sue her sister.

Edith's husband, Clarence Heckman, had been acting as Deanna's business manager. He had placed one of her properties in his name in order to ease Deanna's tax burden; however when she asked him to return the property, she learned the house had been sold. Deanna claimed she hadn't sanctioned the sale and sued both her sister's family and the new buyers. The publicity led to the case being settled out of court; and although Deanna publicly claimed it was all just a misunderstanding, a wedge had been driven between her and Edith.

Meanwhile, Deanna's next film had started production. She told executives that she wanted to take on another dramatic role; however, as Pasternak wrote, "Upon her return to Universal, it was as if Deanna had come full circle back to her adolescent film days." Deanna's wishes were ignored and she was assigned another light romantic comedy.

SOMETHING IN THE WIND (1947)

Something in the Wind was based on an original story by Fritz Rotter and Charles O'Neal called *For the Love of Mary*, a title later used for Deanna's final picture. In the film, Mary Collins (Durbin) is a radio DJ.

She is visited by Donald Reed (John Dall), who explains that payments she had been receiving from his late grandfather were going to stop. Mary is confused and storms off when inferences are made that she was the grandfather's mistress. At home, Mary's aunt Mary (Jean Adair) explains that the payments were hers, from a boyfriend whose family had forbidden their love.

The next day, Donald and his cousin Charlie (Donald O'Connor) kidnap the younger Mary. Angry at being taken against her will, Mary pretends that she was their grandfather's mistress. She claims to be expecting a baby and demands a million dollars to buy her silence. Eventually Mary and Donald fall in love, and after appearing on a television show sponsored by the Reeds, Mary embraces Donald and the movie ends happily.

During the press junket for *Something in the Wind*, a Universal-International press agent concocted a fake organization, the National Association of Disc Jockeys, to promote the movie. Fifty of the country's top DJs were invited to Chicago for a one-day "National Association Conference" with travel and expenses paid. Upon their arrival, the disc jockeys were resentful when they realized the "conference" was primarily a media opportunity for the movie. However, the DJs liked the idea of a National Association, and they surprised Universal-International when they elected several officers. Their mission statement was: "To promote more respect for the profession, improve standards and promote finer disc shows." From then on, the NADJ was a real organization.

Although many of Deanna's fans disliked this new movie, *Something in the Wind* was enjoyed by critics. *The Melbourne Argus* wrote, "Durbin has fresh appeal in this new movie." The *New York Times* called the film, "A light and pleasantly-amusing charade using a studiously contrived plot," praised Deanna's character as "the ebullient, girlish Deanna Durbin of old back again, to warm the hearts of her fans."

Deanna's newer movies weren't a resounding success in North America, but her older pictures were being released overseas to staggering popularity. In Austria, *It Started with Eve* was labeled "social-reactionary" by the newspaper *Neues Osterreich*. The leading man in the film was wealthy, which set a bad example because Deanna "dared hell or high water" to win hand, heart, and purse of such a man in holy matrimony. Despite this critique, the picture ran for twenty weeks in sold-out houses.

Again, Deanna was a hit in Russia. When *His Butler's Sister* started its Russian run, one journalist reported the film "almost started riots among the eager crowds fighting to get into the theaters." According to the reporter, "One Russian militia woman was not important enough to simply demand a seat and did not want to queue. So she offered the employees at one theater where the picture was showing 'special consideration' on her beat if they would give her a ticket."

The reporter mused that one explanation for Deanna's popularity in his country was the fact that she looked young, and Russian film directors "had an unfortunate habit of starring their wives, regardless of their age, in parts calling for eighteen-year-olds." Several Russian fans wrote to Deanna. One of them declared, "Since I heard you sing, I have resolved to live a better life."

Deanna's popularity even reached as far away as Armenia, where she was mentioned in a recently unclassified CIA report about an agent's assignment in that country:

> *Upon arrival in Erivan, I was met by a very persistent Intourist interpreter whose first question was, "Is Deanna Durbin really dead?" Having assured him that such was not the case, he drew her picture from his pocket and addressed it in dulcet tones, confessing that she was the only girl he would ever love and requesting, if I should ever meet her, that I tell his beloved about the "lonely Armenian youth who would always be her slave."*

Back in America, Deanna was growing tired of the pressures of Hollywood. She had lost her longtime champions. She was constantly battling with her studio over the artistic control she had been promised, and she felt unhappy and resentful. She confided in her old mentor Eddie Cantor, telling him she wanted to quit the business. She also confided in her father, who told the *Winnipeg Free Press*, "Deanna never talks about her responsibilities, and she has so many of them. They keep her too busy. In addition to her acting she must keep up her music studies, look after her wardrobe, attend to publicity, and a thousand-and-one details."

Deanna had been "kept too busy" from the moment she first walked through the imposing front gates of MGM on her first day in Hollywood. She was used to being occupied with "a thousand-and-one details," but things were different now that she had Jessica. She didn't want to miss a moment with her little girl, and the one thing she couldn't buy was time.

Deanna tried to successfully balance work and motherhood. A room in her studio bungalow was set up as a nursery so she could run over to see her daughter between takes. She chose Jessica's clothes herself, bringing home three dresses for her daughter's first birthday celebration: one pink, one blue, and "a white one with French knots that would melt a heart of stone."

When Jessica was no longer a newborn, she was left at home with a trained nurse. Deanna recalled, "I can see how much Jessica missed by not having me around. When she was a baby, I was at the studio from six in the morning until eight at night. During that time she was in the care of a nurse, and heaven knows what would happen to her while I was at the studio."

Deanna mourned each moment she missed from Jessica's babyhood. One day, she was on set when she received a phone call from Jessica's nurse. Deanna felt a chill of fear as she reached for the receiver, and when the nurse started to speak, Deanna cut her off. "What, what, what? What's the matter? What happened?"

The nurse responded, in a cheerful and excited tone, "Sure, and Jessica's walkin'." Deanna sighed in relief when she heard her baby was safe. But her relief was tinged with wistfulness. Another milestone missed.

Deanna's beloved dog Tippy had been replaced by a Doberman named Buddy who became Jessica's loyal companion. Initially, Deanna had been a bit nervous about leaving her baby with such a huge dog, but Buddy was calm and devoted to Jessica. William Dozier, one of Universal-International's new executives, thought it was funny to joke about Buddy. He would seek out Deanna with a gruesome tale involving pet dogs, such as, "I just heard about a Doberman Pinscher who looked just like Buddy that ate a five-year-old boy." According to an onlooker, "Deanna would dash to the telephone to make sure everything was okay. Mr. Dozier, who kept a perfectly straight face during the entire proceedings, enjoyed himself immensely."

On most days, Deanna would depart for Universal-International before Jessica awoke. The studio was a full hour away, and often when Deanna arrived home, Jessica was already sleeping. When asked if she missed spending more time with Jessica, Deanna often quoted Gene Kelly's famous line, "What you go through for a lousy fortune!" In truth, Deanna was far less philosophical and regretted her long days at the studio.

And then, Judy Garland had a nervous breakdown. Two years earlier, both young women had been eager new mothers—the toast of Hollywood, in love, and excited about their new daughters. However, while filming *The Pirate* with Gene Kelly during April 1947, Judy's drug addiction spiraled out of control. She missed full days on the set, costing MGM thousands in production costs. Judy then caught Vincente Minnelli in bed with a man. This led to what her studio diplomatically called "an emotional episode," where Judy was placed in a sanatorium. She was eventually able to return to MGM to complete the picture, but later that year she made her first suicide attempt, cutting her wrist with a broken glass.

Several newspaper columnists, including Hedda Hopper, jumped to her defense. Hopper wrote, "People think of her as a slim, dark-haired beauty who can sing and dance like an angel. That's a tribute to her artistry. But Judy Garland, as you or I, is flesh and blood." Hopper went on to reminisce about how Judy had always "struggled for a place in the sun"; how when Deanna Durbin was such a hit with *Three Smart Girls*, it had crushed poor Judy.

Deanna hated that she and Judy were still being compared. She hated that her early success in Hollywood was being blamed for Judy's current troubles. Once again, their lives appeared to be running parallel. Both Deanna and Judy had been betrayed by their second husbands, and both were missing some of the most important months in their daughters' young lives.

The difference was that Judy would rather die than leave Hollywood. She would act in pictures if it killed her—and it almost had. And Deanna, well, she was already thinking ahead to when her six-year contract would expire and deciding what she should do next.

CHAPTER 21

Perhaps (1948)

The trouble is, people set child stars on a pedestal. They expect them to be perfect little darlings, and to remain that way when they grow up. No one can be that good. People criticize when these stars grow up and prove to be human with their own faults.

—DEANNA DURBIN

ON JANUARY 5, 1948, ALMOST A YEAR AFTER FELIX HAD LEFT DEANNA and her baby, Deanna's lawyer officially announced, "Deanna Durbin and Felix Jackson have come to a friendly parting of the ways. The separation is perfectly amicable and can have no particular interest to anyone."

Deanna was feeling less and less comfortable in Hollywood and was less and less inclined for her life to be an open book to the press, her fans, and the executives at Universal-International. As *Photoplay* described, "A delicate but nonetheless stone wall has suddenly been built around the life of Deanna Durbin." The magazine cited a recent trip Deanna had taken to New York. At Grand Central Station, she didn't leave the train until the other passengers had disembarked. Then she exited the station with a police escort, using a freight elevator.

Years earlier, Deanna had been made readily accessible to her fandom, something that directly contributed to her unparalleled popularity. She would meet visiting admirers at Universal, dining with them in the canteen or chatting with them on movie sets. "Should anyone ever ask me if I believe in miracles," one fan wrote after visiting Hollywood, "you may be sure I shall answer most emphatically 'yes,' because my wish came true. I met Deanna."

Even as Deanna made a concerted effort to keep her private life private, fans still adored her. One admirer sent her ten thousand tulip bulbs. Another sent a sweater he had spent almost ten years knitting. However, Deanna no longer offered her fans unlimited direct contact. She insisted on shooting on a closed set, and spent the little free time she had with her child. She didn't feel like the world needed to know and judge every aspect of her personal life. It had been one thing when she was a girl and the press office reported on everything from her sleeping schedule to the food on her breakfast plate. But now, Deanna was an adult—a mother—and she wanted at least some measure of privacy.

Louella Parsons didn't agree. She felt that Deanna had "embarked on a campaign to alienate the friends who had affectionately supported her for years." Deanna's crime, according to Parsons, was a refusal to discuss her separation with Felix Jackson with the press. In a media statement, Deanna stressed that her marital issues were her business and that every aspect of her life shouldn't be given to the public to judge and consume as entertainment gossip.

Parsons, whose career was built upon the judgment and consumption of entertainment gossip, took umbrage with what she considered Deanna's ingratitude. "It was all over town that Deanna was taking a high-handed attitude with her studio; she was running her own show and refusing to listen to wiser heads."

Deanna continued to be annoyed with the studio, frustrated with the movies she was assigned, and tired of feeling like someone else's property. First her parents had "owned" her, then Vaughn and Felix, and now Deanna legally belonged to her studio until the expiration of her contract in 1949. Both Vaughn and Felix had failed her, and Universal-International was failing her, too. It wasn't a matter of "wiser heads"; the issue was that nobody seemed to care about Deanna's happiness. And on top of that, the public—and media—declared the unquestionable right to judge and comment on everything she did. Deanna needed to think, to decide what to do next. But with her shooting and promotion schedule, she barely had time with her own child, much less the space to make important decisions about both of their lives.

Perhaps Louella Parsons had some inkling of this. She usually didn't hesitate to destroy an actor's reputation, but she had always been a staunch supporter of Deanna. "If I hadn't known and liked Deanna since she was fourteen, I suppose I wouldn't have cared. I asked her to come and see me, as she had often done in the past. I wasn't at all sure that she would accept. Neither was I sure that she would talk freely."

Deanna took Parsons's accusations as a warning. She still had several movies to make before the end of her contract, and in Hollywood public opinion mattered. Deanna agreed to a meeting. She smiled and gave the columnist a warm greeting, and then she did exactly what she had declared she wouldn't do: talk about Felix Jackson.

Deanna's statements about Jackson were as carefully prepared as any movie studio press release: Yes, she was happier now. No, the difference in age was never an issue. Deanna spoke about being married to a colleague. "With many couples it might be an ideal arrangement. But it will never be right for me. If you are going to have little temperamental moments—and most actresses do—it is just as well if the man you are married to isn't around to either sympathize or argue with you about them. Working together all day as we did, we found we had no outside interests, no stimulating contacts to bring to even the ordinary dinner conversation. Instead, trivialities of the day became major problems at the dinner table. Or else we knew every detail of the other's day so thoroughly, we had nothing to talk about at all. One of those things leads to arguments, the other to utter and complete boredom. And that is what happened between Felix and me."

Parsons brought up rumors of romantic liaisons with Al Proctor, Deanna's singing coach, and with co-star Vincent Price. Deanna just laughed these off. "Louella," she responded, "there are just two vital issues in my life right now, and neither one is a man. I am completely wrapped up in my two-year-old daughter, Jessica, who is a never-ending source of joy and happiness to me. And I want to make good pictures, fresh pictures, gay pictures. Like the ones that first brought me to stardom."

Parsons was impressed with Deanna's response, and the article she wrote following their meeting ended with the statement, "All this new Deanna is asking, is the dignity of a little privacy while she tries to work out her personal problems. Also, a little patience from all of us who are fond of her while she works hard, hard and harder to give us what we know she can do on the screen. I'm for her. Aren't you?"

Meanwhile, Deanna was making another movie. Films considered for Deanna's next picture included *Song of Norway*, which Universal had bought for $200,000 before the merger as a vehicle for Deanna; *Bloomer Girl* by Harold Arlen and E. Y. Harburg (who had written Judy Garland's signature song, *Somewhere Over the Rainbow*); and the Kurt Weill musical *One Touch of Venus*.

Instead, the next movie Deanna was assigned at Universal-International was *For the Love of Mary*. The film was supposed to be a mature comedy, reasserting Deanna as the popular and appealing young actress the world loved and expected to see on-screen. However, to Deanna, this was just a slightly older version of "a little girl with a big sailor hat on the back of her head." And she loathed every minute of it.

FOR THE LOVE OF MARY (1947/1949)

For the Love of Mary was the second-last movie Deanna made and the final Durbin film released. The story, originally titled *White House Girl* and then *Washington Girl*, was purchased by Universal-International from MGM. Pasternak had originally planned to produce the film for Deanna in 1941; however the movie wasn't made, and when Pasternak went to MGM, the rights went with him. Universal-International, hoping to recapture some of the "Deanna Durbin" magic from the Pasternak/Koster days, decided to revive and develop this earlier idea.

In the film, Mary Peppertree (Durbin) is starting a job as a switchboard operator at the White House. She receives an incoming call from David Paxton (Don Taylor), an ichthyologist who insists on speaking to the president. The next call comes from Mary's former fiancé, attorney Phillip Manning (Jeffrey Lynn), who won't accept that their relationship is over. When the president overhears Mary telling Manning that she would rather stay home than attend a party with him, the president sends Lt. Farrington (Edmond O'Brien), a naval aide at the White House, to escort her to the event.

The rest of the movie is filled with romantic and political confusion. By the end, Mary and Paxton are in love, and Manning and Farrington are given assignments far from Washington. Mary calls the president with the good news about her romance, and Paxton interrupts her conversation with a kiss.

For the Love of Mary was produced by Karl Tunberg and directed by Frederick de Cordova, who later went on to work with Johnny Carson. The movie received mixed reviews. *Variety* called it "a delightful light comedy experience." Bosley Crowther of the *New York Times* saw the film in a much different light. He called the movie "a sly piece of propaganda against the administrators of our government in Washington, where their evident lack of ingenuity is the clue to their basic design. And the simple fact that all this bother of Washington's highest brass is over Deanna Durbin, who is rapidly losing her girlish charm, is a patent attempt to cast aspersions upon the administrators' taste."

Although *For the Love of Mary* was completed on schedule, the movie was put aside for several months before being released. Meanwhile Deanna was assigned to another picture, the last movie she ever made.

UP IN CENTRAL PARK (1948)

Up in Central Park was a movie adaptation of a 1945 Broadway show by Dorothy and Herbert Fields, with music by Sigmund Romberg. Universal bought the film rights in 1946 as a starring vehicle for Deanna. At the time, they announced the movie would be filmed in Technicolor and that it would be produced by Felix Jackson and directed by dance legend Fred Astaire.

But when Jackson left Hollywood and Universal-International couldn't come to terms with MGM, Astaire's studio, plans were revised. Joseph Sistrom was assigned as producer, and William Seiter took over as director. Then the Technicolor lab was hit by a strike, and *Up in Central Park* was delayed for several more months.

Eventually, Universal-International executives decided the film and its star weren't worth the cost of Technicolor. Sistrom was assigned to another project, and Karl Tunberg wrote the screenplay and produced the movie. Dick Haymes and horror icon Vincent Price were cast in leading roles. In Price's words, "I took the part because Fred Astaire was going to direct, but he quit on the opening day of filming. Perhaps he finally read the script."

Up in Central Park is set in New York City in the 1870s. Corrupt political boss William Tweed (Vincent Price) and his Tammany Hall political machine are working to re-elect their candidates. The one voice opposing Tweed's organization is John Matthews (Dick Haymes), a *New York Times* reporter. When Irish immigrant Timothy Moore (Albert Sharpe) and his daughter Rosie (Durbin) arrive in New York, they are brought to Tweed's victory party. At the event, when Rosie overhears Tweed's plan to embezzle the city's coffers, he appoints Moore as Central Park superintendent to ensure Rosie's silence.

Rosie and Tweed become romantically involved; however, Matthews falls in love with Rosie too. With Moore's help, Matthews gains evidence against the political boss, Tweed's corruption is exposed, and he flees. Matthews and Moore discover a disconsolate Rosie wandering through Central Park, and she and Matthews are reunited.

Up in Central Park was released on March 5, 1948. Most of the popular songs audiences loved from the stage production were filmed and inexplicably cut. The *New York Times* praised Deanna's voice, calling it "clear and bell-like, but such a limited repertoire is hardly enough to provide her with a decent workout." The *New York Herald-Tribune* called the movie "one of the dullest shows on record . . . utterly without charm, a still and static bore." *Modern Screen* callously claimed, "They just do not go for Deanna as they did years ago."

In August 1948, just over two months after the release of *Up in Central Park*, Universal-International sued Deanna for $87,083, money the studio claimed was paid as an advance when she was on leave during her pregnancy. The reason why the money had been advanced and why Universal-International wanted it returned was never directly explained. Perhaps Deanna decided she didn't wish to make any more movies and tried to buy out her contract. Perhaps the studio had lost such faith in Deanna that the executives didn't want to pay her for movies they didn't plan to make.

The suit was eventually settled out of court four months later. Deanna's contract was revised to require her to complete (and be paid for) three more films instead of the five previously listed. The revised contract would expire on August 31, 1949, which would scarcely allow Universal-International enough time to make three films, let alone five.

Deanna's next film was supposed to be a joint venture between Universal-International and Scalera Films of Rome, with Goffredo Alessandrini directing. There was also talk of a movie in France. However, the last three movies were never made, and Universal-International quietly stood back until Deanna's contract expired, paying her a $150,000 bonus for the unmade films. Perhaps Universal-International didn't want to work with an actress who clearly no longer wanted to be there. Perhaps the staff at Universal-International considered Deanna "box-office poison" and didn't want to invest in making another Durbin film. Perhaps the new executives forgot that if it weren't for Deanna, there wouldn't be a Universal-International. But for whatever reason, the contract was allowed to run its course.

ESCAPE FROM HOLLYWOOD (1949)

Success, you know, is something that is merely loaned to you. You can keep it as long as you want to, providing you keep on paying the interest due.

—EDDIE CANTOR

After the disappointing reviews for both *Up in Central Park* and *For the Love of Mary*, the press appeared to turn against Deanna. An article in *Photoplay* titled "Babies—Hollywood's Most Expensive Luxury" specifically mentioned both Deanna and Judy: "Even in the days before Liza, Judy Garland never was any Rock of Gibraltar from the point of view of physical endurance or temperament. But lately, certainly, Judy is less dependable as a human being and as a star. Deanna Durbin's downgrade began with the birth of her Jessica, after Deanna had established herself as an adult star."

Perhaps Deanna was angry because her personal life was once again under scrutiny. Perhaps she felt that she couldn't successfully progress past the "Durbin Formula" characters movie audiences still expected. Perhaps she secretly felt the reporter was right that she couldn't balance stardom and motherhood. Or perhaps Deanna just didn't care and was already planning her escape.

In 1949, Deanna filed for divorce from Felix Jackson on the grounds of mental cruelty and desertion. According to Deanna, about a year after their marriage, Jackson had experienced a series of unhappy moods and restlessness. He said he was no longer content to be a married man, that he preferred being single, and that he was "going to do something about it." Deanna's friend, actress Anne Shirley, testified on behalf of Deanna in the divorce proceedings. She claimed Jackson sent her a letter saying, "I couldn't possibly go back, and I won't do it. It's no more Hollywood for me and no more marriage."

On September 1, 1949, after thirteen years in Hollywood, Deanna Durbin walked off the Universal-International lot for the last time. She had not made a picture in sixteen months and didn't even glance back as she drove through the gates.

Deanna's divorce was granted on October 27, 1949, and she was given full custody of three-year-old Jessica. A prenuptial agreement gave Deanna the right to keep her own income. Not long after, Deanna gave her first interview since leaving Universal-International. As she spoke to reporter Bob Thomas, her resentment toward both the studio and Hollywood was clear. At the time of her interview, Deanna had spent the past year sitting out her $350,000/year contract. Although her last two movies had been released, no new films had been shot or even seriously discussed, and Deanna had been paid to sit and wait, ignored by her studio and legally unable to accept work anywhere else. It had felt like a punishment, and perhaps it was.

In the interview, Deanna expressed that she didn't care about fame. "I would like to have people like me because I am just Edna, not Deanna. I would like to walk down a street and have people admire me because of the dress I was wearing or the look in my eye or the bounce of my hair—not because I was a movie star." As for her thirteen-year relationship with Universal-International and the way it ended, she confided, "I must say, they paid well to make me miserable." Deanna added that she had spent the past year studying voice and waiting for word from the studio. It never came. "The public hasn't been clamoring to see my pictures because they know I can't play *Three Smart Girls* any longer. The public knows that, but the studio didn't." Deanna shared her plan to move into a small house with Jessica, to settle down and enjoy life.

And with that, Deanna was free. Truly free, for the first time. She was no longer married, no longer under contract to a movie studio, out from under the watchful eye of parents and producers. Her career with Universal-International was over, but even though Deanna had mostly thrived in Hollywood, she had never aspired to be a movie star. She was a singer before anything else, and her lifelong dream had been to achieve an opera career.

Deanna thought about the offers to audition at the Metropolitan Opera she had received, first as a teenager and then again shortly after Jessica's birth. Perhaps now if she reached out to the opera company, she could be given another chance. The first time, Deanna had felt too young for an opera career, and later Universal hadn't allowed her to accept the offer. Perhaps now she could finally realize her dream.

But no. The world of opera was fraught with at least as many politics as Hollywood, and Deanna no longer had the same confidence in herself and her voice. After the critical reception to her recent movies, she felt the press would be waiting for her to fail. And if she signed a contract with an opera house, she would lose her freedom once again. Perhaps . . . well, perhaps it was all right to let this dream go. Besides, she had Jessica. Deanna had worked since she was a young girl. Perhaps now it was time for her to play. And wouldn't she and Jessica have fun discovering the world together?

Shortly after Deanna's last interview, she and Jessica left for France. Edna Mae, the little girl who had arrived in Hollywood in the rumble seat of an automobile, squeezed in amid bedding and crockery, departed California a wealthy, independent woman, seated in a private berth in the "de luxe" cabin of a 377 Stratocruiser. As suddenly as Deanna had burst onto the Hollywood scene, she left it. For good. And as her plane soared over the dark Atlantic Ocean, Deanna, the most successful child actor in history, became Edna Mae once more, as she slammed the door on Hollywood with a bang heard halfway around the world.

CHAPTER 22

Happily Ever After

I'm the one star who grew up to be happy.

—EDNA MAE DURBIN

DEANNA LOVED PARIS. YES, SHE RECEIVED SOME CURIOUS GLANCES AS she walked down the Champs-Élysées, her blue eyes and auburn hair familiar to many. But for the most part, she was just another tourist fumbling with unfamiliar currency, wandering through the winding streets, and laughing with a small girl while sipping steaming bowls of chocolate.

Deanna rented a flat and started learning French, and soon Jessica could ask for *pain au chocolat* in a perfect Parisian accent. Each morning, Deanna sat on her tiny balcony and watched the sun rise over the rooftops of her *quartier*. She would think back to her time at Universal: how she used to wait by the darkened set between takes, working away at needlepoint, hidden from the bright California sun. She recalled the endless photoshoots and interviews where even her likes and dislikes had been dictated in advance by the Universal press office, how most of her friends had always been adults, telling here what to do and how to act.

Deanna looked at Jessica tearing down the street, chasing pigeons and poodles and dancing in the rain. There was such joy and freedom in her little child. Deanna could feel a sense of joy and freedom in herself, too, growing stronger each day. Her life belonged to her, now. She was alone, but not lonely. And she was free. No movie role was worth giving up this liberty so dearly gained.

The Associated Press ran an article about Deanna's new life in Paris, lamenting her "increasing plumpness." Deanna just laughed it off. "I went to the Louvre," she said, "and saw the beautiful women of the past—they are much fatter than me." By 1950, Edna Mae Durbin—for she thought of herself that way now—had made another discovery: Paris alone was a delight, but Paris with a man by her side was an even more magical place.

CHARLES HENRI DAVID

When my husband and I married we made a deal. He would protect me from spiders, mosquitos and reporters, whilst my job is to protect him from lions, tigers and dinosaurs. And we both came through. For years I have not had to give any interviews, or pose for pictures, while it's been ages since a dinosaur breathed down my husband's neck.

—EDNA MAE DURBIN

Charles Henri David was born on May 4, 1906, in Metz, Germany (now Moselle, France). He built a career as head of the French film production company Pathé, and after leaving the French Army in 1940, he sold one of his stories, *A Fairy Tale Murder*, to Universal. The studio renamed the movie *River Gang* and invited David to California to direct the film. Deanna first met David on the Universal backlot during the filming of *The Amazing Mrs. Holliday*, and he later directed her in *Lady on a Train*.

Back in 1945, Deanna and David had not been romantically linked in the press; however perhaps it was merely an oversight by Hollywood reporters. After narrowly avoiding scandal with Joseph Cotten, Deanna had learned how to conceal the most private aspects of her personal life from public scrutiny.

Soon after Deanna's arrival in France, she and Jessica moved in with Charles David. In America, newspapers began to hint that Deanna was in love again. Deanna officially broke the news of this romance in a "letter from Paris," a public missive she wrote to her fans that appeared in newspapers around the world:

I am living a life of leisure and my neck is stiff from sightseeing. And such sites! My first trip abroad and it's really turned into a good one. Jessica is wonderful and is learning French faster than I. You know that I am planning to be married to Charles David somewhere before

the end of this year. Then off to Germany, where Charles will direct a
picture and I will do more sightseeing. Not to mention all the sauer-
kraut I'll eat.

Eight months later, on December 21, 1951, Deanna married David in
the Sarreguemines City Hall in the northeast of France. They exchanged
vows before the mayor's assistant. It was David's second marriage, and at
the time of the wedding, he was forty-four years old and Deanna was just
under twenty-nine.

The wedding attracted little attention from the local residents and no
crowds gathered to cheer or toss confetti. Deanna wore a simple traveling
suit and answered, *"Oui,"* when asked by the deputy mayor if she wished
to marry Monsieur Charles David. Their only wedding photograph was
a casual snapshot of the couple leaving City Hall, a dramatic contrast to
the 2,500 photographs taken at the Wilshire Hotel reception at Deanna's
first wedding.

Newspapers reported that Deanna made her husband sign a prenuptial agreement, swearing he would never ask Deanna to appear in
another film and promising she could live away from the glitz and glitter
of Hollywood. Despite this, reporters did not believe Deanna would truly
stay tucked away in France, and rumors circulated about which movie she
would choose next and about which studio would sign her.

But Deanna's thoughts were a million miles from Hollywood. The
newlyweds bought an apartment in Paris as well as an old two-story
farmhouse surrounded by a high stone wall in the village of Neauphle-le-
Château, population 1,250, thirty minutes outside of Paris.

A month later, newspapers reported that Deanna was expecting a baby—due the following July, just seven months after her wedding. Again, nobody questioned the early due date; articles just quoted
Deanna, who said if the baby was a girl, she would be named Nora, and
if he was a boy, Peter.

With the announcement of Deanna's pregnancy, media interest
surged once more. An article in the *Reporter* claimed, "Deanna Durbin's
letters to friends say that she'll make a stab at pictures again after she has
her baby." Hedda Hopper seemed to take personal offense at Deanna's

choice to leave Hollywood behind. She wrote in a column, "Look at Deanna Durbin. Now—at twenty-nine—she is reported to be less happy in her third marriage than she hoped to be. And instead of being the bright singing star she should have been, she is almost forgotten."

Hedda was wrong about this bit of news because Deanna was not forgotten. She was, in fact, blissfully content. On June 20, 1951, almost six months to the day after Deanna's wedding, nine-pound Peter David was born at a clinic in Paris.

Although Deanna now lived across the ocean from California, her old friends didn't forget her. Pasternak was genuinely delighted that his Deanna had followed her heart. He recalled, "At last, when I saw her, she had found happiness. She had married once again, for she had found herself, and when I saw her she was radiant, beautiful, glowing with the youthful charm which she always possessed."

Each morning, Deanna toured the town's shops carrying her purse and a tattered brown shopping bag. Her dresses were plain. She wore a simple cloth coat with a tweed patch on the left sleeve. People referred to Deanna as "Madame David," but everyone in the village was aware that a former star lived in their midst.

Local residents helped Deanna and Charles David avoid the media. The mechanic across the road from their house tipped them off when strangers came around. One reporter, who asked two local farmers about the star, was told that they'd never heard of Deanna Durbin. A third farmer referred the reporter to another village, over thirty miles away.

The press didn't give up easily. There were rumors that Deanna would co-star opposite Mario Lanza in *This Night Is Ours*; that she was considering a film with Gracie Fields; that instead of movies, she would appear on the London stage in Aleen Leslie's new play. However, these rumors abated as Deanna remained ensconced in Neauphle-le-Château.

Deanna wasn't a recluse. She attended the theater and art museums in Paris. At first, she discouraged visitors, but when it became clear that she was genuinely not interested in returning to Hollywood, gossip and media interest eventually died down, and Deanna and Charles David opened their house to guests.

As Deanna explained, "I have succeeded in attaining privacy and peace only through being most uncooperative in meeting press. The press has accepted this attitude of mine most understandingly. Please let my fans enjoy the Deanna Durbin of years ago and keep this fairytale character from any 'what's happened to her' story. I have found my fans wonderfully understanding in my happily shedding Deanna Durbin to live the wonderful and exciting private life of Edna Mae David."

Deanna publicly vowed never to make another personal appearance and announced that she would give no more interviews. Ever. And with that, Deanna Durbin was, in essence, dead, allowing Edna Mae David a clear path to happiness.

LEGACY

I had a lot of dreams when I came to this country and being in opera was one of them. But sometimes we all wake up.
—DEANNA DURBIN, *UP IN CENTRAL PARK*

Deanna never appeared in another movie, and she didn't sing publicly again. The magnitude of this sacrifice can be difficult to fully understand, and is almost overwhelming when one considers what was lost.

Deanna's voice was truly a special gift. It had matured into a rich sound with a compelling emotive quality to each note. She made music come alive in a way that few singers could hope to achieve. Deanna's childhood and adolescence had been committed to shaping and developing her rare instrument, and unlike Judy, who just a few years later destroyed a voice that should have been reaching its peak, Deanna's voice was better than it had ever been. And to just give that up . . . the decision must not have been easy. Or perhaps it was. Deanna's talent, after all, was hers to use and hers to waste. And perhaps she didn't consider it a waste, to save her soaring voice for the few people she loved.

Despite maintaining a very private life, throughout the decades Deanna and her films were featured in books, songs, and movies, and several icons of the twentieth century were influenced and inspired by the life and films of Deanna Durbin.

Dancing actress Carmen Miranda, known as the "Brazilian Bomb-shell," described her childhood: "When there is a Deanna Durbin picture, all the girls dress just like her. Rio de Janeiro is then filled with little South American Deanna Durbins in dresses like she wore, with their hair like she fixes hers."

As a young girl in Athens, legendary opera diva Maria Callas would watch Deanna's films. She was "entranced by that child star's utterly perfect voice" and vowed that someday she, too, would sing. Dame Sister Mary Leo in New Zealand was so taken with Deanna's vocal technique that she trained her students to sing in this way, including famous opera singers Malvina Major and Kiri te Kanewa.

Russian musician and conductor Mstislav Rostropovich, often considered one of the greatest cellists of the twentieth century, publicly acknowledged Deanna's influence on his career. "She helped me in my discovery of myself. You have no idea of the smelly old movie houses I patronized to see Deanna Durbin. I tried to create the very best in my music, to try and recreate, to approach her purity."

In an interview, Angela Lansbury credited part of her vocal success to Deanna's movies, saying, "I always did my best singing as a child after seeing a Deanna Durbin movie." When Indian filmmaker Satyajit Ray was awarded a 1991 Honorary Academy Award, which he accepted from his hospital bed in India, he recalled, "When I was a small, small schoolboy, I was terribly interested in the cinema. Became a film fan, wrote to Deanna Durbin. Got a reply, was delighted."

In 1991, Georgi Skorochodow, a lecturer at the Moscow Film Institute, wrote a letter to Deanna Durbin on her seventieth birthday:

On the silver screens of our country, we have seen your films since 1939. For each performance, all tickets were sold out. I give lectures and the most popular are on your films. This year, in June and July, we had a retrospective of your films. Each ended with a discussion about your part and how you played it. The cinema was packed every time. All this shows that you are very well-remembered and very much loved in our country. Let me wish you the best and express to you greetings from Moscow and your innumerable fans.

In addition to her prints at Grauman's Chinese Theatre, Deanna Durbin was awarded a star on the Hollywood Walk of Fame at 1722 Vine Street. It was one of the original 1,500 stars installed in 1960, the Walk of Fame's inaugural year.

Deanna is referenced in music satirist Tom Lehrer's 1965 live album *That Was the Year That Was*. In the introduction to the song "Whatever Became of Hubert?" Lehrer says, "Vice President Hubert Humphrey had been relegated to 'those where-are-they-now' columns: Whatever became of Deanna Durbin, and Hubert Humphrey, and so on."

Deanna is also mentioned in several novels, including *Trout Fishing in America* by Richard Brautigan, *A Guest in the Homeland* by Vadim Mesyats, *Reading Chekhov: A Critical Journey* by Janet Malcolm, *The Exeter Blitz* by David Rees, and *Petros' War* by Alki Zei.

Canadian author Beatrice Thurman Hunter's *As Ever, Booky* is part of a trilogy describing her childhood in Depression-era Toronto. In the book, Hunter devoted an entire chapter to her obsession with Deanna Durbin:

> *Ever since I'd seen my first silent moving picture at the Kingswood in Birchcliff years ago, I'd been mad about movies. So when Glad, Ruth and I went downtown to see a Christmas special called* Three Smart Girls, *we could hardly wait to get there. The newspaper ad read:* Scintillating young Canadian soprano, Deanna Durbin, sings her way right into your heart! *Well, did she ever. She was just fifteen, the perfect age for an idol. And what a name—Deanna Durbin!*

The characters start a fan club, buy Deanna Durbin dresses, write a fan letter to Hollywood, receive an autographed picture from the movie star, and even enter a Deanna Durbin look-alike competition.

Although Deanna's name did appear in the occasional song, book, or speech, these occurrences were few and far between. From her position as a shining beacon to a generation of young women, Deanna quietly slipped into the past. The star system that had created Deanna Durbin ended, and the Golden Age of Hollywood faded.

But what of all the people who figured so prominently in Deanna's life and career? What happened to her children, to Ada and James Durbin, to Eddie Cantor, to Joe Pasternak and Henry Koster?

Deanna's two children, Jessica and Peter, grew up in France. Jessica eventually moved back to California, where she married and gave birth to a son. At a young age Peter was an accomplished pianist, recording tapes of Mozart and Schubert and accompanying Deanna at home as she sang. He went on to study medicine at the Paris University, building a career in the medical field.

Ada and James stayed in California. Thanks to Deanna's generosity, the overworked housewife and the frail blacksmith who seemed fated to an early death had the sort of retirement they would have never dared imagine. James took up flying as a hobby, and Ada bought him a two-motored, four-seater Stinson plane. The couple flew to Winnipeg to visit relatives, to Mexico for a dinner-dance. They were healthy and happy until Ada died in 1972 and James in 1976.

Eddie Cantor went on singing, writing, and composing. He was one of the first stars to appear on television, where his scheduled song, "We're Havin' a Baby, My Baby and Me," was considered too risqué by network censors. Never one to bow to convention, Cantor bluntly refused to change the song. When the number was aired, with the sound cut and picture blurred on the "racy" lines, it became the first instance of television censorship. Cantor published several books and was honored by a balloon figure in the Macy's Thanksgiving Day Parade. He worked in show business until he died in 1964, and he adored every minute onstage.

Henry Koster became one of MGM's most respected directors. His films included *The Bishop's Wife* (1947), the classic comedy *Harvey* (1950), *Flower Drum Song* (1961), and *The Singing Nun* (1965). After retirement, Koster changed his focus to art, painting a series of portraits of the movie stars he'd directed. He eventually became close again with Deanna, seeing her on her rare visits to California. Koster died in 1988.

Joe Pasternak produced over 105 films in his career, earning over $400 million for his studios. At MGM his films included *Seven Sweethearts* (1942), *Presenting Lily Mars* (1943), *Two Girls and a Sailor* (1944), and *Anchors Aweigh* (1945). Pasternak made stars of both Kathryn Greyson and Esther Williams and worked with Frank Sinatra, Gene Kelly, and of course, Judy Garland. After fourteen years at MGM, Pasternak set up the independent production company Euterpe with MGM's former vice president, Sam Katz, and produced another string of successful pictures. Well-known and well-respected throughout Hollywood, Pasternak remained close to Deanna. They spoke often, and he visited her several times in France. Pasternak died in 1991.

And then there was Judy. When Deanna moved to France and left Hollywood behind, the parallel paths she and Judy Garland had been traveling finally diverged for good.

While Deanna and Jessica discovered the wonders of the City of Light, wandering through misty evenings by the Seine, Judy's life became darker. She was suspended from the movie *Annie Get Your Gun* for showing up late to the set and missing film shoots, and later she was removed from the film entirely. In June 1949, while Deanna and Charles kissed under a streetlamp near Montmartre, Judy survived a suicide attempt when she attempted to cut her own throat with the shattered edge of a water glass.

In September of 1950, Deanna laughed over her attempts to order groceries in her halting French and navigated cobblestoned streets in high heels. She and Charles motored through the sunny French countryside, spring air perfumed with roses, searching for the ideal house for their growing family. In Hollywood, despite earning more than $100 million for her studio, being considered MGM's greatest asset, and having recently completed Pasternak's hit film *Summer Stock*, Judy Garland was "granted an early release" from her studio contract, likely because of her increasingly erratic behavior.

Judy was a fighter, and she never quit. She continued living in the spotlight, through marriages and divorces, onstage collapses, and suicide attempts. She pushed her remarkable voice until it became a quavering mockery of its one-time brilliance. Even if performing was slowly killing her, in Judy's eyes, a life out of the spotlight wasn't any life at all.

After Judy's first breakdown in 1947, Deanna had publicly defended her childhood friend. She had explained to reporters, "People criticize when Judy Garland and Vincente Minnelli have their marital troubles. 'Why can't they have a normal married life?' they say. Judy has a great talent, one of the greatest in our business. That's why she can't conform to other peoples' ideas of 'being normal.'"

This time Deanna didn't comment to the press, but perhaps she spoke directly to Judy. Perhaps she sympathized with Judy and recalled how she, too, had been driven from her studio. Perhaps Deanna reminded Judy of how MGM had built her into a legend, but how in doing so, had crushed an earnest little girl with a remarkable talent. Or perhaps Deanna didn't feel an offer of support would be helpful from someone who, even then, was still being constantly brought up in newspapers and magazines as Judy's more-talented rival.

Judy went on to star on the concert stage and appeared on television several times, including as a guest on *Tonight with Jack Paar*. In 1962, Paar asked her if Deanna was "still around." Judy answered, "Well, her eyebrow still is!" Later, Paar asked Judy what she used to call Deanna in those days, and Judy said, "Hairy!" which elicited a big laugh from the studio audience. Then, as the laughter died down, Judy quietly said, "Edna" in a wistful tone that suggested she too regretted the closeness they'd lost.

Once, when Judy was a guest on Merv Griffin's talk show, she recalled how she had phoned Deanna when performing in London.

"What are you doing in London?" Deanna asked.

"I'm in England for some concerts," Judy said.

"My God!" Deanna exclaimed. "Are you still in the business?"

Judy often made fun of her fellow celebrities, but her offhand comment to Paar and brief anecdote to Griffin were taken as further proof that the two singers still nurtured resentment toward each other. For reporters and fans, these stories kept alive a rivalry that may have never truly existed.

Judy kept making movies, including *A Star Is Born* (1954), considered by many to be her masterpiece. She married twice more and performed several iconic concerts. But she just couldn't leave the stage—or the drugs that enabled her to meet the rigorous demands of her career—behind.

Judy Garland died in London on June 22, 1969, less than two weeks after her forty-seventh birthday. She was found by her fifth husband, discotheque manager Mickey Deans, in the bathroom of their Belgravia house. Even in Judy's *New York Times* obituary, Deanna was mentioned as the story was recounted about how Louis B. Mayer "was determined to give Miss Garland a major build-up" by starring her in *The Wizard of Oz*, and how Mayer making Judy a star was directly attributed to him losing Deanna to Universal.

When Deanna recalled Judy, it was not as a former friend or a lifelong rival, but instead as a skilled fellow actress, admired and respected. "Right from the start Judy had an immense talent. She was a professional and had been on the stage since she was two. Her later story is tragic, but I'm certain she could never have given it up. She needed an audience as she needed to breathe."

Deanna did not have a tragic story, and she remained fulfilled throughout the years. And yet, of these two talented ingénues who dared to grow up, it is Judy who is the most widely remembered. Decades after her death, her voice is instantly recognizable, and her presence and music is as vivid as if she were still performing on the worldwide stage. So why did one singing juvenile fade into near obscurity during her lifetime and the other blaze even more brightly decades after her death?

As one reporter mused, "Deanna was not a topic of sensation—except for her talent. About Judy there are legends. She always made news. People wanted to write and talk about Judy because she was explosive and unpredictable." Joe Pasternak saw Deanna and Judy as two different types of singers who elicited different emotions from their audiences. "When I saw Judy, I wanted to dance and sing with her. When I saw Durbin, I wanted to kiss her and fall in love with her and just sit back and listen."

A *Picture Play* article that compared the stars at the height of their careers expressed, "Deanna has many assets to help her. But Judy has that flaming quality that has colored the lives of many stars before this, has made them capture the public's affection. Deanna has grown beautiful and her voice is as exquisite and pure as a bird's singing at eventide. Judy has grown beautiful and her voice is as throbbing and tortured as the voices of all women in love."

Perhaps it is Judy's "flaming quality" that has allowed her to live on so vividly—that has allowed her to live on so vividly and has kept her memory fresh. Or it was the air of tragedy that clung to her. Judy suffered loneliness, despair, and abuse, and yet she still smiled and sang through her tears to touch hearts and bring happiness to generations of moviegoers.

But what of Deanna, the girl with a voice "as exquisite and pure as a bird's singing at eventide?" Who not only had the strength to survive Hollywood, but who was strong enough to leave it without a backward glance; the woman who built a new life and lived six decades of happiness in obscurity. What happened to her?

CHAPTER 23

Six Decades of Obscurity

You can order your own happiness . . . because happiness isn't an accident. It doesn't come from the outside. It's your own private property.
—EDNA MAE DURBIN

IN THE YEARS AFTER LEAVING HOLLYWOOD, DEANNA RESISTED NUMER-ous offers to perform again. She was approached to star in MGM's film versions of Cole Porter's *Kiss Me, Kate* (1953), a remake of Grace Moore's hit *One Night of Love* (1934), the film *Melba* (1953), and a movie based on Sigmund Romberg's operetta *The Student Prince* (1954). Deanna was also offered roles in theatrical productions, including an invitation to star in the West End production of *Kiss Me, Kate*. Deanna was Alan Jay Lerner's first choice to portray Eliza Doolittle in the 1956 Broadway cast of *My Fair Lady*, and Lerner even paid Deanna a personal visit where he tried to convince her to accept the role.

Deanna was offered $100,000 to appear in the movie *The Opposite Sex* (1956), and was considered for a film version of Puccini's opera *La Bohème*. She was also desperately wanted by Desi Arnaz as a performing partner, was approached by Sir Thomas Beecham, and received numerous invitations to sing at Las Vegas casinos. But Deanna firmly refused every offer to perform.

In the six decades that followed her retirement, the world received only the occasional glimpse of Deanna's private life. A press quote here, an interview there—words to search out and treasure for the millions who still loved her.

In October 1952, Deanna briefly returned to Hollywood for the first time since leaving for Europe two-and-a-half years earlier. She planned to see her parents and to sell her empty Beverly Hills home before returning to France. But from the moment Deanna's French liner, *Ile de France*, docked in the New York harbor, reporters started buzzing about a comeback.

Deanna tried to set the record straight. "I have had enough," she firmly told the eager reporters thronging the dock. "I don't want to go back. I have completely retired from any professional work. I've enjoyed taking care of my two children so much that I want to do just that. I enjoy living without motion pictures. I have a husband and family and that's enough. When I left I didn't think I was through with my career. I didn't want to make any definite decisions. But now I have."

When asked about the numerous movie offers she had received, Deanna replied, "I'm not interested. I keep up my singing lessons, but just for my own enjoyment. I'm happy. I certainly am." She smiled once more at the press, now a confident and sophisticated woman, radiant with love and happiness. "I had shared with the world the girl, Deanna. But the woman—Edna Mae—she belongs to me."

And with that, the interview ended, and Deanna considered any question about her return to public life unequivocally answered. The *New York Post* drove the point home, writing:

> *Deanna Durbin, who sang her way to stardom as the "ideal teenager" of the late 1930's, is now singing the praises of obscurity. She's living down what she calls the "concocted Durbin personality" that appeared on the screen. She's being herself for the first time. She loves it.*

In 1958, a reporter wrote to Deanna to request an interview. The request was firmly turned down, but Deanna wrote a long letter in response. The reporter asked for permission to publish the note, and it was printed in dozens of papers across America.

In the letter, Deanna assured her fans that she was content with her new life and that she had thrown herself wholeheartedly into the role of wife and mother. She drove the family car around the countryside and did most of her own shopping. Her one luxury was a part-time maid to clean the house. She and Charles David made frequent trips to the theater, attended dinner parties, and took vacations in Switzerland.

She wrote she would not change it for the world. Although she no longer performed, Deanna still practiced singing for an hour each morning:

> *The most exciting thing at the moment is six-year-old Peter's studying piano. We go into Paris once a week for lessons. I get a tremendous kick out of singing with him to help him practice.*
>
> *You press people must be sick and tired of quoting former Holly-wood personalities as saying such things as, "I don't plan a comeback ... I'm not bitter with Hollywood, but I was never happy making pictures," and so on. But I do mean it.*
>
> *My fans sat in the dark, anonymous and obscure, while I was projected bigger than life on the screen. Fans took home an image of me and studio press agents filled in the personal details. They invented most of them and before I could resist, this worldwide picture of me came back stronger than my real person and very often conflicted with it. How could a young, unformed girl fight this publicized image of herself while still trying to develop her real, still-growing personality?*
>
> *I was a typical thirteen-year-old American girl. The character I was forced into had little or nothing in common with myself—or with other youth of my generation, for that matter. I could never believe my contemporaries were my fans. They may have been impressed with my "success," but my fans were the parents, many of whom could not cope with their own youngsters. They sort of adopted me as their "perfect" daughter.*
>
> *Just as the Hollywood-produced pin-up industry represents sex to many dissatisfied people, I represented an idealized daughter to the millions of frustrated fathers and mothers. They could, with their tick-ets, purchase twice a year new stocks of sweetness and innocence.*

In 1961, Deanna turned forty. To mark the occasion, she and Charles David granted a brief interview to Hollywood reporter Bob Thomas.

David mused, "You'd think after twelve years, the idea would get across that Deanna does not want to work anymore. The French understand it. When we go to an opening in Paris, the photographers wink and look the other way. But the foreign journalists don't understand this and we continue getting inquiries."

Deanna described her new life outside Paris. "I cook and I garden. Before I came here, I couldn't boil water. Now my husband says I am a good French cook. Our gardener died, so I had to take over his job. I also sing. But now I sing only for myself and I sing the songs I want, not what I'm told to sing."

During the interview, Thomas asked Deanna if she was planning a comeback. She said, "I can't seem to convince people that I have retired. But I have. It's not that I don't like acting. I did. What I didn't like was the publicity, the invasion of my private life. A person needs to have an identity of his own. When you're a star, it's virtually impossible. That's something I never got used to."

In 1963, after a trip to France, Joe Pasternak reported, "Deanna looks great, and she surprised me by saying she still keeps up on her singing practice. Sort of jokingly, I asked her if she would give up her life in a lovely country place outside Paris to make another movie for me. She said, 'Sure, if you can find the right script.' Deanna's delightful and sings like a bird. And she's on her way back. When I find a good script for her, she'll come back."

In 1967, film historian Anthony Slide wrote an article about Deanna Durbin's career for *Films in Review* and sent it to Deanna. Her reply read:

> *I never had any feeling of identity with the "Deanna Durbin" born from my early pictures and from a mixture of press agents, publicity and fawnship. . . . As I often wonder, I cannot see why, after so many years, it still matters to write about Durbin. I know that years ago my life was everybody's business and that the concoction of screen image and publicity created a sweet monster, which the real person I was had a lot of trouble to fight and to overcome eventually.*

*The fact that even today with the world's terrifying problems peo-
ple are still interested in the synthetic old Durbin of the thirties only
shows what escape from reality I must have meant. I may still have
some good physical resemblance with that "Deanna Durbin," but this
living self has no authority to comment on the biographical dates of a
past that was never my own.*

In 1972, a French producer was nearly killed after he attempted to scale
the walls of Deanna's estate. The purpose of this unwanted visit was to
convince Deanna to make a comeback. In 1980, rumors started circulat-
ing in the press that Deanna had aged into a "well-rounded matron."
Although she had not communicated with reporters in years, Deanna
sent a photograph to film historian William Everson. The photo, which
was later printed in *Life* magazine, was a casual snapshot taken by Charles
David showing Deanna in a gray turtleneck sweater with curly, shoulder-
length auburn hair. Although she was older, Deanna's smile was the same,
sunny and playful.

A letter accompanying the photograph read, "After so many years of
happy oblivion, I can still pass under the Arc de Triomphe without holding my breath."

In 1982, MCA Records in Britain released a "new" disc, *The Best of
Deanna Durbin*. It became a bestseller and instantly the public's interest
in Deanna was revived. What was she doing now? Was she still singing?
Was she even still alive?

Journalist David Paskov decided to travel to Neauphle-le-Château
and write an article about Deanna, to "unravel the mystery of Deanna's
disappearance." In a town where the population had slowly grown to
around 2,000, the locals weren't helpful. The butcher claimed that he
hadn't seen Deanna for two or three years. He said she was just an ordinary person, "just like you or me."

At the local newsstand, the owner disappeared when Deanna's name
was brought up. "He won't come back until you're gone," an assistant
said. "Twenty years ago, we were asked not to talk about her, and we
won't." The postmaster said that he had never seen Deanna, but that every

day she received fan mail from all over the world. The amount varied, but there was always something.

At Deanna's house, Paskov rang the doorbell, vainly hoping that Deanna herself would answer. Instead, he was met with ferocious barking from Sully, one of Deanna's two dachshunds, and Charles David opened the door. He was dressed in a dark blue cap and a green waterproof countryman's jacket.

David, too, generally avoided reporters. But something about Paskov caught his fancy and they began to chat. David explained, "When we got married Deanna said, 'Either I'm going to be married to the studio or I shall lead a normal married life.' And that's what we have done."

David described how Deanna's daughter Jessica lived in the South of France and how their son Peter was an accomplished pianist and lived in Washington. He allowed Paskov to peek through the gate, revealing a garden with wide lawns, rustling trees, and gravel paths dotted with rubber balls from Deanna's dogs. David laughed and declared, "I tell everybody that I keep her in a dungeon at the bottom of the garden."

He paused and then said, "You know, her movies still have a special something. She was a very good actress, not just a singer. But she has turned her back on Deanna Durbin. It isn't her now. And for her fans, she wants them to remember her that way, the way Deanna Durbin was."

Paskov thanked David and departed. A few days later, a letter arrived for him from Deanna. It was signed, "Globetrotting Recluse." She wrote, "It's surprising, and I have to admit satisfying, that after 33 years of retirement the interest in Deanna Durbin not only remains but is shared by an entire generation of young friends. It is this image of the young Durbin that I have tried to protect."

This playful, almost maternal sentiment from Deanna toward her younger self was a noted shift in attitude. Perhaps time had erased some of the bitterness Deanna felt toward Hollywood and the "ideal" girl she had been groomed to be. Perhaps the thought of her still-loyal fans made Deanna reconsider her vow to efface herself completely from the public eye. Perhaps she was simply curious about what would happen. Whatever brought on the change of heart, one year later Deanna agreed to her first in-person interview since leaving Hollywood, with movie writer David Shipman.

When they met, Deanna greeted Shipman and said, "I knew that sooner or later I would give an interview and decided that I would do it with you. I admire you as one admires a scientist who, with a few bones, manages to reconstruct an entire dinosaur. So, I am curious to see what you'll make with the bits and pieces I offer you today."

Deanna assured Shipman, "I did not hate show business. I loved to sing. I was happy on the set. I liked the people with whom I worked and after the nervousness of the first day, I felt completely at ease in front of the camera. I also enjoyed the company of my fellow actors, the leading men who were so much older, like Herbert Marshall, Melvyn Douglas, Franchot Tone, Walter Pidgeon, Joseph Cotten, Vincent Price and Robert Cummings. I did two films with my special friend, Charles Laughton. Working with these talented men helped me so very much and I grew up much faster than the average teenager. What I did find difficult was that this acquired maturity had to be hidden under the childlike personality my films and publicity projected on me.

"I hated being in a goldfish bowl," she went on. "If I went to New York, I had to stay in my hotel room or go everywhere under guard, whisked away in a big black limousine, terrified that the fans running alongside would get hurt in the traffic. My mother and I were once mobbed in Texas. The police lost control of the crowd and my mother suffered two broken ribs from people trying to reach me. I have never been so frightened. They put me in the town jail for safety and to avoid the mob still waiting at the station, they flagged the train down in the middle of nowhere, where I got on safely."

Deanna described growing up in a Hollywood studio: "It was drummed into me that I must never have sex with a man before I was married, and then the next day I was off to the studio where a very different set of rules prevailed. I must admit that it was lovely to be asked and even lovelier to be able to say no . . . or yes . . . part of the fun of being asked meant that I wasn't a little girl anymore.

"And that is why I wanted to look glamorous. I couldn't wait to wear low-cut dresses and look sultry. I remember the day when Philippe

Halsman from *Life* magazine came to my home. He said he was going to photograph me 'looking like an angel.' I answered that I may not know how I did want to be photographed, but if there was one way I certainly did not want to be photographed it was looking like an angel! He laughed, and the picture he took more than satisfied me. I'll admit that for some of my public all of this must have been hard to understand."

After the interview, Shipman wrote:

> *I could not imagine her ever being more contented than she is now. The waste of her talent is in the past, even if, at a cheerfully admitted sixty-one she looks a mere thirty-five . . . she is not only like the young Deanna, but uncannily like: candid, sensible, completely without affectation, concerned and captivating company. Like all great stars, and despite her particular qualities, she is mysterious. She is Deanna Durbin—one of the best-loved of all stars.*

In 1990, Deanna and Charles David moved to 10 Rue du Vivier in Paris. Four years later, Deanna was quoted in the magazine *American Movie Classics*, "I was extremely flattered to hear that my films are requested and happy to know that my work is still enjoyed." She then provided her address for fans to send correspondence.

In the 1990s, Deanna started regularly answering fan mail. She signed the letters "Deanna," which was telling, as decades before she had declared her movie persona "dead." Perhaps Deanna agreed with Shipman that "the waste of her talent is in the past." Perhaps she realized that even if she had continued performing, at this point her career would likely have been over. Perhaps, as she lost Joe Pasternak, Eddie Cantor, and the other friends of her youth, she gained a new appreciation for the fans who had remained loyal for over half a century. Perhaps, once the bitterness about what Deanna considered her "stolen girlhood" faded away, something gracious and even nostalgic took its place.

Those who received correspondence from Deanna Durbin treasured her letters. To the organizer of a film festival, she wrote:

I am proud of my work and want to assure you that I loved my career. It was far from easy to give it up. Since the showing of my films on TV and video, my mail bag is splitting its seams. It's great to hear from the older, faithful friends and the amazing reaction from the young and very young makes me feel like I'm being discovered all over again!

Deanna composed notes to thank her fans for sending her gifts—for yes, Deanna's admirers still sent tributes to their beloved star: "Dear Win, Many thanks for the little heart with my name embroidered on it oh so prettily. Also, the perfumed sachets. All your warm thoughts were most welcome."

And she penned letters to her young fans—a new generation, not yet born when Deanna's movies were first released: "Dear Brad, Such a kind and flattering letter! The image of you sitting with your grandfather watching your favorite DD films touched me very much. To know that my work is still being enjoyed makes me truly happy."

Joe Gonsalvez from Oakville, Ontario, was one of the fans who regularly corresponded with Deanna. "I have adored Deanna for over sixty years. Fifteen years ago, I wrote to her and to my surprise she wrote back and sent me a lovely photo. We kept in touch ever since and I still get a note per year which I am very grateful for. When she was moving, she gave me her post office box number. It is one thing to answer a fan's letters, but to advise him of a change of address is a rare courtesy, especially from a woman in her 70s who has no secretary."

The Deanna Durbin Devotees, formed back in the 1930s, had segued into the Deanna Durbin Society, which advertised itself as "the only appreciation society which is authorized by Deanna Durbin." Just as in the 1930s, members received a "twelve-page newspaper of superb quality, three times a year," and there was a British convention "once a year over a weekend, where members socialize and everyone enjoys a selection of Deanna films." The Deanna Durbin Society included fans from all over England, Australia, as well as from Winnipeg, Deanna's hometown.

On March 1, 1999, Charles David died in Paris with Deanna by his side. After her husband's death, Deanna wrote to her long-running fan club, explaining why she would no longer answer correspondence:

> *This is not easy for me to do for many reasons. One of the most important is the tremendous amount of mail I receive I cannot possibly answer. But it seems wrong to have people writing so kindly, not receiving an answer and not understanding why. There simply are not enough hours in a day.*

However, these devoted fans did not require an answer. They understood, and they kept writing. It was fitting, then, that during the week of April 17, 2013, when Edna Mae Durbin died, her death was announced to the world by the Deanna Durbin Society. They were given the news by her son, along with a message that later appeared on the front page of the Society's newsletter:

> *Deanna Durbin David died a few days ago. Over the years, my mother was deeply touched by the marks of affection expressed by her many admirers. She was also extremely thankful to the Deanna Durbin Society for the respect shown to her privacy. This is why I now wish to ask you to kindly share the news of our loss to all. Indeed, spring will be very late this year. . . .*
> *Sincerely, Peter H. David*

Overnight, newspapers burst with glowing tributes to the once-beloved luminary of Old Hollywood. Deanna's movies were replayed, and her rise to stardom was retold in magazines and online. Obituaries appeared in the *Guardian*, the *Hollywood Reporter*, and the *New York Times*. On comment pages and message boards, the rivalry with Judy was brought up and debated, fans once again arguing hotly about which young woman was prettier, a better singer, a more-talented actress.

And then, Deanna once again faded into relative obscurity, a footnote to a time in Hollywood that had long passed. The mention of the name "Deanna Durbin" only brought puzzled looks, and at best, a vague sense of recognition. But Deanna is one star who should not be forgotten. Watched today, many of her movies seem simple and saccharine, and there are thematic elements that did not age well. But Deanna shines, and there is a magic to these films that time cannot dilute.

Deanna Durbin is unique among actresses in that although her life was not tragically cut short, she will never grow old. Aside from the one photograph in the 1980s, the only images we have show Deanna as a sprightly teenager or an attractive young woman. As admirer Geoff Milne wrote in the *Winnipeg Free Press* decades after Frank Morriss retired, "Seen today, Deanna's films are as fresh as the day they were made. They are happy films, full of bright, frothy entertainment, bubbling with fun. They came as a breath of fresh air when first seen in the cinema—they still come as a breath of fresh air."

Joe Pasternak once had a conversation with Deanna, where she mused that nobody would want her even if she did return to Hollywood. She said they would have surely moved on, past her and her movies.

"Darling," Pasternak responded, "you amuse me. You talk about *they*—the audience—as though they get finished with people and throw them away as a child discards old toys. I'll tell you one of the few secrets learned from the theater. The public is never 'through' with a star. It's always the star who is through with the public. People say there's a new generation of moviegoers and they don't remember the great stars of last year. But listen, the thing that made the audience of last year love you will make the audience of this year love you."

An article from *Classic Images* illustrated Pasternak's point: "We continue to love Deanna even after she no longer was able to return our love. In her films, she had worked a special magic that the biggest stars of her day simply could not match. Whenever she smiled or sang or even spoke, she immediately put you at ease. No matter what was going on in this troubled world, a few moments with Deanna could make everything seem better."

Over eight decades have passed since the release of Deanna's first film. The world is still troubled, and magic is hard to find. But it does remain, in the sunny smile of a mischievous sister in *Three Smart Girls*; in the loving devotion of a daughter in *One Hundred Men and a Girl*; in a remarkable voice that bridges time, trilling of love and passion and joy. Deanna's movies are still magic, and for this reason, they will never completely be forgotten.

According to Joe Pasternak, "Greatness does not fall from a true star like a cloak. It is in the very marrow and bones of their being. And Deanna can never lose what God has given her. One day, I hope, she will call me and say, quite simple, 'Joe, I'm ready.' That will be all I need to know."

Deanna didn't ever call. Just like a fairytale, she had found her happy ending. In her castle in France, she danced through the years of her life in a whirl of happiness and love. But now the ball is over and the lights have dimmed. And so, as is fitting in a fairytale, Deanna's story ends with the words the Brothers Grimm used once the quest was complete, the prince had been found, and love had triumphed over all: "And they all lived happily together, until their deaths."

Notes

Chapter 1
1. This dubious honor was later revised by the Universal publicity department as the "Prettiest Baby Award."
2. Some reports say $100, some $125, others $150.

Chapter 2
1. Schumann-Heink died on November 17, 1936, at the age of seventy-five.
2. Another story is that *Every Sunday* was used to decide which singer would remain with MGM; however as the movie was produced after both Judy and Deanna's initial studio contracts expired, this is likely not the case.

Chapter 3
1. Anschluss: the annexation of Austria into Nazi Germany.

Chapter 7
1. In 1936, a house was built for actress Danielle Darieux. However, after making just one movie, *The Rage of Paris*, she broke her seven-year contract and returned to France.

Chapter 8
1. The penny later disappeared, likely pried out by a fan.

Chapter 9
1. When World War II began, a receipt for a donation of three pounds and sixpence to the Red Cross took the place of dues.

Chapter 10
1. This was the first time Deanna's actual age was publicly mentioned.

Chapter 12
1. *It's a Date* was remade at MGM in 1950 as the movie *Nancy Goes to Rio*, starring Jane Powell and directed by Joe Pasternak.

CHAPTER 13

1. In 1934, Hollywood adopted the Hays Code, a set of production directives voluntarily adopted by all the major studios.
2. In Spanish countries, Deanna sang the final song in Spanish; for the British release, it was replaced with "There'll Always be an England."
3. An American burlesque dancer.
4. These celebrations were held in conjunction with the "March of Dimes," a fundraiser that was named and heavily promoted by Eddie Cantor.

CHAPTER 15

1. A photograph of an attractive, often scantily clad woman.

CHAPTER 17

1. Joseph Cotten, *Vanity Will Get You Somewhere: An Autobiography.* In Orson Welles's biography, published forty years later, Welles addressed the affair: "What Hedda was doing was printing that (Cotten) was balling Deanna Durbin, which he was. In cars, in daylight, where everybody could see."

CHAPTER 19

1. This was in addition to the "died in childbirth" rumors circulated in prison camps.
2. At that time Judy Garland was not well known in Japan, and *The Wizard of Oz* was not released there until 1954.
3. In 1965, Judy Garland married her fourth husband, Mark Herron, in the same venue.

CHAPTER 20

1. Deanna was third on the overall list, which was headed by Abbott and Costello at $469,170. Judy also had an impressive salary by this time, with a weekly salary of $5,619.23 and a guarantee of $300,000 per year with a bonus of $150,000 for each film she shot.

BIBLIOGRAPHY

BOOKS

Atkins, Irene Khan. *Henry Koster*. Metuchen, NJ: The Scarecrow Press, 1978.

Basinger, Jeanine. *The Star Machine*. New York: Knopf, 2008.

Blanchard, Jim. *Winnipeg 1912*. Winnipeg: University of Manitoba Press, 2005.

Boller, Paul, and Ronald Davis. *Hollywood Anecdotes*. New York: Morrow, 1987.

Brautigan, Richard. *Trout Fishing in America*. Berkeley, CA: Four Seasons Foundation: 1967.

Clarke, Gerald. *Get Happy: The Life of Judy Garland*. New York: Random House, 2000.

Davis, Ronald. *Just Making Movies*. Jackson: University Press of Mississippi, 2005.

Hautzig, Esther. *The Endless Steppe*. New York: Scholastic Book Services, 1985.

Heisenfelt, Kathryn. *Deanna Durbin and the Adventure of Blue Valley*. Atlanta, GA: Whitman Publishing Company, 1941.

———. *Deanna Durbin and the Feather of Flame*. Atlanta, GA: Whitman Publishing Company, 1941.

Hunter, Beatrice Thurman. *As Ever, Booky*. Toronto: Scholastic Canada, 1985.

Lejeune, Caroline Alice. *Chestnuts in Her Lap, 1936–1946*. London: Phoenix House, 1947. Print.

Malcolm, Janet. *Reading Chekhov: A Critical Journey*. New York: Random House, 2002.

Melnick, Jeffrey. *A Right to Sing the Blues: African Americans, Jews, and American Popular Song*. Cambridge, MA: Harvard University Press, 2001.

Mesyats, Vadim. *A Guest in the Homeland*. Northfield, NJ: Talisman House, 1997.

Monti, Carlotta. *W. C. Fields and Me*. Hoboken, NJ: Prentice-Hall, 1976.

Pasnak, Kristine. *Edna Mae and the Child Star*. Ottawa, ON: Carleton University, 2003.

Pasternak, Joe. *Easy the Hard Way*. New York: G.P. Putnam's Sons, 1956.

Rees, David. *The Exeter Blitz*. London: Hamish Hamilton, 1978.

Shipman, David. *Judy Garland: The Secret Life of an American Legend*. New York: Hyperion, 1993.

Weinstein, David. *The Eddie Cantor Story: Jewish Life in Performing and Politics*. Waltham, MA: Brandeis University Press, 2017.

Zei, Alki. *Petros' War*. New York: E.P. Dutton, 1972.

Zierold, Norman. *The Child Stars*. New York: Coward McCann, 1985.

MOVIES

Armstrong, Samuel, codirector. *Fantasia*. Walt Disney Productions, 1940.

Berkeley, Busby, director. *Babes on Broadway*. Metro-Goldwyn-Mayer, 1941.

Borzage, Frank, director. *His Butler's Sister*. Universal Pictures, 1943.

Butler, David, director. *Pigskin Parade*. 20th Century-Fox, 1936.

Capra, Frank, director. *You Can't Take It with You*. Columbia Pictures, 1938.

Chaplin, Charlie, director. *The Kid*. Charles Chaplin Productions, 1921.

Cukor, George, director. *A Star Is Born*. Warner Bros., 1954.

David, Charles Henri, director. *Lady on a Train*. Universal Pictures, 1945.

De Cordova, Fred, director. *For the Love of Mary*. Universal-International, 1948.

Del Ruth, Roy, director. *Broadway Melody of 1938*. Metro-Goldwyn-Mayer, 1937.

Edison, Thomas, director. *Widow at the Races*. Edison Studios, 1917.

Feist, Felix E., director. *Every Sunday*. Metro-Goldwyn-Mayer, 1936.

Fleming, Victor, director. *The Wizard of Oz*. Metro-Goldwyn-Mayer, 1939.

Green, Alfred E., and Jack Pickford, directors. *Little Lord Fauntleroy*. United Artists, 1921.

Griffith, D. W., director. *Orphans of the Storm*. United Artists, 1921.

Hand, David, supervising director. *Snow White and the Seven Dwarfs*. Walt Disney Productions, 1937.

Julian, Rubert, director. *The Phantom of the Opera*. Universal Pictures, 1925.

Koster, Henry, director. *First Love*. Universal Pictures, 1939.

———, director. *It Started with Eve*. Universal Pictures, 1941.

———, director. *One Hundred Men and a Girl*. Universal Pictures, 1937.

———, director. *The Rage of Paris*. Universal Pictures, 1938.

———, director. *Spring Parade*. Universal Pictures, 1940.

———, director. *Three Smart Girls*. Universal Pictures, 1936.

———, director. *Three Smart Girls Grow Up*. Universal Pictures, 1939.

Kosterlitz, Hermann (Henry Koster), director. *Das Abenteuer der Thea Roland*. Georg Witt-Film, 1932.

———, director. *Das häßliche Mädchen*. Avanti-Tonfilm, GmbH, 1933.

———, director. *Frühjahrsparade*. Universal Pictures, 1934.

———, director. *Kleine Mutti*. Universal Pictures, 1935.

Lamont, Charles, and Ray Nazarro, directors. *Baby Burlesks*. Universal Pictures, 1931–1933.

Lang, Walter, director. *The Blue Bird*. 20th Century-Fox, 1940.

Leisen, Mitchell, director. *The Big Broadcast of 1937*. Paramount Pictures, 1936.

Ludwig, Edward, director. *That Certain Age*. Universal Pictures, 1938.

Manning, Bruce, director. *The Amazing Mrs. Holliday*. Universal Pictures, 1943.

Milestone, Lewis, director. *All Quiet on the Western Front*. Universal Pictures, 1930.

Minnelli, Vincente, director. *The Clock*. Metro-Goldwyn-Mayer, 1945.

Niblo, Fred, and B. Reeves Easton, directors. *Ben Hur: A Tale of the Christ*. Metro-Goldwyn-Mayer, 1925.

Ryan, Frank, director. *Can't Help Singing*. Universal Pictures, 1944.

———, director. *Hers to Hold*. Universal Pictures, 1943.

Seiter, Norman, director. *I'll be Yours*. Universal-International, 1947.

———, director. *It's a Date*. Universal Pictures, 1940.

———, director. *Nice Girl?* Universal Pictures, 1941.

———, director. *Up in Central Park*. Universal-International, 1948.

Sidney, George, and Busby Berkeley, directors. *Annie Get Your Gun*. Metro-Goldwyn-Mayer, 1950.

Siodmak, Robert, director. *Christmas Holiday*. Universal, 1944.

Sistrom, Joseph, director. *Something in the Wind*. Universal-International, 1947.

Smallwood, Ray, director. *Camille*. Nazimova Productions, 1921.

Spielberg, Steven, director. *Jaws*. Universal Pictures, 1975.

———, director. *Jurassic Park*. Universal Pictures, 1993.

———, director. *Schindler's List*. Universal Pictures, 1993.

Swift, David, director. *The Parent Trap*. Walt Disney Productions, 1961.

Taurog, Norman, director. *Mad about Music*. Universal Pictures, 1938.

———, director. *Presenting Lily Mars*. Universal Pictures, 1943.

———, director. *Skippy*. Paramount Pictures, 1931.

Wallace, Richard, director. *Because of Him*. Universal Pictures, 1946.

———, director. *The Under-Pup*. Universal Pictures, 1939.

Walters, Charles, director. *Summer Stock*. Metro-Goldwyn-Mayer, 1950.

Whale, James, director. *Show Boat*. Universal Pictures, 1936.

MAGAZINES AND NEWSPAPER ARTICLES
Articles are listed chronologically within each chapter.

Prologue

"Crowds Greet Her." *Winnipeg Free Press*, April 3, 1937: 3.

Chapter 1: Early Life

"Schumann-Heink in Hollywood." *Jefferson City Daily Capital*, October 1, 1935: 4.

"14-Year-Old Girl from St. Vital Is Signed for Movies." *Winnipeg Free Press*, February 1, 1936: 3.

"Honor Rarely Bestowed." *MacGregor Herald*, March 25, 1936: 3.

"Deanna Durbin." *Hanover Evening Sun*, August 3, 1936: 10.

Associated Press. "13-Year-Old Girl Opera Possibility." *Evening Huronite*, October 6, 1936: 1.

Lockett, Doris. "No Modern Cinderella? Look at Deanna Durbin." *Centralia Daily Chronicle*, March 6, 1937: 10.

Sulecki, Robb. "Deanna Durbin: In Remembrance." *Classic Images*, December 2013: 76–79.

Cassidy, Christian. "Singer Became One of World's Biggest Stars." *Winnipeg Free Press*, September 27, 2015: A6.

Chapter 2: From MGM to Universal

Harrison, Paul. "Radio Listeners Won't Believe Film Songstress Is Only 13." *Blytheville Courier News*, October 16, 1936: 2.

"Simple Funeral to Be Held for Mme. Schumann-Heink." *Syracuse Herald,* November 18, 1936: 1–2.

Churchill, Douglas. "One Smart Girl." *New York Times,* September 19, 1939: 115, 188.

Walker, Rosalind. "Durbin vs. Garland." *Picture Play,* April 1940: 28–29, 78.

Thomas, Bob. "Judy Garland, Deanna Durbin Contrast Study." *Washington Record-Herald,* June 25, 1969: 11.

Chapter 3: Two Smart Men

Kennedy, Tom. "He's Her Boss." *Screenland,* March 1939: 36.

Asper, Helmut G., and Jan-Christopher Horak. "Three Smart Guys: How a Few Penniless German Émigrés Saved Universal Studios." *Film History* 11, no. 2 (1999): 134–53. Accessed April 13, 2021. http://www.jstor.org/stable/3815318.

Chapter 4: Three Smart Girls

"Dream of Singer Will Be Realized by His Daughter." *Winnipeg Free Press,* November 20, 1936: 1.

Bordages, Asa. "Lights of New York Awe Cinderella Advancing Swiftly in Her Career." *New York World-Telegram,* November 27, 1936.

"Coming Friday to the Garrick." *Winnipeg Free Press,* January 6, 1937: 4.

Morriss, Frank. "Granny Sheds Tears of Joy as Deanna Sings Her First Movie." *Winnipeg Free Press,* January 8, 1937: 3.

"Deanna Durbin in Gay Musical at the Garrick." *Winnipeg Tribune,* January 9, 1937: 16.

"Wonder Singer in Garrick Film." *Winnipeg Free Press,* January 9, 1937: 23.

Kilgallen, Dorothy. "Young Star Has Desire to Sing Grand Opera." *New York Evening Journal,* January 11, 1937.

"Second Week for Garrick Picture." *Winnipeg Free Press,* January 16, 1937: 14.

Nugent, Frank S. "The Screen." *New York Times,* January 25, 1937: 22.

Graham, Sheilah. "Studios Kowtow to Adolescent Players of 'Awkward Age.'" *Salt Lake City Telegram,* February 8, 1937: 7.

McStay, Angus. "Four Smart Girls." *Macleans,* September 1, 1937: 12, 31.

Morriss, Frank. "Here There and Hollywood." *Winnipeg Free Press,* September 26, 1946: 5.

Chapter 5: Jenny Lind in Short Socks

Lewis, Frederick. "The Private Life of Deanna Durbin." *Liberty,* Spring 1937.

"Honor Rarely Bestowed." *Hamiota Echo,* March 24, 1937: 3.

Thompson, Jack. "Deanna of the Golden Voice Plans to Make Debut at Metropolitan Opera within Three Years." *Winnipeg Tribune,* April 2, 1937: 1, 5.

"Why Deanna Durbin Quit Singing." *Radio Guide,* July 31, 1937: 11, 16.

Eustace, Edward J. "Deanna Durbin, Spinster." *New York Times,* September 12, 1937: 211.

Rawles, Obera. "Hollywood Finds Deanna Durbin Normal Girl as She Begins Her First Picture." *Evening Independent,* November 5, 1937: 14.

"When the School Bell Rings on a Movie Lot." *Lima News*, January 16, 1938: 31.

Townsend, Leo. "Good News." *Modern Screen*, October 1938: 65.

Parsons, Louella. "Studio Teachers Are Only Real Bosses in Hollywood." *San Antonio Light*, October 16, 1938: 33.

Graham, Sheilah. "Deanna Durbin Plans Metropolitan Debut." *Winnipeg Tribune*, August 1, 1939: 1.

"Now, Deanna!" *Modern Screen*, February 1940: 56.

"Strictly Personal." *Modern Screen*, August 1940: 37.

"She Taught the Stars." *Titusville Herald*, June 24, 1980: 4.

Chapter 6: One Hundred Men and a Girl

Nugent, Frank S. "The Screen: A Symphony and Deanna Durbin Are Starred in the Roxy's '100 Men and a Girl.'" *New York Times*, September 18, 1937: 15.

Morriss, Frank. "Winnipeg's Wonder Child." *Winnipeg Free Press*, September 22, 1937: 3.

"Music and Deanna Durbin." *Adelaide Advertiser*, April 18, 1938: 5.

Zeitlin, Ida. "Their Boss Tells on 2 Smart Girls." *Screenland*, March 1940: 24.

Chapter 7: Durbin-Daffy

"Deanna Durbin Coming to Winnipeg." *Winnipeg Tribune*, March 22, 1937: 1.

"Deanna in Accident." *Brandon Daily Sun*, March 26, 1937: 6.

"Deanna Thrilled by Visit." *Winnipeg Free Press*, March 30, 1937: 3.

"Deanna Comes Home." *Winnipeg Free Press*, April 3, 1937: 3, 14.

"Underpriviledged Children Guests of Shrine Circus." *Winnipeg Tribune*, April 3, 1937: 9.

"Fireside Reunion." *Winnipeg Free Press*, April 5, 1937: 3.

Morriss, Frank. "Deanna Durbin's Agent." *Winnipeg Free Press*, April 10, 1937: 19.

United Press. "Deanna Drinks Nothing but Water at Cantor's Anniversary Party." *Winnipeg Free Press*, October 30, 1937: 4.

"Winnipeg's Deanna Signs New Contract." *Winnipeg Free Press*, November 9, 1937: 3.

Graham, Sheilah. "Deanna Durbin, 15 Today, Will Be Up to Her Ears in Work Until She's 22." *Winnipeg Tribune*, December 4, 1937: 1.

York, Cal. "Cheap at 55." *Photoplay*, April, 1938: 93.

Siegel, Norman. "Home Sweet Home in Hollywood." *Cleveland Press*, March 14, 1941.

Chapter 8: Prints at the Chinese Theatre

"Talent Scout Suing on Durbin Earnings." *Motion Picture Daily*, July 29, 1937: 2.

"Deanna's Agents Sued." *Motion Picture Herald*, August 7, 1937: 88.

Parsons, Louella. "Grauman to Play Himself in Film." *Charleston Gazette*, November 26, 1937: 7.

Zigmond, Helen. "Our Film Folk of Hollywood." *Indianapolis Jewish Post*, February 25, 1938: 7.

"Deanna Durbin Looks at New York." *Life*, March 14, 1938: 32.

Evans, Delight. "Reviews of the Best Pictures." *Screenland,* April 1938: 52.

D'Arne, Wilson. "Deanna Does It Again." *Picturegoer Weekly,* April 2, 1938.

McGinley, Alfred. "Screen 'Homecoming' Triumph for Deanna." *Winnipeg Evening Tribune,* April 13, 1938: 6.

"Sweet as a Lily." *Winnipeg Free Press,* April 14, 1938: 5.

"Deanna Durbin Honoured by Grauman Theatre." *Perth West Australian,* April 22, 1938.

"Deanna Durbin Follows in Footsteps of Movie Great." *Brisbane Courier Mail,* April 28, 1938: 10.

York, Cal. "Gossip of Hollywood." *Photoplay,* May 1938: 45.

"Mad about Music Review." *Motion Picture Herald,* May 7, 1938.

Evans, Delight. "An Open Letter to Deanna Durbin." *Screenland,* June 1938: 19.

Parsons, Louella. "Deanna to Reach Film Maturity Gradually." International News Service, July 23, 1938.

"Durbin's Tune Tutor Awarded 1/3 Commish." *Variety,* August 3, 1938: 4

Parsons, Louella. "Deanna Durbin Gets Jenny Lind Role." International News Service, August 24, 1938.

Harrison, Paul. "Harrison in Hollywood." *Kingsport Times,* October 4, 1938: 9.

Morriss, Frank. "No Cinderella." *Winnipeg Free Press,* October 27, 1938: 8.

Nugent, Frank S. "The Screen." *New York Times,* November 24, 1938: 37.

"Deanna Durbin Scores Hit in 'Mad about Music.'" *New York Commercial Advisor,* March 28, 1939: 3.

Chapter 9: Deanna Durbin Devotees

Gillespe-Hayek, Annabelle. "Who Said 'Awkward Teens'?" *Silver Screen,* August 1937, 30–31.

Parsons, Louella. "Judy Garland Gets Dorothy Role in Film." *San Antonio Light,* February 25, 1938: 14.

Churchill, Douglas. "Hollywood Ponders a Paradox." *New York Times,* August 21, 1938.

"Deanna Fans Have a 'Devotee' Club." *Life,* October 3, 1938: 33.

Spencer, H. E. "Deanna Fan Club Growing." *Winnipeg Free Press,* October 18, 1938: 4.

United College Press. "Soph Sees Deanna Durbin Movie 141 Times." *Muhlenberg Weekly,* November 2, 1938: 2.

Ross, Ann. "Shots and Angles." *Macleans,* November 15, 1938: 72–73.

Hollywood Parade. "Mrs. Durbin Has a Word to Say about Film Fans." *Adelaide Advertiser,* November 26, 1938: 13.

United Press. "Star Seeks to Legalize Name." *Nevada State Journal,* December 26, 1938: 2.

"Fan No. 1." *Butte Montana Standard,* January 1, 1939: 27.

"Deanna Durbin Prize Contest." *Screenland,* March 1939: 20.

Jay Gordon, editor. *Deanna's Diary,* vol. 3, no. 4 (First Quarter 1940).

"Film Fans Help Red Cross." *Fremantle Mail,* April 12, 1941: 21.

Chapter 10: Academy Award

Morriss, Frank. "Ham off Deanna's Menu." *Winnipeg Free Press*, January 31, 1939: 4.

Associated Press. "Bette Davis and Spencer Tracy Again Win Academy Awards." *Lincoln Star*, February 24, 1939: 2.

Parsons, Louella. "Deanna's Romance Upsets Hollywood." *Charleston Gazette*, April 23, 1939: 10.

"Deanna Durbin and 'Glamour.'" *Perth West Australian*, May 19, 1939: 2.

United Press. "Court Studies Durbin Million $$ Contract." July 1, 1939.

"2 Camp Taylor Boys to Shove Off for California in 18-Foot Canoe." *Courier-Journal*, August 7, 1939: 9.

Mann, May. "Gloria Jean Is Successor to 'Cinderella' Durbin." *Ogden Standard Examiner*, September 3, 1939: 12.

"Youth Reach Coast without 'Busting.'" *Courier-Journal*, December 26, 1939: 2.

Chapter 11: The Kiss

Zeitlin, Ida. "Will Deanna Marry an Older Man?" *Screenland*, July 1939: 28–29.

"Flyers Honor Deanna Durbin." *Hammond Times*, September 10, 1939: 54.

Othman, Frederick, "First Screen Kiss for Deanna Durbin." *Winnipeg Free Press*, October 9, 1939: 7.

Nugent, Frank S. "Screen in Review: First Love." *New York Times*, November 9, 1939: 27.

McGinley, Alfred. "Deanna Durbin Delightful in Romance Film." *Winnipeg Tribune*, November 24, 1939: 14.

"British Selections in All Star Poll." *Motion Picture Herald*, December 30, 1939: 18.

"Review: First Love." *Photoplay*, January 1940: 58.

Lee, Philip. "Oh, to Be a Star!" *Winnipeg Free Press*, October 10, 1940: 3.

Chapter 12: A Dash of Sophistication

Brandt, Harry. "Dead Cats." *Independent Film Journal*, May 4, 1938.

"28 Changes of Costume." *New York World-Telegram*, December 30, 1939.

"Cupid Strikes." *Modern Screen*, February 1940: 83.

Morriss, Frank. "Deanna's Newest Role." *Winnipeg Free Press*, March 23, 1940: 16

Nugent, Frank S. "The Screen in Review: It's a Date." *New York Times*, March 23, 1940: 18.

Churchill, Douglas O. "A Comic's Comeback." *New York Times*, March 24, 1940: 111.

Kahn, Alexander. "School Days for Deanna." *Hollywood Wire Service*, April 2, 1940.

Copeland, Elizabeth. "Reel News from Hollywood." *Richmond News Leader*, April 15, 1940.

"Deanna Durbin Sends Recordings to Soldiers." *Winnipeg Free Press*, May 21, 1940: 6.

"It's a Date—Deanna's Best!" *Silver Screen*, June 1940: 78.

"Strictly Personal" *Modern Screen*, August 1940: 37.

"Extras Breathe Thanks When Deanna Durbin Production Is Started." *Winnipeg Tribune*, September 3, 1940: 4.

"Hollywood's Fan Mail." *Modern Screen*, October 1940: 12.

Crowther, Bosley. "The Screen in Review: *Spring Parade*." *New York Times*, October 4, 1940: 29.

Morriss, Frank. "Lilting and Lovely." *Winnipeg Free Press*, October 12, 1940: 15.

"*Spring Parade*." *Modern Screen*, December 1940: 15.

"Life on the Newsfronts of the World." *Life*, December 16, 1940: 24.

Marsters, Ann. "Deanna's Really in Love." King Features Syndicate, 1940.

Associated Press. "Deanna Durbin Looks to Altar." 1940.

"Deanna, Engaged, Now Cast with Boyer." *Salt Lake City Telegram*, March 3, 1941: 7.

Horak, Jan-Christopher. "'*Spring Parade* (1940)': Imperial Austria Lives Again (at Universal)." *Modern Austrian Literature* 32, no. 4 (1999): 74–86. Accessed April 13, 2021. http://www.jstor.org/stable/24648887.

Chapter 13: The Greatest Love Story

Trumbull, Stephen. "Crowds Jam Premiere to See Deanna Who's Not in Film." *Miami Herald*, January 1941.

Parsons, Louella. "Deanna Durbin Set for Good Will Tour." International News Service, January 17, 1941.

"Fairy Story Finale." *Winnipeg Free Press*, January 31, 1941: 6.

Harrison, Paul. "Aging Deanna Gets Even More Fan Mail Now She's Engaged." *Winnipeg Tribune*, March 11, 1941: 13.

"This Week in Hollywood." *Movie and Radio Guide*, March 14, 1941: 7.

Crowther, Bosley. "The Screen in Review: *Nice Girl?*" *New York Times*, March 27, 1941: L29.

Associated Press. "Deanna's Love Story is Told." April 11, 1941.

Creelman, Eileen. "Deanna's 'Man' in Dither at Prelim." *New York Sun*, April 11, 1941.

Creelman, Eileen. "Picture Plays and Players." *New York Sun*, April 16, 1941.

"Old Winnipeg Friends of Durbins Receive Invitations to Wedding." *Winnipeg Tribune*, April 18, 1941: 15.

Associated Press. "Deanna Durbin on Honeymoon." April 19, 1941.

"Deanna Durbin Weds." *Daily News*, April 19, 1941: 1.

Muir, Florabel. "Deanna Durbin Weds Only Beau in Church Ceremony." *Daily News*, April 19, 1941: 4.

St. Johns, Adela Rogers. "Hollywood's Greatest Love Story." *Photoplay*, June 1941: 42.

Muir, Florabel. "Their Star Took a Husband." *Sunday News*, October 12, 1941: 68.

Whittaker, Otto. "Anna Sklepovich, 'The Cinderella Girl.'" *Bluefield Daily Telegram*, February 6, 1972: 28.

Chapter 14: Greetings from Mussolini

"Death for the Race Defilers." *Der Stürmer*, January 18, 1938.

Associated Press. "Deanna Durbin on Honeymoon." April 19, 1941.

Greenhow, Tom. "The Man Deanna Durbin Is Getting." May 1941.

"Dearest Deanna." *New York Times*, June 6, 1941: 42.

Graham, Sheila. "Deanna Settling Down to Happily Wedded Life." *Winnipeg Tribune*, June 7, 1941: 21.

Parsons, Louella. "Marriage Won't Hurt Judy's Career." *Cedar Rapids Gazette*, June 8, 1941: 42.

Phillips. H. I./Associated Newspaper. "The Once Over." *Hagerstown Morning Newspaper*, June 12, 1941: 8.

Othman, Frederick. "Deanna Durbin Building a House." *New York World-Telegram*, June 13, 1941.

"Mussolini Is Suddenly Very Disturbed about Welfare of American Youth." *Arizona Independent Republic*, June 16, 1941: 42.

Howard, George. "What Deanna Durbin Expects of Marriage." *Hollywood*, July 1941: 20.

Graham, Sheilah. "Blames Deanna's In-Laws." *Newark News*, October 1941.

Crowther, Bosley. "The Screen in Review: *It Started with Eve*." *New York Times*, October 3, 1941.

"*It Started with Eve*." *Morning Telegraph*, October 3, 1941.

"*It Started with Eve*." *New York Herald-Tribune*, October 3, 1941.

"Deanna 'Strikes,' Is Cut Off Payroll." *Daily News*, October 17, 1941: 6.

Morriss, Frank. "Deanna and Her Co-Star." *Winnipeg Free Press*, November 8, 1941: 6.

Procter, Kay. "What's Keeping Deanna Durbin off the Screen?" *Hollywood*, March 22, 1942: 23.

Chapter 15: Camp Tour

"Laddie, Grieving Dog, May See His Master Today." *Empora Gazette*, February 10, 1941: 1.

"Laddie to Live, Doctors Say." *The Sandusky Register*, February 12, 1941: 1.

"Laddie's Dead." *The Lowell Sun*, February 14, 1941: 1.

"Army Private Gets Replacement for Laddie." *Havre Daily News*, March 7, 1941: 2.

United Press. "Owner of Laddie Gets Another Dog," *Klamath News*, March 7, 1941: 1.

"Deanna 'Strikes,' Is Cut Off Payroll." *Daily News*, October 17, 1941.

Othman, Frederick. "Marriage Publicity Wears Off, So Deanna Starts Studio Fight." *Amarillo Globe*, October 17, 1941: 3.

Parsons, Louella. "Universal Confirms Rumors of Deanna Durbin Suspension." International News Service, October 17, 1941.

United Press. "Deanna Durbin to Entertain Soldiers." December 15, 1941: 4.

Mantle, Burns. "Trailing This Soldier Show Reporter Hears Deanna Durbin Sing." *Daily News*, February 17, 1942: 375.

Graham, Sheilah. "Back from Camp Tour." *Newark News*, March 10, 1942.

Crocker, Betty. "Deanna Durbin's Victory Dinner." *Hollywood*, May 1942: 12.

Procter, Kay. "Deanna Durbin: My Army Camp Tour." *Hollywood*, June 1942: 22.

"Souvenirs from Army Camp Tour Flood Deanna Durbin." *Salt Lake Tribune*, July 7, 1942: 6.

Graham, Sheilah. "Back from Camp Tour." *Newark News*, October 3, 1942.

Henderson, Jessie. "Fun on the Farm." *Photoplay*, August 1943: 17.

Lyne, Louis A. "Someday: Letter." *Photoplay*, August 1943: 26.

Nugent, Frank S. "Super-Duper Epic: Hollywood Canteen." *New York Times*, October 17, 1943: 56, 156.

Durbin, Deanna. "Happiness." *Photoplay*, November 1943: 47.

Procter, Kay. "Canteen Anecdotes from a Canteen Hostess." *Photoplay*, November 1943: 84.

Evans, R., and J. J. Loeb. "Peggy the Pin-Up Girl." 1944 (song lyrics).

Chapter 16: Deanna in WWII

"Movie Memos." *Hollywood*, January 1941: 12.

"Cunningham Sees Deanna Movie." *Winnipeg Free Press*, April 2, 1941: 4.

"Film Fans Help Red Cross." *Freemantle Mail*, April 12, 1941: 21.

"Deanna Durbin Made Honorary Colonel of Veteran Society." *Hartford Courant*, July 6, 1941: 17.

Hollywood. "RAF Pilot Writes Deanna Durbin from Nazi Prison." *Hartford Courant*, July 13, 1941: 15.

"Dutch R.A.F. Pilot Writes to Deanna." *Winnipeg Tribune*, September 27, 1941: 21.

Sampas, Charles. "Cavalcade." *Lowell Sun*, October 15, 1941: 53.

"Private Howard Jones." *Valparaiso Vidette Messenger*, July 25, 1942: 4.

Wood, Leslie. "A Letter from Hell to Hollywood." *Screen Guide*, August 1942: 4.

"Star Inspires New Organization." *North Hollywood Valley Times*, August 10, 1943: 1.

Blair, Eunice, and Patrice Schoonmaker, editors. *Deanna's Diary*, 1943

"Pilot Engen Redeems Pledge to Film Star Deanna Durbin." *Argus-Leader*, July 17, 1945: 4.

Brody, Rochard. "Anne Frank's Cinema." *New Yorker*, July 11, 2012.

Berger, Joseph. "Recalling Anne Frank." *New York Times*, November 4, 2014: 14.

Chapter 17: War-Themed Movies

United Press. "Carole Lombard's Body and 21 Others Found." *Sunday Times Signal*, January 18, 1942: 1.

"Markey, Montgomery Meet in Solomons." *New York Times*, February 14, 1943: 51.

Parsons, Louella/International News Service. "Deanna Cast in New 'Smart Girls' Picture." March 18, 1943.

T.S., "The Screen in Review: *Presenting Lily Mars*." *New York Times*, April 30, 1943: 25.

"Brief Reviews: *His Butler's Sister*." *Photoplay*, September 1943: 23.

Associated Press. "Deanna Durbin Seeks Divorce." *Ogden Standard Examiner*, October 14, 1943: 13.

Morriss, Frank. "Mr. Cotten Has a Kiss for Deanna." *Winnipeg Free Press*, October 14, 1943: 21.

Associated Press. "Deanna Durbin Ends 'Important' Marriage." *San Antonio Express*, December 15, 1943: 8.

Crowther, Bosley. "The Screen: *His Butler's Sister*." *New York Times*, December 30, 1943: 13.

Parsons, Louella, "Divorce for Deanna." *Photoplay*, January 1944: 18.
Flanley, Barbara. "Deanna at the Crossroads." *Screenland*, February 1944: 30.
"Hedda Hopper, Columnist, Dies." *New York Times*, February 2, 1966: 32.

Chapter 18: The "Nightclub Singer"
"Deanna's Mother Turns Sod at Site of Model Home." *Winnipeg Free Press*, April 28, 1944: 3.
Crowther, Bosley. "The Screen: *Christmas Holiday*." *New York Times*, June 29, 1944: 16.
"Deanna Durbin Model Home News." *Winnipeg Tribune*, August 21, 1944: 2.
Wilson, Elizabeth. "Deanna Has Her Fling." *Screenland*, September 1944: 48.
Morriss, Frank. "Emoting by Deanna." *Winnipeg Free Press*, October 21, 1944: 19.
"Durbin Rejects Offer of Concert Date to Do Movie." *Port Arthur News*, December 3, 1944: 25.
"Deanna Gets Slap in Movie Scene." *Blue Island Sun Standard*, December 7, 1944: 9.
"Star Helps Him Realize Ambitions." *Madison Wisconsin State Journal*, December 10, 1944: 2.
Parsons, Louella/International News Service. "Louella Parsons." *New York Journal American*, December 17, 1944.
"Deanna Durbin in Hoopskirts to Make Her Technicolor Debut." *New York Herald-Tribune*, December 24, 1944.
Crowther, Bosley. "The Screen: *Can't Help Singing*." *New York Times*, December 26, 1944: 22.

Chapter 19: Two New Mothers
"Cover Photo." *Yank*, January 1945: 1.
Shaffer, Rosaline. "Deanna Durbin at 23." *Cedar Rapids Gazette*, January 21, 1945: 31.
"Durbin Picture Stirs Manila." *New York Times*, April 3, 1945: 5.
Macpherson, Virginia/British United Press. "Deanna Durbin Having Fun in Role of Bachelor Girl." *Winnipeg Free Press*, April 5, 1945: 8.
United Press. "23-Year-Old Singing Star and Husband, 43, Elope in Nevada." *News-Herald*, June 14, 1945: 14.
Hopper, Hedda. "Deanna Durbin Elopes with Film Producer." *Los Angeles Times*, June 14, 1945: 1.
United Press. "Durbin to Wed Producer." *Santa Cruz Sentinel*, June 13, 1945: 15.
Todd, John. "In Hollywood." *Hammond Times*, September 11, 1945: 24.
Crowther, Bosley. "The Screen: *Lady on a Train*." *New York Times*, September 15, 1945: 21.
Wilson, Elizabeth. "Deanna Talks about Her Marriage." *Screenland*, October, 1945: 40.
Holliday, Kate. "30,000,000 Gal." *Macleans*, December 15, 1945: 10, 26.
"Brief Reviews: *Lady on a Train*." *Photoplay*, January 1946: 25.
Crowther, Bosley. "That Old Question: Because of Ham." *New York Times*, February 3, 1946: 131.
"Deanna Durbin Has Daughter." Associated Press, February 7, 1946.

Pryor, Thomas M. "By Way of Report: Brief Encounter with Deanna Durbin." *New York Times*, April 21, 1946: 51.

"Inside Stuff." *Photoplay*, May 1946: 16.

Skolsky, Sidney. "Husband Picks Her Lovers." *New York Post*, November 14, 1946: 12.

Chapter 20: Highest-Paid Woman in America

"Miss Durbin Sues Sister." *Boston Post*, June 3, 1946.

"Miss Durbin to Do 'For Love of Mary.'" *New York Times*, December 7, 1946: 27.

Parsons, Louella. "Deanna Leaves Second Mate." International News Service, January 6, 1947.

"Abbott, Costello Top Income List." *Los Angeles Times*, January 8, 1947: 2.

T.M.P. "At the Winter Garden: *I'll Be Yours*." *New York Times*, February 22, 1947: 15.

"Smith Clan Honors Canadian Film Star." *Winnipeg Tribune*, April 17, 1947: 35.

Hopper, Hedda. "Breakdown." *Modern Screen*, June 1947: 41, 102.

Squire, Nancy Winslow. "Call Me Mama." *Modern Screen*, June 1947: 49, 101.

"Deanna's Poppa Has an Old-Home Week." *Winnipeg Free Press*, June 5, 1947: 8.

McGaffin, William. "Today in Russia: Escape from Troubles Offered by Theatres." *Winnipeg Free Press*, July 22, 1947: 7.

A.W. "At the Winter Garden: *Something in the Wind*." *New York Times*, August 29, 1947: 14.

Kilgallen, Dorothy. "If I Were Queen." *Modern Screen*, January 1948: 20, 73.

Chapter 21: Perhaps

"Price to be Tweed in '*Central Park*.'" *New York Times*, July 5, 1947: 15.

Parsons, Louella. "Good News." *Modern Screen*, April 1948: 8.

T.M.P. "The Screen in Review: *Up in Central Park*." *New York Times*, May 27, 1948: 29.

"*For the Love of Mary*." *Variety*, September 1, 1948: 14.

Crowther, Bosley. "The Screen in Review: *For the Love of Mary*." *New York Times*, September 23, 1948: 37.

Parsons, Louella. "No Help Wanted." *Photoplay*, October 1948: 42.

Brady, Thomas F. "U-I Settles Its Row with Miss Durbin." *New York Times*, November 15, 1948: 21.

Johnson, Erskine. "She Did It Before and She Can Do It Again." *Modern Screen*, February 1949: 38–39, 87.

Thomas, Bob/Associated Press. "Deanna Durbin Points Out Problems of Child Stars." *Reading Eagle*, November 21, 1949.

Maxwell, Elsa. "Babies—Hollywood's Most Expensive Luxury." *Photoplay*, April 1950: 32–33.

Chapter 22: Happily Ever After

Reuters. "Movie Star Bares Troth." *Windsor Star*, May 25, 1950: 12.

Thomas, Bob/Associated Press. "Deanna Durbin to Extend Europe Stay." *Daily Advertiser*, December 17, 1950: 27.

Associated Press. "Deanna Durbin Marries." *New York Times*, December 22, 1950.

Associated Press. "Deanna Durbin Expecting Child." *Orlando Evening Star*, January 27, 1951: 1.

Hopper, Hedda. "Act Your Age, Joan!" *Photoplay*, October 1951: 48.

Thomas, Bob/Associated Press. "Served Her Time, Family Needs Her Now Stays at Home." *Medicine Hat News*, December 19, 1952: 5.

"Eddie Cantor Dead; Comedy Star Was 72." *New York Times*, October 11, 1964: 1.

Lehrer, Tom. "Whatever Became of Hubert?" *That Was the Year That Was*. LP, Reprise, 1965.

"Judy Garland, 47, Found Dead." *New York Times*, June 23, 1969: 1, 31.

"The Song of Slava." *Washington Post*, February 27, 1983.

"Henry Koster, 83, Director of '*Harvey*' and '*Bishop's Wife*.'" *New York Times*, September 27, 1988: 47.

Associated Press. "Movie Producer Joe Pasternak Dies at 89." *Eureka Times Standard*, September 17, 1991: 23.

Rickey, Carrie. "Filmmaker Satyajit Ray Introduced India to the World." *Salt Lake Tribune*, April 26, 1992: 102.

Chapter 23: Six Decades of Obscurity

Carter, Gene. "She Shed Glamour and Wears a Patched Coat Now!" *New York Enquirer*, March 10, 1957.

Hudgins, Garvin. "Deanna Durbin: Obscurity and No Regrets." *New York Post*, April 13, 1958: 58.

Thomas, Bob/Associated Press. "Really Retired." *Newark Evening News*, July 14, 1961: 16.

Associated Press. "Pasternak Is Trying to Lure Deanna Back Onto Screen." *New York Morning Telegraph*, March 29, 1963.

Mosby, Aline. "Deanna Durbin: Lady of Leisure." *New York World-Telegram*, April 20, 1963.

Ringgold, Gene. "Deanna Durbin." *Screen Facts* #5, 1963.

Christiansen, Richard. "Deanna's Back—On Discs." *Chicago Daily News*, October 3, 1971.

"French Producer Nearly Killed." *Daily Mirror*, February 10, 1972.

Dorn, Norman. "Denna Durbin—She Gave It All Up for Obscurity." *Datebook*, November 5, 1978.

Graham, Lee. "Deanna Durbin in 1979." *Hollywood Studio Magazine*, December 1979.

"Note from Deanna Durbin." *New York Times*, April 22, 1980: B8.

Shipman, David. "Interview." 1983.

Dalton, Andrew/Associated Press. "Obituary: Hollywood Star Deanna Durbin." *Newsday*, April 2013.

The Deanna Durbin Society Newsletter #123, Spring 2013.

INDEX

Acknowledgments and Author's Note

As a performer and a music historian, I have researched, written, and toured shows on a variety of topics: from the "lost" knitting songs of WWI and WWII to the lives and music of Vera Lynn, Noël Coward, Edith Piaf, and Jacques Brel. I had always wanted to do a show about Deanna Durbin, but when the time came to write the script, I was surprised to find that no biographies of Deanna existed. Instead, my research included watching her movies, poring over archived scrapbooks, searching newspaper databases, and ordering fan letters and movie magazines online. The more I uncovered about Deanna, the more I felt there needed to be a book written about her life, to tell her story and preserve her legacy.

I hope this book will give modern readers a glimpse of what it was like to grow up, live, and work in the world of Old Hollywood. Although my initial intention was to research and write exclusively about Deanna, I quickly discovered that it would be impossible to do this without including a fair amount about Judy Garland, a fellow ingénue whose life and career were inextricably interwoven with Deanna's, and that their stories couldn't be properly told without bringing in the other "players" who created and steered their careers.

So, in the end, this book tells many stories. But primarily, it is the biography of Deanna Durbin that I was hoping to find when I began researching my show *Ingénue*. I am so proud and honored to share her story after so long, as Deanna's singular talent and the love her movies inspired deserve to be remembered.

I'd first like to thank my agent, Alice Martell, for taking a chance on this book, and to editors Rick Rinehart and Melissa McClellan from Lyons Press for working tirelessly to get it out into the world.

I would also like to thank:

My mum, Karen Gall, for her editing skills and advice throughout (even when I didn't want to hear it!) and my late father, Gerald Gall, whose books on the Canadian Legal System made me want to be a writer someday, too.

I'm so grateful to Jem Rolls for spending a good chunk of his pandemic beach exile in Gokarna, India, reading and editing the manuscript, to Allison K Williams for her generous guidance. I'd also like to thank my fellow "Triumverate" members: Eden Ballantine and Shelby Bond, as well as Bennett Paster, Monique Salazar, Simon Caine, and Winona Richardson for their advice and support throughout.

A special thanks to Hisato Mastsuyama for being so generous with his collection of "Durbiana," including most of the photographs in this book. To Barry Berkman, Tina Kazan, and Chrisstache Ross for their photography and photo editing skills. Also thanks to Jeffrey Macklis, whose generous hosting allowed me to complete my in-person NYC research just before the pandemic hit.

Also, thank you to fellow creatives Keith Alessi, Erika Conway, Suzanne Bachner, Bob Brader, and Bremmer Duthie for the encouragement and artistic inspiration.

Thanks to Wendy Gall and Amelia and Isadora Sharfstein, my own "Three Smart Girls." And finally, my wee bird Colette, because writing a book is a lot more fun—albeit sometimes perilous—with a tame sparrow napping on the keys and pecking at anything that moves.